Grant Park

GRANT PARK

—

THE EVOLUTION OF

CHICAGO'S

FRONT YARD

—

Dennis H. Cremin

Southern Illinois University Press
Carbondale

Southern Illinois University Press
www.siupress.com

Copyright © 2013, 2023 by the Board of Trustees,
Southern Illinois University
All rights reserved. Cloth edition 2013.
Paperback edition 2023
Printed in the United States of America

26 25 24 23   4 3 2 1

Cover illustration: Buckingham Fountain, Chicago, Illinois. Photographs in the Carol M.
  Highsmith Archive, Library of Congress, Prints and Photographs Division.

ISBN (paperback) 978-0-8093-3910-5

The Library of Congress has catalogued the hardcover edition as follows:
Cremin, Dennis H.
Grant Park : the evolution of Chicago's front yard / Dennis H. Cremin.
  pages cm
Includes bibliographical references and index.
ISBN 978-0-8093-3250-2 (cloth : alkaline paper)
ISBN 0-8093-3250-7 (cloth : alkaline paper)
ISBN 978-0-8093-3252-6 (ebook) (print)
ISBN 0-8093-3252-3 (ebook) (print)
1. Grant Park (Chicago, Ill.)—History. 2. Chicago (Ill.)—History. 3. Chicago (Ill.)—Social life
and customs. 4. Social change—Illinois—Chicago—History. 5. City planning—Illinois—
Chicago—History. 6. Community development—Illinois—Chicago—History. 7. Landscape
architecture—Illinois—Chicago—History. 8. Chicago (Ill.)—Buildings, structures, etc.
9. Urban parks—United States—Case studies. I. Title.
F548.65.G73C74 2013
977.3'11—dc23   2012038099

Printed on recycled paper ♻

SIU
Southern Illinois University System

To my parents, Howard and Eleanore Cremin,
and
Rebecca, Emma, and Julia

Contents

Illustrations

Preface to the Paperback Edition: Chicago's Front Yard

As another day begins in Grant Park, bikers and runners start to make their way across sidewalks and paths out toward the lake front. With the din from the morning traffic building, passersby might look up to appreciate the classical facade of the Field Museum or watch the light play along the curtain of the earliest skyscrapers from the late 19th century mixed now with the newest ones of glass and metal along the western side of Michigan Avenue. More than a century after its beginning, Grant Park is still a central place to gather. The 309-acre park is decidedly in the city, and of the city, yet it feels set apart. It is a destination separated from the concrete, the chaos and the cacophony of urban life. In a world that often feels fragmented by neighborhoods and business districts, religious faiths and political parties, the park has been a cohesive center. It remains Chicago's Front Yard.

As city planners began to build for the needs of the 21st century, members of the city government and the Chicago Park District refashioned parts of the park and its spectacular lakefront to uses more suited to the changing needs of the population. Designers created Maggie Daley Park in the northeast section of the park with its skating ribbon and climbing structures, acknowledging the trend of outdoor active space that reflects today's park usage. Millennium Park's Crown Fountain by Jaume Plensa had already been relegated as such, however unintended by the park planners or the artist. The streaming fountain during the summer can look like an expensive wading pool, with hundreds of children at play in the basin between the lighted pillars. Cloud Gate by Anish Kapoor, nicknamed The Bean because of its shape, is actively explored from far, near, and even underneath. It has become the iconic photo stop of Chicago, surpassing the Picasso sculpture in Daley Plaza as a symbol of the city.

Through programming, Grant Park now attracts a younger crowd of people between 16 and 24 years old. With a move to revitalize its brand in 2005, Lollapalooza, the once travelling musical event, found a home in Grant Park. Though the four-day event requires temporarily fencing off large areas of the park, which challenges the park's original designation as "forever, open, clear and free," it has created a central location for more than 100 bands to perform each year on multiple stages. While it has been a success in terms of audience response and revenue, the festival puts considerable stress on the park's landscape, surrounding traffic, and efforts to provide security. Almost 400,000 people each year brave the changeable July weather to see headliners like Lady Gaga and Foo Fighters. They have also enjoyed Chicago's Mavis Staples, Kanye West, and Chance the Rapper. The mega event has also shined a light on lesser known acts such as Le Butcheetts, Tove Lo, and DJ Moore Kismet.

As in the past, the park has continued to be a location for protest. With the murder of George Floyd on May 25, 2020, demonstrations were quickly organized across the United States and around the globe. In Chicago, the summer was punctuated by disorder, looting, and fractious demonstrations in Grant Park. While the majority of the protests were peaceful, some devolved into violence, frequently from opportunistic looters and groups outside the main protest groups. In the months that followed, factional debates arose over the phrase Black Lives Matter, with competing versions such as All Lives Matter and Blue Lives Matter. Chicago's Mayor Lori Lightfoot and the Chicago Police Department were occasionally overwhelmed by the events. In the park, violent skirmishes occurred near the Christopher Columbus statue, which protestors attempted to topple. Ultimately, the Chicago Park District removed the Columbus statue and boarded up its base.

Grant Park also continued to be the place to celebrate Chicago's sports champions. Approximately 5 million fans reveled when the Chicago Cubs won baseball's World Championship in 2016 by defeating the Cleveland Indians. Often labeled the "lovable losers," the Cubs had not won the World Series since 1908, or even appeared in one since 1945. On a beautiful sunny day, double decker buses proceeded to a stage at the south end of Grant Park. The team featured popular players Anthony Rizzo, Chris Bryant, and Ben Zobrist, the series' Most Valuable Players. Then, in 2021, the Chicago Sky rolled through the WNBA playoffs and won the league's championship. The team defeated the Phoenix Mercury in the finals and made their way to Millennium Park to celebrate at the Jay Pritzker Pavilion. Candace Parker, Allie Quigley, Courtney Vandersloot, and the final's Most Valuable Player Kahleah Copper led the team. As in the past, Chicago's basketball champions celebrated in Grant Park.

It is safe to say that Grant Park is now revered as a public space. Visitors from around the world enjoy its open spaces, festivals, and major museum exhibitions. In 2021 a diverse crowd viewed exhibitions at the Art Institute of Chicago of Bisa Butler's art quilted portraits, featuring images of African Americans crafted out of fabric from Africa, and Kehinde Wiley and Amy Sherald's official portraits of former President Barack Obama and Michelle Obama. In 2022, the Field Museum of Natural History replaced its old exhibit on Native Americans with a new permanent exhibit entitled Native Truths: Our Voices, Our Stories. The goal of the exhibit is to reflect on the past, from the earliest history of peoples on the land here through today's thriving Native communities.

From its roots as sacred land of Native People, Chicago has evolved into the vibrant, leading city of the Midwest. Grant Park embodies the civic spirit and the vision of many planners and advocates and has adapted to Chicagoans and visitors. It has become beloved and it continues to evolved to meet the ever-changing needs of the city.

Preface to the Cloth Edition

Chicagoans have visited their lakefront park from its earliest days, looking out at the great blue expanse of Lake Michigan and turning to gape at the sprawling settlement on the lakeshore. More than just a place for recreation, Grant Park, as it came to be called, proclaimed the city's greatness. This book examines how the park's landscape changed over time and how Chicagoans transformed it into Chicago's high cultural center.

Chicagoans first set aside a narrow, nearly mile long section of shoreline east of Michigan Avenue in 1836 for a public park and over a century created an expansive landscape. Some of the park is fashioned from rubble from the Great Chicago Fire of 1871, but systematically filling in the lake provided the vast majority of land. In fact, the expansion of Grant Park into the lake provided a template for filling in the rest of the much-vaunted lakefront.

Chicagoans rave to visitors about their lakefront and how it was saved for the people. What the natives often don't realize is that the lakeshore has been filled in and landscaped. In the nineteenth century, most of the lakefront was sold, some of it given over to use by railroads. It was with the filling in of the lakeshore and the vision of the Plan of Chicago (1909) that the new lakefront emerged. As it has done many times over its history, Chicago re-created itself and fashioned its spectacular lakefront. While many people quickly call to mind the audacity of reversing the Chicago River, they are less likely to point to the transformation of almost the entire lakefront as a park. Grant Park is revealed as one of the most engineered parks in the world.

Being next to the business and governmental center of Chicago's Loop, Grant Park has garnered a great deal of attention. Given Chicago's role as the burgeoning metropolis of the Midwest, the city had the financial resources to reenvision its park many times. Some parts of the park were altered for temporary events, while others became the location for permanent struc- tures. Edward Bennett, architect and coauthor of the Plan of Chicago (1909), provided the design for the park with his Revised Plan of Grant Park (1925), and by the end of the Century of Progress Exposition (1933–34), the park took on its definitive form. The northern section features the Art Institute of Chicago, the Buckingham Fountain and the Congress Street entrance dominate the middle, and the Field Museum anchors the southern section. Roadways, footpaths, bridges, and water and electrical systems tie together the entire park's large lawns and formal, linear gardens. Recent additions, although spectacular, including the Museum Campus on the south and Millennium Park on the north, did little to transform the overall plan of the sizable park.

The study of urban parks can be traced to the history of cemeteries and battlefields. This book has been informed by historic preservationists who first took historic homes as their point of departure but eventually expanded their scope to landscapes, business districts, and regions. This book reflects this approach as well as trends in urban history. In this context, Grant Park reveals a great deal about Chicago, its planners, business leaders, and inhabitants. In many ways, Grant Park served and serves as a display case for the city and a calling card to visitors. It exposes a great deal about how some Chicagoans wish to be perceived by the outside world.

This book focuses on built features of the park. Although landscape designs that were not executed sometimes are examined, this is not a com- prehensive planning history of the park. Rather, it examines how the land- scape actually changed and how the park was used. As a result, it provides a comprehensive narrative history of the park, a survey spanning 175 years, focusing on significant events and developments. For people paging through the book, the transformation in the landscape and the variety of uses should be readily apparent. More elusive is what these changes mean in the context of the city's history.

By "reading" the physical landscape of the park and its monuments, it is possible to gain insight into the cultural history and values of the Chi- cago community. For example, in the 1890s, patriotic citizens erected a monument to General John A. Logan, one of Illinois' leading volunteers during the Civil War and member of the Grand Army of the Republic, the leading post–Civil War veterans' organization. Around 1900, Chicagoans rededicated Lake Park in honor of Ulysses S. Grant, Civil War general and president. The statue of Abraham Lincoln was cast in 1908, although it was not unveiled in the park until 1926. Taken in concert, Grant Park commem- orates the American Civil War at a time when many of the combatants were passing away and the nation faced new challenges. A cultural reading of the landscape reveals a theme of the centrality of community sacrifice that is embedded in the park's meaning in the past and is still a component of the park's symbolism.

This book also surveys how Chicagoans changed this public land from an often unsightly neighborhood park into a landscape of regional, national, and international significance. The transformation of the park was by no means direct, and the current appearance is the result of a great number of plans, efforts, court battles, and compromises. In the wake of the World's Columbian Exposition of 1893, civic leaders advocated for a permanent "White City," the popular name for the exposition. They envisioned a place that could evoke the glory of the fair and would over several decades provide a place for high culture within the city.

Although a part of the city center, the park has offered an alternative to the built-up urban environment. While the city has been crowded and full of commerce and industry, the park has furnished open space and a home for nonprofit organizations. Although the lines between commercial and nonprofit uses of the park have often been blurred, the park has remained largely an open area reserved for recreation and edification through the arts.

Over its history, the park has provided the staging area for a variety of events, including the entry of Lincoln's funeral train into the city in 1865, political rallies, and music festivals. It is world renowned for cultural institutions, among them the Art Institute of Chicago, Field Museum, and Grant Park Music Festival. A site for major celebrations, the park hosted Pope John Paul II's open-air Mass, supplied a place for the Chicago Bulls to celebrate their championships, and provided the site for President-elect Barack Obama's victory speech. It has also seen its share of protest, such as the demonstrations related to the 1968 Democratic National Convention with the chant, "The whole world is watching." Taken as a whole, Grant Park's history is intimately intertwined with that of the city. It is Chicago's front yard.

Acknowledgments

Many people and institutions aided in the preparation of this book. I thank Dr. Patricia Mooney-Melvin of Loyola University Chicago for all her help in the early stages, for introducing me to the field of public history, and for her encouragement. I offer deep appreciation to Lewis Erenberg and Theodore Karamanski, both of Loyola University Chicago, for their keen insights and thoughtful comments. I also thank the faculty, staff, and administration of Lewis University and the College of Arts and Sciences for their ongoing support. In particular, I appreciate the assistance of the chairs of my department, Dr. Ewa Bacon, who also read the manuscript, and Br. John Vietoris. I have enjoyed the fine support and leadership of Dean Angela Durante and Dean Bonnie Bondavalli. I also thank the Christian Brothers Order and in particular Br. James Gaffney, president of Lewis University.

Added to the long list of people who read all or significant parts of the manuscript are Maureen Brennan, Angela Cotta, Donna DeFalco, Robert Fried, Mark Schultz, and Carol Summerfield. I appreciate their keen insights and willingness to discuss the history of the park. I thank Julia Bacharach Sniderman, Chicago Park District, for her willingness to help a colleague. I appreciate the steadfast friendship of Russell Lewis of the Chicago History Museum. I also thank Karl Kageff and the staff at Southern Illinois University Press.

This work would not have been possible without the editing and computer skills of my wife, Rebecca Cremin. Finally, I thank my daughters, Emma Catherine and Julia Camille. Their enthusiasm has made my study of parks a joy.

Grant Park

1

Early Park History: Lake, Land, and Place

Grant Park's history stretches back to the earliest days of Chicago and is closely linked with the community's development. Centrally located south of the Chicago River and adjacent to the emerging central business district, the park often became embroiled in the commercial ventures and civic plans of the city. Chicagoans have, from the beginning, used it as a showplace and a cultural center.

As early as 1835, the Village of Chicago benefitted from state and federal governmental support for improvements to the mouth of the Chicago River and the construction of the Illinois and Michigan (I&M) Canal. These public-works projects would have a significant and long-lasting impact on Chicago and the public land that would one day become Grant Park.

Internal Improvements, Speculation, and Public Land

From its outward appearances in the 1830s, Chicago did not portend much for the future. Harriet Martineau, a novelist and journalist in Chicago, wrote, "Chicago looks raw and bare, standing on the high prairie above the lake shore. The houses appeared all insignificant, and run up in various directions, without any principle at all."[1] While some did find beauty in the Illinois prairie, others found it monotonous, with its long horizon devoid of significant hills or stands of trees. Chicago's location at the mouth of the Chicago River meant it was swampy in the winter and prone to flooding at all other times of the year. It made up for this detractor by its favorable location near a mid-continental divide that separates the Great Lakes, which drain into the Atlantic Ocean, from the great watershed of the Mississippi River, which empties into the Gulf of Mexico. Community boosters asserted that the route through Chicago provided the most direct water link across the continent by connecting New York City, New York, to New Orleans, Louisiana, right through their settlement.

On August 12, 1833, the settlement's three hundred residents established themselves as the Town of Chicago. With their water route in mind, these early community supporters said that Chicago had "natural advantages" and boasted that it was just a matter of time until Chicago would take its place as a leading American city.[2]

Since statehood, in 1818, Illinois had called for the federal government to support the construction of the Illinois and Michigan Canal.[3] As its name implies, the canal would connect the navigable part of the Illinois River to Lake Michigan via the Des Plaines and Chicago Rivers. To businessmen, the lure of a network of waterways that could link the nation was enthralling. Although other canals had opened up trade to the west, the proposed canal at Chicago, ninety-six miles long, provided an almost direct route from the Great Lakes to the mid-continent. The first canal surveyors traveled north from Saint Louis and, in 1829, platted the ends of the proposed canal at the settlements at Chicago and Ottawa. When workers completed the canal in 1848, one ending point remained Chicago, but the other was located at LaSalle, Illinois.

One of the primary difficulties for the construction of the canal was the financing of the project. Like the Erie Canal in New York, the project would require considerable investment and a great many laborers' work. In Illinois, workers with picks and shovels would dig a canal that was six feet deep and sixty feet wide for most of its length. In a spectacular show of support for the internal improvements of Illinois, in 1827, the federal government backed the construction of the canal by granting the State of Illinois the right to sell "odd-numbered 640-acre sections of land within five miles of the proposed canal."[4] Surveyors platted these sections of land for sale, and new arrivals seeking jobs and land soon came to "subdue and populate" the young state.[5] Once the government sectioned off land, private investors attempted to profit from it.[6] The canal commissioners eventually controlled about 284,000 acres dedicated to financing the canal construction with the interest on the bonds.[7] Finally, in 1835, they had raised almost enough money to start work on the canal.

Significantly, Chicago also had gained federal support to build a breakwater to improve the mouth of the Chicago River, which served as the Port of Chicago. By building a breakwater into Lake Michigan, the river's mouth would no longer be clogged with sand, and a clear, straight entrance would be engineered. The ability of Chicagoans to attract such improvement and notice from the federal government portended a bright future for the community. Engineers set to work in 1833 with the construction of two piers that extended hundreds of feet into the lake. The project, which took a number of years to complete, required a great deal of modification and upkeep.[8]

Given the federal involvement, the village became the focus of significant interest from investors, especially from the east. Arthur Bronson, a New York investor, and Gurdon Hubbard, an early traveler and businessman, bought land for both short-term gain and long-term investment.[9] Throughout the 1830s, the demand for real estate remained high, and even allowing for the boom-and-bust cycles that were typical of the period, land values increased.[10] The ability of community boosters to attract investment became a self-fulfilling prophecy that gave credence to their claims of Chicago's greatness.

Martineau describes Chicago in the midst of land fever, "[T]he streets were crowded with land speculators, hurrying from one sale to another. A negro, dressed up in scarlet, bearing a scarlet flag, and riding a white horse with housings of scarlet, announced the times of sale. At every street corner where he stopped, the crowd flocked around him; and it seemed as if some prevalent mania infected the whole people. The rage for speculation might fairly be so regarded."[11] In the midst of this mania, local residents expressed a desire to set aside some public land for their use.

It is in this era of optimism and rapid land sales that Chicagoans in 1835 made their request for public land. At first, the village government ignored requests, but they persisted.[12] The federal government owned a large tract of land around Fort Dearborn, a soon-to-be decommissioned U.S. fort located at the mouth of the Chicago River and the lake. Local residents looked to this area for public land. On November 2, 1835, Chicagoans met at the First Presbyterian Church for their weekly meeting where the topic of the Fort Dearborn tract, which would eventually be sold at public auction, was raised again. The group set forth a resolution for twenty acres on Lake Michigan that would be "reserved in all time to come for a public square, accessible at all times to the people."[13] The local populace had made their formal request.

The following year, I&M Canal commissioners Hubbard, William F. Thornton, and William B. Archer, exercising their significant power to finance the work on the canal, divided up the canal land in Chicago (see fig. 1.1). By 1836, the commissioners had sold 375 lots in Chicago, earning $1,355,755. In this optimistic climate, workers began construction on the canal on July 4, 1836.[14] The commissioners also may have been well-disposed toward the request for public land from Chicago, and in a significant action for the history of the city, they set aside part of this land as a public ground.[15]

The canal commissioners sold much of the land in fractional section 15 in 1836, but they did not subdivide a long, narrow area along the lakefront. Between what became known as Monroe and Eleventh Streets, an area of ten city blocks would become the historical core of this public land. Lois Wille, author of a highly influential book on Chicago's lakefront, and others have long maintained that the real estate adjacent to this public land sold for a higher price because it would have an unobstructed view of the lake.[16]

Three years later, in 1839, the federal government sold the Ford Dearborn addition, in section 10 of the town plan, just north of the public land. Again, surveyors set aside an area east of Michigan Avenue between Randolph and Madison Streets as public ground (see fig. 1.2). Taken all together, the public ground ran about a mile along the shoreline from Randolph to Eleventh Streets.[17] The commissioners designated this on their map as a "Public Ground—A Common to Remain Forever Open, Clear, and Free of Any Building, or Other Obstruction Whatever."[18]

Another piece of public land was set aside west of Michigan Avenue between Randolph and Madison Streets that would one day be designated as Dearborn Park. It has a separate history, but in the 1890s, it would become the site for the Chicago Public Library, which later was rededicated as the Chicago Cultural Center.[19] From these complicated land transactions emerged the practice of designating areas in Chicago that could be developed into parks.

Before It Was Public Land

When the public land was set aside in 1836 and 1039, people had already been putting the land to use. One of these people was William Crawford, who erected a building for a brewery on fractional section 15 on the shore of Lake Michigan, which was part of the state's canal land that was sold in 1836. Crawford noted that the land had been reserved and transferred "over to the town of Chicago for the use of its citizens as public ground." Although he had no title to the land, he maintained that he built the structure "with the full purpose and intention of purchasing the lot when offered

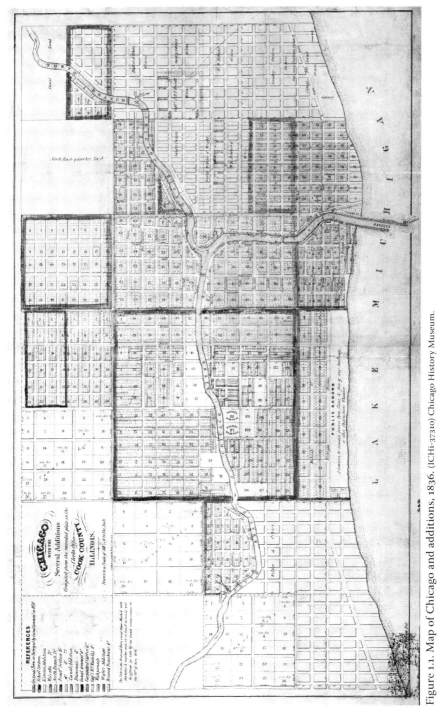

Figure 1.1. Map of Chicago and additions, 1836. (ICHi-37310) Chicago History Museum.

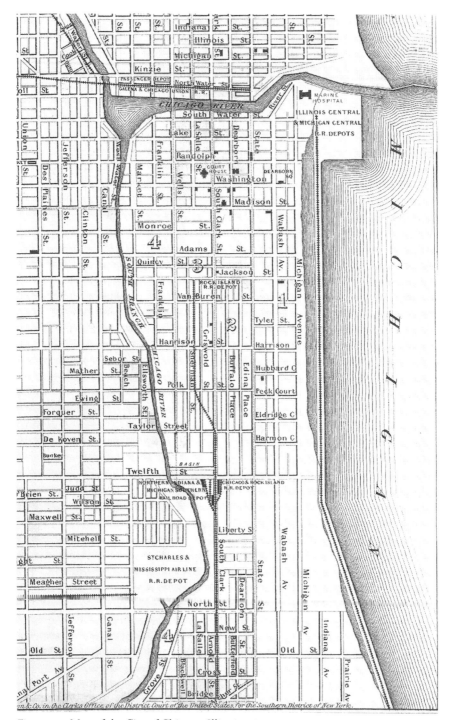

Figure 1.2. Map of the City of Chicago, Illinois, 1855. Courtesy of the Howard and Lois Adelmann Regional History Collection, Lewis University.

for sale." He petitioned the Chicago Common Council to keep his building on site until at least July 1838. Crawford believed that given his expense and trouble, he should not have to move it, but, rather, "as buildings are scarce and far between where he has located it, it cannot possibly be an injury or inconvenience to any person." It appears that the petition was denied, but it is unclear when this structure was removed.[20] So, for the first time, I&M Canal commissioners' designation of public ground thwarted a private businessman's plans. Although Crawford was squatting on the land, the council's denial demonstrates the importance of this designation in the earliest days of the developing settlement. For his part, Crawford is remembered as the first brewmaster in Chicago. In 1835, he was listed as the only brewer on the list of the ninety-five businesses in the growing community.[21]

Even with the land set aside in 1836 not being sectioned for sale, some businessmen wanted to use the land for commercial purposes. On August 28, 1837, John P. Chapin petitioned the Chicago Common Council to allow him to erect a hay scale on the vacant ground south of Randolph Street, making it clear that he did not want to "interfere with any of the public ground." While the common council did not permit the use, the request again demonstrates the desirability of this land for commerce.[22]

Apart from commercial interest, at least one early resident called the public land home. Jonathan Young Scammon, an early settler who arrived in Chicago in 1835, told of someone who had lived on the lakefront. At the sale of lots in the Fort Dearborn addition in 1839, Scammon bought a lot and built a home at the northwest corner of Randolph Street and Michigan Avenue around 1840. He continued to live at the site until after the Great Chicago Fire of 1871. Scammon recalled that a man named Handy once owned a house "of hewn timbers" and a garden in the area that was designated public ground in 1839. It had been built on the lakeshore prior to the "Forever Open, Clear, and Free" designation. Scammon believed that the house was either removed or washed away in one of the storms that eroded the shoreline.[23] So the designation of the area as public ground shifted the use from business and residential purposes.

Early Chicagoans incorporated their city on March 4, 1837. Between 1830 and 1840, Chicago's population increased from around one hundred to almost five thousand.[24] The citizens needed to preserve their open land. It emerged as a borderland between the increasingly built-up harbor area to the north beside the Chicago River and the budding residential area west of the lakefront. As the stories of Crawford, Chapin, and the eyewitness testimony of Scammon make clear, residents of Chicago had various uses and designs for the public land.

Lake Park in the City

On April 29, 1844, the common council designated the area bounded by Michigan Avenue on the west, Randolph Street on the north, and Park Row (Eleventh Street) on the south as Lake Park.[25] As their community continued to develop at an impressive rate, some civic-minded individuals saw the need for additional park land. Mayor James Curtiss said as much in his 1847 inaugural address: "[S]carcely a city in the Union, perhaps in the world is so poorly provided for in this respect."[26] In a move perhaps reflecting the lack of improvement of their existing park, the city in 1851 again dedicated its public grounds on the lakefront as Lake Park.[27] The double dedication may reflect that the settlement was still close enough to "nature" that green space attracted little attention. After all, prairie and agricultural fields lay only a short wagon ride from the center of town. In addition, property owners showed little interest in assuming the cost of park improvements or spending money benefiting only the part of the city at the lakefront.[28]

People did use Lake Park for leisure activities in the 1840s and 1850s, taking the "healthful" air and enjoying views of the lake. The few park proponents argued that the "natural" setting of the parks, especially the open space and fresh air, served to aid health. A small group of people often linked their concerns over sanitation issues, such as clean water, the disposal of refuse, and the spread of disease, to the need for open spaces. By midcentury, sanitarians in the United States championed parks as "the lungs" of the city, which could provide healthful air to the populace as well as an area of moral uplift and beautification. The wealthy residents of Chicago built homes west of Lake Park on Michigan Avenue, centrally located with the lake view. It is not surprising, therefore, that this locale became the place to see and be seen.

As early as the 1840s, Lake Park, sometimes called Lake Front Park, became an area where people promenaded singly or in small groups. In a city known for business activities and profit, the promenade, as historian Daniel Bluestone notes, "offered the benign vision of a coherent social order coalescing around shared leisure and shared urban space." Promenading reached popularity first in Europe and then in the United States. Though this activity was often associated with the societal elite of the city, it did attract devotees from the emerging middle class as well. While the working class and poor might have been attracted to the scene, the main participants took this opportunity to dress in their finery. Given their advantage of resources and leisure time, both the upper and the rising middle class came to champion public grounds as a result of their recreational interests. In this context, some of the tensions related to immigration, industrialization, and urbanization might have been reduced. Promenading humanized a society undergoing sizable transformations by providing an area in which to see, and perhaps even talk with, one another.[29] The health benefits and stylishness of walking along the lakefront helped make a case for parks and their improvement.

Erosion at Lake Park

While people enjoyed their lakefront park, it was threatened by lake erosion. One unintended result of the harbor improvements at the mouth of the Chicago River was the erosion of the lakefront at Lake Park.

Early maps and descriptions make note of the significant spit of land created as the Chicago River turned south as it entered Lake Michigan. The shoreline at Chicago had a considerable lateral movement of sand towards the south, which often silted up the mouth of the river. In 1835, the Army Corps of Engineers carried forward a major internal improvement by constructing two piers to keep the entrance to the Chicago River free of sand. The piers transformed the lakeshore by halting the movement of sand north of the pier and starving the shoreline south of it of protective sands. Unintentionally, the Army Corps of Engineers had created additional shoreline erosion south of the Chicago River that threatened Lake Park.

By the late 1840s, the north pier extended nearly three-quarters of a mile out into the lake, and the government had spent almost a quarter of a million dollars on dredging. The city reported that winter storm surges had washed up onto Michigan Avenue, and the property owners inland from Lake Park voiced their concern to the city. The situation had deteriorated to such an extent that the future of the lakefront land was in doubt.[30] The city appealed to the federal government for dikes and breakwaters to protect the shoreline. These pleas, however, yielded little action.

Chicago's richest families lived in this district, and they exerted their influence to save their homes and the park. If Chicago's common council did nothing, the city could lose its exceptional public ground to erosion. The *Chicago Democrat* newspaper asserted in 1849, "[N]o common property would be left to the great mass of that portion of our citizens who now make it a resort for exercise, fresh air, bathing and pleasant pastime."[31] If the park was preserved, the city could improve it and create "a place of general resort for our citizens during the summer evenings, where they will be enabled to enjoy, not only the benefits of a delightful promenade, but also the sanitary advantages which the invigorating breezes from the Lake, generally prevailing at that time, will impart to the system."[32] Faced with the encroachment of the lake, some citizens pledged their financial support toward this cause. The city moved to protect the lakeshore, but its efforts failed due to the scale of the daunting task. At this point, the Illinois Central Railroad offered its assistance and considerable resources to preserve the lakeshore.[33] Eventually, the city and the railroad reached a compromise that would, in the short term, remedy the problem of lakefront erosion and, in the long term, would significantly influence the history of the city and its lakefront.

The Illinois Central on the Lakefront

Business leaders formed the Illinois Central Railroad (IC) in 1850, and the railroad flourished because of its ample federal land grant, which drew on the model of the financing of the Illinois and Michigan Canal. By 1856, the railroad had seven hundred miles of charter line in Illinois, making it arguably the world's longest railroad. During the winter of 1851–52, the IC started negotiations to gain access to the Chicago River in the city. Although the railroad planners would have preferred to enter the city farther to the west, the company determined that the most direct route to the river was along the lakefront. The erosion of Lake Park provided the opportunity to take this route, as the railroad offered to build a breakwater to protect the lakeshore south of the river in exchange for direct access to the Chicago River.[34]

The Chicago Common Council discussed the prominent role that the IC could play within the city. Some Michigan Avenue residents lobbied for the IC to have expanded access to the lakefront, but others objected. Chicago's city government supported the railroad's proposal because the residents who lived away from the lakefront opposed increased taxes for an improvement that would not have a direct benefit for the entire metropolis.[35]

Even though they stood to gain from the improvements to be made by the IC, some local residents were concerned about the noise and the loss of their unspoiled lake view, as well as the probable soot from locomotives.[36] Yet, in December 1851, the city approved a petition from the "Illinois Central officials requesting the right to place its tracks along the shoreline from Hyde Park north to the Chicago River."[37] The railroad was already beginning to transform the city's landscape, and it would soon change the lakefront. In the process, the IC and the other railroads played a role in the transportation revolution that altered the way people and goods were moved around the nation.

Along the lakefront at Lake Park, the IC constructed tracks on offshore piers. The railroad would be protecting its track as well as the lakeshore. On June 14, 1852, the city granted the railroad permission to proceed with the plan. This proved to be a significant development in the history of Lake Park, as the Illinois Central obtained a "300-foot right-of-way north of 12th

Street" offshore from the park.[38] The newly built railroad breakwater and trestle created a sizable lagoon offshore. Citizens soon utilized the lagoon for sailing and boating in the summer and ice skating in the winter.

The IC bought land between the Chicago River and north of Lake Park. It built an enormous terminal, outbuildings, and a number of lines of track. It also expanded its holdings by filling in the lake bed between the Chicago River and Randolph Street. The company constructed a terminal larger than its immediate needs demanded, knowing it would soon grow into the building (see fig. 1.3). The railroad completed its station and headquarters between Water and Randolph Streets in 1856 and, in doing so, further altered the lakefront.[39]

Figure 1.3. Illinois Central freight depot and grain elevators, 1858. (ICHi-05211) Chicago History Museum.

Despite the Illinois Central's early efforts to build breakwaters, their offshore track continued to be threatened by storms. In 1856, the IC stated that "at and near Chicago the protective works along the lake shore had been much shattered by severe storms, and in some places totally destroyed; while the gradual inroads of the lake, south of the city, had reached such a point that further protection was absolutely necessary." The restoration of the line was completed in 1857, and the IC stated in its annual report that "6997 lineal feet of crib and pile breakwater have been built or re-built along the lake shore at Chicago, placing beyond injury a part of the track which has heretofore been seriously damaged by almost every storm."[40] The railroad protected the shoreline from erosion and saved Lake Park. In the process, the IC capitalized on its access to the mouth of the Chicago River and filled in the shoreline of Lake Michigan for additional land for operations, including the creation of an area for track and the exchange of rolling stock.

While the shoreline that made up Lake Park had been largely unaltered, people looking out toward the lake now viewed a train trestle and a lagoon between the tracks and shore. For a few Michigan Avenue property owners, their worst fears had been realized. While the lakeshore had been saved, they had lost their unobstructed lake view, and visitors seeking the healthful air might have to look elsewhere. In the context of nineteenth-century industrialization, some undoubtedly looked out from Lake Park and gloried in the noisy engines issuing black smoke with their long line of cars as evidence of commerce and industry.

An Early Proposal for Lake Park

Once the railroad protected the lakefront, there were calls to improve the park property and make it into an area "similar to the Battery of New York," which had been military land that was converted into a park through the use of landfill.[41] On August 19, 1853, the *Daily Democratic Press* printed an article that proved to be visionary, calling for the improvement of Lake Park: "A Splendid Park—in Imagination—the necessity of parks for the health and happiness of our citizens has of late frequently occupied our attention. We have one in our eye, *that is to be* at no very distant day one of the finest in the wide world. . . . We allude to the space between Michigan Avenue and the Illinois Central Railroad."[42] The article goes on to set out an image for a public space, much in the spirit of the early boosters.

The anonymous journalist suggested making land by filling in the shoreline. The Illinois Central had already filled in areas north and east of Lake Park, in part to protect the area from erosion and storms but also to create valuable real estate. The journalist proposed filling in the area between Michigan Avenue and the railroad tracks. Civic taxes would pay for this project, which would be spread over the future population of more than half a million people.[43] In nineteenth-century America, especially in cities growing up adjacent to water, this kind of landfill program was common.

The journalist continued, "Imagine if you please that whole space filled up, covered with a rich green ward, lain out tastefully in walks and lawns, filled with our splendid American forest trees, evergreens and choice shrubs and flowers, here and there a fountain sparkling in the sunbeams, and the whole surrounded by a neat iron fence, and where else could you find a spot more enchanting!" The article closes with a call for a philanthropic individual, someone who had made considerable money in Chicago, to pay for the park improvements.[44]

The journalist's vision of the potential for Lake Park may have arisen out of some of the practical concerns of the day. At midcentury, as America experienced an explosive period of urbanization, city dwellers felt a need for green space. It may be that the journalist was thinking about the need to find a way to bridge America's agrarian past with its increasingly urban present. This view is in accord with others who argued for parks as a way to promote public health and provide recreational areas. In either case, the journalist makes a strong case for increasing the landfill and giving it over to an expanded Lake Park.[45]

Despite the lack of a formal improvement to Lake Park in these years and the arrival of the Illinois Central, visitors wrote favorably of the Lake Park area. As one anonymous author wrote in *Putnam's Monthly Magazine* in 1856, "Michigan avenue, the favorite street for private dwellings, on the south side, runs directly on the lake shore on a sort of bluff formed by the action of the winds and waves. It is something more than a mile in length, and has an elevation of twelve or fourteen feet above the water. The houses are built only on the west side, leaving the view of the lake entirely unobstructed. There are many fine private residences on this street, and one, belonging to the Roman Catholic bishop of the diocese, might, both in size and style, be fairly ranked as a palace."[46] What is noteworthy is that this viewer, with his focus on the residential area, left out any mention of the railroad and paid scant attention to Lake Park itself (see fig. 1.4).

Figure 1.4. Lake Park, 1850s. Carte de visite. (ICHi-21402) Chicago History Museum.

Another, more vivid account was made by Edward L. Peckham a year later. His account of his trip to the West includes an entry for Saturday, June 6, 1857:

> Michigan avenue is the only street where one can walk in safety, and in (is) the avenue of the city. It is wide and runs parallel with the shore of the lake. It is adorned by many beautiful private residences, and commands a grand view of the ocean-like waters, with its numerous steam and sail vessels moving hither and thither. Some near enough to hear the cry of the sailors, others hardly discernable on the distant verge. I strolled down to the shore (which is composed of a fine glass house land) and with my leather drinking cup, imbibed freely from the huge Michigan bowl, and also thoroughly washed my linen gloves. Land on this street is selling at $5.00 per square foot, an unheard of price, but then, only rich people can live here. Indeed it is the only street fit to live in.
>
> The only objection to this place, by some, is the Michigan Railroad [now the Illinois Central] which is built on spiles, immediately in front, about 200 or 300 feet from the shore and on a line with it.[47]

This descriptive account underscores the significant cost of property in the area and Michigan Avenue's relationship with Lake Michigan.

Until the 1850s, the park was made up of the narrow strip of shoreline, with a high fence that resembled ones used for equestrian enclosures, that separated it from Michigan Avenue. An elevated plank walkway close to Michigan Avenue invited people to stroll. Substantial residences lined the western edge of Michigan Avenue, claiming the space as a neighborhood park. Yet, Lake Park and the city would undergo significant changes in the decade to come.

Lake Park in the 1860s

If it is true that Chicago came of age in the 1890s, then the 1860s were part of a tempestuous adolescence marked by peaks and valleys. By the beginning of the Civil War in 1861, Chicago was one of the fastest growing metropolises in the United States. Businessmen opened the Union Stock-yards in 1865, and Chicago emerged as the premier city of the Midwest. The impact of this growth was again observable on the city's lakefront.

Living just a few blocks from Michigan Avenue, the working poor claimed the park as their own front yard and an escape from their often crowded quarters. As one participant reminisced of his time in the park in 1862, "[O]n every pleasant Sunday afternoon, almost the entire unattached population would be there on parade, or otherwise lending itself to the filling up of a rather gay and festive scene . . . rather more warmly than the staid people whose fine mansions faced the esplanade thought either necessary or seemly." The population of the nearby boardinghouses would often stay in the park late and filled the grassy areas of the park. The upper-crust residents were not happy with this view. As journalist Frederick Francis Cook reminisced, "[T]here were no signs warning possible trespassers to 'keep off,' the green places were generally pretty well worn."[48]

One contemporary publication, *Chicago Illustrated*, featured high-quality lithographs by the Chicago Lithography Company depicting different parts of the city's center, including Lake Park. The illustrated thirteen-part series, written by James W. Sheahan, served as booster literature for Chicago in the late 1860s. The editors selected a cover image that showed Lake Park with a railroad train on the raised offshore tracks. One hundred years before the Sears Tower (now Willis Tower), this panorama came to symbolize the city.[49]

The first issue of *Chicago Illustrated* includes a description and image of the Illinois Central's depot, highlighting the neighborhood around Lake Park, such as the Terrace Block or "Marble Terrace" on Michigan Avenue south of Van Buren Street. Chicagoans proclaimed the residence one of the finest in the city. Reflecting its elite status, Lieutenant Governor William Bross and Judge H. T. Dickey resided at the Terrace Block.[50] The Terrace Block and structures like it reflected Chicago's newfound refinement. While *Chicago Illustrated* celebrated the structure as one of distinction, some Chicagoans derided it as ostentatious, and nearby boarders disparaged the elitism associated with the "Marble Terrace." After the Civil War, the nouveau riche of the dawning Gilded Age became noted for conspicuous display and was often denounced for their extravagance.[51] What also may have drawn attention to the building was that its scale was out of proportion to surrounding residential structures.

In the 1860s, Lake Park and the surrounding area became increasingly part of the city center. As Cook reminisced, "[L]ate in the sixties this guileless Eden [Lake Park] was ruthlessly invaded; and thereafter practical interest[s] claimed it more and more for their own." He continues to describe the change as "the old boardinghouses had nearly all disappeared—and finally because parks everywhere presented rival attractions, the old 'Lake Front' knew its crowds no more."[52] All of Chicago was undergoing significant changes in the 1860s, but Lake Park declined as a neighborhood park. A few blocks to the west, merchants started to transform State Street into a model retail center. Although industry and shipping still flourished along and around the Chicago River, it became less significant to the cityscape, as Calumet Harbor, twelve miles to the south, was developing into a new center for industry and freight by 1869.[53]

With the decrease in use by residents and reduction in the number of wealthy neighbors, the park began to show signs of urban decay. Visitors to Lake Park saw a worn, narrow, grassy area, occasionally littered with refuse, with a view more of the Illinois Central trestles than of the lake beyond.

In 1861, the Board of Public Works took over managing Lake Park and other grounds, thereby having the power to "open or improve any park upon the approval of the council." In 1863, the city extended these powers to the Chicago Common Council, which soon exercised its new jurisdiction. The council subsequently banned all parties "from encroaching on land or water west of a line four hundred feet east of Michigan Avenue."[54] Given the significant activities of the Illinois Central Railroad on the lakefront at Lake Park, the common council may have been defining the park's boundaries and sending the IC a clear message to respect the park's borders, though they did little else to maintain or improve the park.

The Board of Public Works budgeted for some improvements in 1863, setting aside money for the enhancement of Jefferson Square, Dearborn Park, and Lake Park, but funding park improvements was rare. During and immediately following the Civil War, the city government set aside little money for park upkeep. Parks were not a high budget priority. As a result, the parks fell into further disrepair. The situation became so dire that the Board of Public Works was "without the means even of repairing their fences, or of keeping the cattle out of them."[55] The writer of *A Stranger's and Tourists' Guide to the City of Chicago*, an early tourism book from 1866, did not even include Lake Park in the listings. In fact, the park lands were becoming so unsightly that Lake Park was known as a site for dumping refuse of all kinds rather than as a park.[56]

Chicagoans, faced with the need for better and more open land, discussed the creation of a larger park system. The city was starting to spread well beyond its wildest projections. New parks would be placed on the outskirts of the city and provide the periphery with green space and anchors for real-estate development. Within a few years, Chicago passed from a city of few, poorly maintained parks to a national leader in park development with the creation of the South Park Commission. The commission would eventually handle the development of Lake Park and drive the formation of the Lincoln and West Park Commissions.

But Lake Park's central location helped it to regain attention and drive efforts to improve the park. Significantly for the future of Lake Park, the local Democratic Party selected Lake Park as the site for its party's 1864 national convention. With the construction of a temporary amphitheater, the park provided the stage for a discussion about the Civil War, politics, and the future of the United States. While nearby Dearborn Park had been the site of the River and Harbor Convention in 1847, the Democratic National Convention delegates used Lake Park in a decidedly unexpected way.

The Democratic National Convention of 1864

The City of Chicago hosted its first major national political event in 1860 when the Republican Party held its national convention in a temporary structure called the Wigwam at Lake and Market Streets in Lake Park. In an event that still resonates with importance, the Republican National Convention's delegates selected Illinois' Abraham Lincoln as its candidate. Given the events of the Civil War that followed, this is perhaps the most significant political convention in the history of the United States.

Just four years later, in the depths of the Civil War, the Democratic Party selected Chicago as the site of its major convention. Scheduled to meet in early July 1864, the party faithful delayed for a month to gauge the leanings toward peace from the costly war among the populace. Finally, the organizers opened their convention on August 29 in Lake Park. Chicago's Democratic Mayor, Francis Cornwall Sherman, hosted the convention and its related festivities, which ran through August 31. Modeled on the Republicans' choice of venue in 1860, the Democrats convened in another temporary structure popularly referred to as the Wigwam (see fig. 1.5).

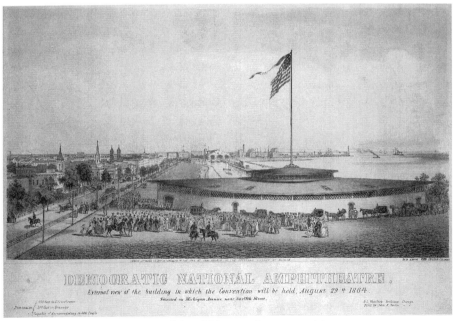

Figure 1.5. Democratic National Amphitheatre, August 29, 1864. Lithograph by Charles Shober. (ICHi-01981) Chicago History Museum.

The term *wigwam* was commonly used in this period to refer to a political headquarters and was taken from a Native American term for a specific type of house the Great Lakes Indians built. Erected on the southern end of Lake Park at Michigan Avenue and Park Row by private subscription, this Wigwam featured a low-pitched canvas roof that covered a sizable wooden circular structure.[57]

Sanford B. Perry and other property owners who lived adjacent to the park on Michigan Avenue argued that the Wigwam of 1864 violated their property rights and, for a time, attempted to block the construction of the building. However, the injunction did not halt the construction, as the courts allowed the barn-like edifice in the park as a temporary structure.[58] Although this decision did not attract much notice at the time, Michigan Avenue property owners gained the right to review and comment on development within Lake Park, setting an important precedent for temporary structures built within the park.

While the Civil War continued to rage, the convention opened on August 29, 1864. The Democratic Party, which had been internally divided during the presidential election of 1860, was somewhat better organized in 1864 with few of the disruptive Southern Democrats attending the convention. Nonetheless, issues surrounding states' rights and the degree of opposition to Lincoln still split Northern Democrats. The most controversial segment of the party was the Copperheads, who desired a prompt end to the war and immediate peace with the South.[59] In general, the Democrats had come to Chicago to defeat Lincoln, but given the context of the war, their critical discussions could easily have crossed the line into treason.

Their criticism of the federal government during the war helps to explain some of the tension in Chicago as the delegates entered the city. City officials were concerned about the possibility of trouble, including fears that Southern sympathizers might set fire to the city.[60] Yet, despite all of their forebodings, the convention ran without major incident. As the *Chicago Tribune* glowingly wrote: "[I]t was fortunate it was held in Chicago, where we can receive and attend to vast assemblages in a manner that challenges the admiration of other cities. It has been handsomely done by our local committees and their emulation of the great Chicago Republican Wigwam of 1860, has accommodated in a charming breezy location on the lake shore a vast concourse of people, witnesses of the struggle for Democratic supremacy." In the end, even the decidedly Republican *Chicago Tribune* had high praise for the convention and even more, though not surprising, for Chicago. Its brief account also notes that the location was well suited for the meeting of a large crowd.[61] The central location and access to transportation made Lake Park an ideal location for the convention. In addition, it carried over a tradition of democratic interaction in the public sphere, though the whole affair was circumscribed by the Civil War.

The business of the convention was conducted in an orderly fashion, and, yet, misadventure ensued. Perhaps the result of hasty construction, the crowded gallery in the Wigwam gave way, and a number of delegates fell more than ten feet. Fortunately, no one was seriously hurt. Furthermore, boisterous activity around the hotels, especially the Sherman House, Tremont House, and Court House Square, caused disturbances.[62] These locations, which were the sites of contentious debates and large torchlit parades, provided the potential for disorder. In the end, however, the delegates and other political activists left the city with no lasting damage. The convention came to a climax with the selection of General George Brinton McClellan as the Democratic candidate.[63]

Lake Park, though trampled by those attending the convention, returned to its previous appearance once workers removed the Wigwam. Because the city park had hosted a national convention, it became far more integral to the city as a place of display and a place for civic gatherings than it previously had been. In addition to its proximity to hotels and transportation systems, it also featured cool lake breezes that could provide a respite, especially in the summer months. Lake Park remained a neighborhood park, but the space, by virtue of its location, portended much for the future.

Lake Park and Lincoln's Funeral Train

Less than a year after the delegates of the Democratic National Convention met in Lake Park, the Board of Public Works used the park as a staging ground for one of the nation's saddest chapters as it participated in the twenty-day journey of Lincoln's funeral train from Washington, D.C., to Springfield, Illinois. With the bloody Civil War finally over, John Wilkes Booth assassinated President Lincoln at Ford's Theatre on April 14, 1865. What followed was an epic journey of transporting Lincoln's body across the country to its final resting place in Springfield. Lincoln's funeral train provided a shared event of public commemoration and national mourning that focused the country's collective anxiety and sorrow after the long war marked by the shared calamity of the loss of over six hundred thousand lives.

During its long journey, the train made a number of stops. At each one, the ritual of mourning was repeated. Men removed the slain president's body from the train, processed to a public area, displayed the body in state for a public viewing, and processed back to the train. The train made its slow but steady progress, and mourners lined the track at all hours as it made its way. Chicago, the burgeoning metropolis of the Midwest, held a memorial that was second in size only to that of New York City.

Lincoln's body arrived on Chicago's lakefront on Monday, May 1, at 11:00 A.M. with only the sound of the train bell ringing (see fig. 1.6). The stop in Chicago was especially poignant as just five years before, in 1860, the Republican Party had nominated Lincoln as its presidential candidate in Chicago. When the train stopped on the trestle along Lake Park, the Veteran Guard descended newly constructed stairs to ceremoniously transfer the coffin to a dais in the park, where workers had erected a large structure of three Gothic arches draped in black that identified the area where the body would lie (see fig. 1.7).[64] The arches had a number of appropriate mottos on them, including "An Honest Man's the Noblest Work of God" and "Faithful to Right: A Martyr to Justice." Chicagoans could see the temporary construction from a considerable distance, given the unobstructed view provided by the park.

Although it had rained for the days preceding the arrival of the Lincoln train, the skies cleared as his body was brought into Lake Park at Park Row. The rain, however, limited the number of mourners who made their way to Chicago for the public memorial. Although city workers did their best to scrape and clear the streets, the route of the public procession was muddy. The *Chicago Tribune* reported that at Lake Park and Michigan Avenue, "[E]very window was filled with faces, and every door step, and places filled with human beings. . . . The whole of the large space to the east of Michigan Avenue—Lake Park—was jammed full even to on the water's edge."[65]

The mournful pageantry in the park included thirty-six young women dressed in white making their way around the dais that bore the coffin. Each placed a single flower on the elevated platform.[66] From Park Row,

Figure 1.6. Lincoln funeral train at Chicago. Abraham Lincoln Presidential Library and Museum.

the body was placed in an elaborately decorated horse-drawn wagon. The procession made its way up Michigan Avenue to Lake Street and on to the Court House with people lining the route to be near their martyred leader.[67] At the Court House, Lincoln lay in state while a long line of mourners, estimated at around seven thousand an hour, streamed past the coffin.[68]

On Tuesday at 8:00 P.M., Chicago's dignitaries gathered again, and the eight black horses pulled the hearse to the Saint Louis and Alton Railroad depot. Lincoln's body had been in the city for thirty-four hours. Lincoln's body next headed to Springfield through the Illinois prairies that had been transformed in his lifetime into some of the most productive agricultural lands in the nation. Lincoln was on his final trip home.

Within two years, the park had featured the Democratic National Convention and served as the staging area for Lincoln's funeral train that drew tens of thousands of people to Chicago's lakefront. Chicagoans had begun to use Lake Park as a site of national significance, and this would allow them to consider an elevated purpose for the park within the city.

Figure 1.7. Lincoln funeral arch, Lake Park, Chicago. Abraham Lincoln Presidential Library and Museum.

The Larger Context: Plans for the North, West, and South Park Commissions

In the late 1850s, the seeds for three new park districts were planted that would provide Chicago with more and better-maintained public space. Although initially faced with resistance, the independent park commissions pushed for the power to appropriate lands through the use of tax monies, which eventually led to a phenomenal increase in park lands. In 1861, park commissioners set aside the land that would one day become Lincoln Park. Landowners and real-estate speculators, often enticed by the increased real-estate values of land near parks, made additional appeals for park land. In 1864, the city set aside sixty acres on the lakeshore, north of an old cemetery, on the outskirts of the city, and named the area Lake Park, overlooking the fact that the park between Randolph and Twelfth Streets east of Michigan Avenue already had the name. At the same time, Chicagoans continued to debate the creation of park-district commissions and the range of their legal powers.[69]

By the late 1860s, the South Park Commission had extensive plans for its park. The state legislature formulated a land bill in order to appropriate real estate. Despite a history of a lack of popular support, the legislature ratified the bill February 24, 1869, allowing "for the location and maintenance of a Park in the towns of South Chicago, Hyde Park and Lake."[70] The South Park Commission secured legal recognition for the appropriated land and, in 1869, hired Frederick Law Olmsted and Calvert Vaux, the landscape architects who had designed New York's Central Park. In the same year, the Lincoln and West Division Park Commissions were created by the state legislature, which permitted them to buy tracts of land for their parks, just as the South Park Commission had.[71]

By 1871, these parks were being established on the edge of the city limits, providing green space for Chicago's outlying areas. The state's ultimate goal for these commissions was to create a boulevard system that would someday link the three parks. Lincoln Park to the north was accessible by public transportation or by foot, but the other parks were reachable to those in the center of Chicago only by commuter trains. Chicago went from having few public parks to providing a model for other park districts in the nation. It was in this context of concern for parks and their design that the city began to plan the landscaping of the parks already within the city center.[72]

A Plan for Lake Park

In 1868, the Board of Public Works advanced a plan for the improvement of Lake Park. The board intended to fill in the area between the former shoreline and the railroad with material that was either free or available at a small price. Although this would fill in part of the lake that had been used for leisure activities, such as boating, it had the benefit of significantly extending the size of the park. The board already had created four acres of land by filling in the lake.[73]

By 1870, the Board of Public Works published new plans for the improvement of Lincoln, Union, Jefferson, Vernon, Ellis, and Lake Parks for the benefit of the public. The board's plans included a landscape map for each park, which not only would enhance the use and beauty of the park landscapes but also include public restrooms and watering troughs for animals. A proposed "Plan of Lake Park" encompassed the area from Michigan Avenue to the Illinois Central trestle by filling in the lake.[74]

The "Plan for Lake Park" was not ascribed to any one planner, yet the layout was in line with other parks that were designed during these years. The South Park Commission had already hired Olmsted and Vaux in 1869 to devise the plan for Jackson Park on Chicago's South Side. All of these plans used curving pathways, structures, and water. William Le Baron Jenney, who created a plan of Chicago's Central Park (now Garfield Park), approached his designs in a similar fashion and reflected aspects of Olmsted and Vaux's layout for Chicago's South Park Commission.[75]

Another contemporary landscape designer active in Chicago at this time was Horace William Shaler Cleveland. Cleveland had moved from Massachusetts to Chicago in 1869 and had begun to work with William M. R. French, a civil engineer. Cleveland, like Olmsted and Vaux, helped bring west the landscape sensibilities of easterners, such as Andrew Jackson Downing, the first great landscape designer in the United States.[76]

Cleveland immediately set to work on the promotion of public spaces. He wrote in favor of the larger park districts on Chicago's periphery, lauding Chicago's vision in setting aside these lands. He also broadly expressed his views on parks and their use. According to Cleveland, "the primary object of a park is to minister to the health and recreation of the citizens; to provide a place for the indulgence of such rational pleasures and amusements, public gatherings and displays, as are inadmissible in the ordinary thoroughfares of the city, and the first duty of those who have the work in charge, is to make such arrangement of the natural and artificial objects of attraction, and such a disposition of the roads, walks, and open spaces, as may best serve that end; and nothing should be admitted as a permanent feature, which conflicts, or tends to the disturbance of the sense of rest and refreshment."[77] Cleveland's view, resonant of an increasingly popular perspective of his contemporaries, declared that parks provided sanitary and moral uplift to the population.[78]

Cleveland emphasized the distinction of the park as a separate space from the crowded city.[79] The park plans published by the Board of Public Works also reflected these prevailing views. The board continued to make improvements to the parks' grounds and reported in 1871 that "Lincoln, Union, Jefferson, and Ellis Parks have been so far improved and beautified as to be very attractive places of resort."[80] Lake Park's design called for a long pond at the center of the park that would be dotted by islands. This plan would have only partially filled in the lagoon that existed between the shore and the railroad trestle.[81]

The Board of Public Works outlined the utility of its Lake Park plan in 1871: "The advantages of the work are beginning to be appreciated by the community. During the pleasant weather, thousands of people daily resort to this locality for the purpose of recreation, and to breathe the pure, healthful, and invigorating air of the lake." The board anticipated that four more years of work on the project would "be sufficient to fill the entire basin and complete the present designs, so that 'Lake Park' will have a local 'habitation' as well as a 'name,' and be an ornament to the city."[82] The planners realized, however, that filling in the lakefront would prove to be both expensive and time consuming.[83] The Great Chicago Fire of 1871 would alter all of these plans.

An Imbroglio on the Lakefront

At the same time that the Board of Public Works had been improving Lake Park, the state had entertained the possibility of selling the park to the Illinois Central and other railroad companies in what was popularly known as the "lakefront steal." Since the early 1850s, there had been tension in Chicago over the placing of the Illinois Central's railroad tracks offshore. The "steal" was another chapter in the lengthy conflict surrounding Lake Park.

In the late 1860s, the newly founded South, Lincoln, and West Park Commissions struggled under the weight of their initial organization and buried themselves in ongoing litigation. Several park advocates proposed selling some of Chicago's smaller parks in the city center in order to help support the new park commissions. To alleviate budget concerns, the Illinois State Legislature moved to sell Lake Park and some of the area around it to the Illinois Central, Michigan Central, and Chicago, Burlington, and Quincy Railroads for the construction of a union terminal. The railroads paid $800,000 for the land and were positioned to gain a prime location for their terminal, while the City of Chicago earmarked the money to pay off the debts of the South, Lincoln, and West Park Commissions. The park advocates assumed that there would be less opposition to the sale if the money was going to help pay for other parks.[84] Accordingly, the state legislature passed an act in 1869 to give the City of Chicago "all the right, title and interest of the State of Illinois to the property" in question.[85]

The tract included the area four hundred feet wide from Michigan Avenue to Monroe Street on the north and Park Row on the south. In addition to the land that composed Lake Park, the sale also included submerged land, which extended up to a mile out into Lake Michigan. Ultimately, the railroads bought the rights and title to this land. The $800,000 was to be put into a park fund, which was to be equally divided among the park commissions.[86]

The sale of Lake Park created fierce opposition. General interest among Chicagoans must have been high because the *Chicago Tribune* published the entire transcript of the mass meeting held to discuss the "Lake Park Question." During the meeting, the sale of the land was attacked on both legal and public-interest fronts. The legal arguments ranged from the right of the Illinois legislature to sell the land, which had been set aside by lawful authority, to the right of the state to sell the submerged land, which legally was asserted to be part of the park.[87] Other arguments were stated in strictly financial terms, as the act would have "permitted the Illinois Central, the Chicago, Burlington and Quincy, and the Michigan Central railroads to pay only $800,000 for land valued at $2,600,000 or more."[88]

At the meeting, a number of speakers referred to the importance of the land for the healthful air it provided to those who worked and could not easily leave the center of the city. Lieutenant Governor Bross, who lived on Michigan Avenue at Lake Park, stated, "[O]ur clerks, our laboring men, our serving girls, on Sunday and every evening of the year, when it is pleasant are found in crowds on Michigan Avenue, enjoying the beauty and freshness and health of that lake." Other speakers focused on aesthetic issues.[89] In the eyes of outraged Chicagoans, the park's benefits far exceeded its monetary value.

One speaker questioned the railroad's intentions and alleged that the earlier landfill efforts attracted the interest of the railroad. He explained that the Board of Public Works had "been engaged for the last year or two in gathering up the mud and dirt which accumulates on the streets, and has been dumping it into the lake between the shore and the Illinois Central track and have in that time made a large quantity of land. The railroad companies have seen this work going on, and they have taken it into their heads that it would be a very nice thing to get possession of that land." The railroads, it was additionally argued, desired the land for purely speculative purposes, as the park was situated in a prime location.[90] All of this conjecture only served to increase the opposition to the sale of the park land. It also reflected the general distrust of the railroad in this era.

In 1869, the city government, in response to popular opposition to the "steal," found a way to back out of the sale. Governor John M. Palmer had objected both to the political chicanery that pushed the act through the legislature as well as to the unspecified rights that the act would give the railroad over the lakefront. As a result, after the legislature passed the act, he vetoed it.[91] However, "[o]n April 16, 1869, the State Legislature passed, over the veto of the Governor, an act which conveyed, in fee, to the city of Chicago, all the right, title and interest of the State of Illinois to the property." The three railroad companies, in accordance with the act, paid the first of four equal quarterly payments within three months after the passage of the act. These payments were made, but the city comptroller held them in trust rather than placing them in the general city coffers.[92]

The governor's veto failed to stop the sale; instead, a provision had been written into the bill of sale that offered the city another way out of the deal. The city, bending to the popular opposition, did not accept the money and quitclaim. The Chicago, Burlington, and Quincy and the Michigan Central withdrew their portion of the money shortly after deposit. The Illinois Central, however, left the money with the trustee for many years and brought the matter to court. Finally, in 1892, the U.S. Supreme Court ruled that the Illinois Central had no claim to land and water as defined in the 1869 act.[93]

In a little more than thirty years, Chicagoans had created the most prosperous and fastest-growing city in the Midwest. From its earliest days, the city's inhabitants had advocated for public ground. With Lake Park, some of the city's most influential residents built homes that made this park their front yard. Amid the tension of rapid industrialization, residents and visitors alike enjoyed this break from the city grid that afforded a view of Lake Michigan.

Lake Park symbolized the inherent contradictions of this ambitious western city. On the one hand, Chicagoans celebrated the machines, the factories, the feats of engineering that delivered prosperity—theirs was the great new industrial American city. On the other hand, they felt a need to demonstrate to their East Coast cousins that Chicago had culture, too. Parks suggested gentility, leisure, civic largesse, and a concern for public welfare. For these and other reasons, Chicago became a national leader in urban park development, and Lake Park was central to that effort.

2

Lake Park: A Cultural and Civic Center

While embers still smoldered from the fire that destroyed thousands of buildings, killed three hundred people, and left one hundred thousand city residents homeless, on October 11, 1871, the editors of the *Chicago Tribune* boldly announced, "The people of this once beautiful city have resolved that CHICAGO SHALL RISE AGAIN." Indeed, the paper reported, dauntless believers in the city's resurrection were already clearing the rubble and making plans for rebuilding (see fig. 2.1).[1]

In Lake Park, people gathered to fight the fire, took refuge from the flames, and even saved some of their prized possessions. But even as the commercial district moved into a row of cramped wooden buildings, and wagons filled the lagoon with the old city's scorched remains, civic leaders envisioned another role for the park. There, Chicago would display a concern for the healthful recreation of its citizens, its achievements in industry and the arts and sciences, and its readiness to take its place in the governance and defense of the United States. Lake Park would be expanded

Figure 2.1. Destruction of Chicago by fire, October 1871. Lithograph by Thomas Kelly. (ICHi-02956) Chicago History Museum.

and take a central role as the new city's front yard. After the Great Chicago Fire of 1871, Chicagoans acted quickly to solidify their city's position as the Midwest's largest metropolis and national transportation center, a position it had gained during the Civil War.

A Temporary Main Street

Chicago's parks had largely escaped the fire; in fact, many had functioned as firebreaks, slowing the spread of the blaze. On the eastern edge of the fire, some of the fiercest firefighting took place in the residential areas adjoining Lake Park.[2] Afterward, these open spaces provided a staging area for hundreds of refugees and merchants while decimated sections of the city were cleared of debris and rebuilt.

At Lake Park, the Board of Public Works allowed businessmen to erect temporary structures (see fig. 2.2). The board leased the property in Lake Park for around $750 per year for "a corner lot, and $500 for an inside lot, each having a frontage of twenty-five feet, and a depth of two hundred feet." It granted businesses the ability to construct a building of one story and to be on the lots for "one year or more at the discretion of the board."[3]

Soon, hastily built wooden structures stretched in a line for a mile along the eastern side of Michigan Avenue. These structures were generally one story, except where "the owner has carried up the walls to twenty feet, the limit named in the permit, and thus obtained two low stories."[4] The residential property owners of the area, who may have been opposed to any kind of construction on the site, tolerated this temporary use of the land in light of the emergency.

In the months after the fire, the controversy involving the railroads and Lake Park rekindled. The city had been dealt a devastating blow by the fire. Many people suddenly lost their homes and became unemployed. It was in this climate that legislation popularly known as the "lakefront steal" became

Figure 2.2. Temporary businesses in Lake Park after the Chicago fire, ca. 1872.
(ICHi-38984) Chicago History Museum.

a topic of debate once again. The city was now somewhat better disposed toward the railroads and their financial interest in the lakefront, as the Illinois Central railroad offered much-needed funds and the possibility of jobs in building a new train terminal.

After the fire, the railroads made a new proposal to the city to buy just the land in Lake Park, "three blocks of ground east of Michigan Avenue and north of Monroe Street," for a new central depot.[5] This was a far different proposal than the large scale "lakefront steal" of 1869. In this case, the railroads reduced the amount of land and did not include the riparian rights but tendered the same amount of money: $800,000.[6] In light of the needs of the city at the time, the *Chicago Tribune*'s position was that the city needed those funds to rebuild. Workers in Chicago would also benefit from the construction of a new central depot, as would their families, who could be taken off the relief rolls.[7] Despite much discussion, the land was not sold, and a depot was built on the site.

The lack of a sale may have been influenced by a group who contested the possession of any segment of park land for use by the railroad. This group enlisted the help of the Attorney General of the United States to file information in the U.S. Circuit Court for the Northern District of Illinois; the information would block the city from granting land for a depot or the railway companies from building one. The group gained an injunction from the court that barred the railroads from building a depot.[8] Although the city could have gained short-term economic benefit from this sale, public opinion helped block the action.

As reconstruction progressed and permanent business locations were completed, the temporary structures were removed from Lake Park, and the land became an open space once again. Thanks to landfills created by the fire's debris, the park had expanded over the entire area between the shore-line and the Illinois Central train trestle. According to one source, "5000 cubic yards of rubbish [were] being dumped in daily in the first month" after the fire. As a result, approximately forty acres of new land were created, far exceeding the fill called for in the earlier "Plan for Lake Park."[9]

Just to the north, in July 1873, the city turned over the management of Lincoln Park to commissioners the governor appointed, creating the core of what became the Lincoln Park Commission. With this shift in the oversight of Lincoln Park, Lake Park became the largest park under the jurisdiction of Chicago's Board of Public Works. Also in 1873, the board spent $4,383.48 on Lake Park's 42 1/9 acres.[10] Lake Park was becoming one of Chicago's most important parks at a time when the Board of Public Works acknowledged the value of open, public spaces. In the annual report for 1874, the board stated that "citizens eagerly seek the recreation to be enjoyed in these public 'breathing places.'" Further, the board noted that for many city dwellers, the new parks on the city's periphery were too far away to be easily used, while the parks in the city center brought "symmetry and beauty" to Chicago.[11]

In addition to these established uses, after the Great Fire, the city could argue that the parks were not only attractive but also utilitarian. As the Board of Public Works stated, "[T]hese places of free recreation have both a practical and an aesthetic value, and in both uses the city would be greatly benefited by an increase in their number." It further reported that the parks served as fire breaks in the dense city center, and they could be used as areas for "relief and protection to large numbers of people." In addition, the parks had long provided a refuge in hot weather, as the city's residents flocked "to the green sward and cooling shade to obtain the rest and refreshment otherwise inaccessible to those accustomed to grimy toil and poorly ventilated dwellings." Finally, the parks served to cultivate the populace. As the board noted, "[T]he beauty of the parks exercises a refining influence, and they contribute at once to the general security and health, as well as to individual improvement." The board insisted that any money spent on the parks "affords a generous return."[12]

The Inter-State Industrial Exposition

In the months after the fire, many of Chicago's business leaders desired to demonstrate to the world that Chicago had arisen phoenix-like from the flames. A group of Chicago's civic and business leaders, including hotelier Potter Palmer and George D. Laflin, called for the construction of a large exposition building in 1873 to house a "state fair and trade show," which would bring attention to Chicago and its wares. Given its central location, expanded land area, and previous successes as a site for temporary businesses, the civic leaders had Lake Park in mind. In February 1873, they established the parameters of the exposition to be held that coming September. They hoped "that the products of mechanical, artistic, and industrial skill, and raw and finished articles of commerce would be exhibited there in a systematic manner." The exposition would also feature "musical and other popular entertainments," and it was hoped a group would "inaugurate a live-stock exhibition to be held in the vicinity of Chicago during the term of the Exposition."[13] The leaders desired to display all that there was to celebrate in Chicago.

Business leaders were drawing on a worldwide trend of expositions, which were popular in the nineteenth century. The earliest fairs were held in Paris in 1834 and again in 1844. These "Expositions des produits de l'industrie francaise" (Expositions of products of French industry) set the precedence for the great fair held in London in 1851. The London exhibition had the sizable title of the "Great Exhibition of the Works of Industry of

All Nations," although most people called it the Crystal Palace Exhibition after its landmark building.[14]

Civic boosters were learning that a successful exposition, large or small, would bring attention and renown to the host city. Businessmen, inventors, and people in the arts and sciences used the large gatherings to meet, exchange information, and sell their goods. In the Midwest, the earliest fair was the Cincinnati Industrial Exposition of 1870. This event, like the one to follow in Chicago, became an annual feature that continued for nineteen years. It became known as the "National Exhibition of Manufactures, Products, and the Arts."[15]

Aware of Cincinnati's success, Chicago's civic and business leaders advocated for something that would combine aspects of a trade show, arts and entertainment venue, and convention center under one glorious roof. Perhaps drawing upon the earlier success of the postfire boardwalk, city leaders raised a subscription of $150,000 to pay for the initial costs of a fair with the continuing expenses to be borne by the entertainments, which accompanied the commodities to be displayed. Additional funds could be raised by costs to display other performances or special events.

The city would contribute to the arrangements by making the land available free of charge. Planners selected Lake Park above Congress Street. The City Council on May 28, 1873, allowed "that portion of Lake Park lying between Monroe Street on the north and Van Buren street on the south, as a site for the exposition and grounds." The centrality of the site was attractive as it was "near the heart of the city, near the central termini of all the street-car and omnibus lines, as well as within from two to ten minutes walk of all the principal hotels, and all the railway depots and steamboat landings of the city."[16]

The exposition's organizers wanted to attract a large number of repeat visitors to the displays. According to the exposition's planners, "the business man, the mechanic, the clerk, the laboring man, and their families" could easily have access to the exposition, without incurring the cost of traveling. The exposition's proponents asserted that because of its central location, these groups could also attend the festivities several times, perhaps in the evening. Additionally, business leaders noted, people could attend "without infringing on the hours of labor or business, and interrupting the city's industries." Part of the attraction for visitors near and far was to see if Chicago had indeed risen from the flames of the Great Fire.[17]

Architect William W. Boyington designed the exhibition's large iron-and-glass building. Boyington had already designed Chicago's Water Tower, which survived the disastrous 1871 fire. He had also gained renown for his Joliet Prison (1858) and other high-profile commissions.[18] The exhibit's structure drew inspiration from the 1851 Crystal Palace in London. The edifice, erected in only ninety days, opened on September 25, 1873. The main building featured twenty-three thousand square feet of exhibition space with few interior supporting columns. The building's highlight was a grand dome, which was beyond the main entrance at Adams Street, sixty feet in diameter and forty feet in height. The architect also designed a great number of skylights that helped to illuminate the vast interior.[19]

An audience of twenty thousand attended the inauguration of the "Inter-State Industrial Palace." The festivities opened with speeches by a number of prominent men including N. S. Bouton, the exposition's chairperson, as well as Mayor Lester L. Bond, Governor John L. Beveridge, and Senators John A. Logan and Richard J. Oglesby. W. F. Coolbaugh, vice president of the exposition's board of directors, suggested that the event heralded "the coming triumph of New Chicago." According to Coolbaugh, the exposition was "an enterprise undertaken with no selfish or mercenary purpose, or expectation of individual gain, but, in the belief that the agricultural, manufacturing and commercial interest of the northwest, as well as the promotion of the arts and sciences, required some fit place in which might be exhibited the trophies of our skill and industry."[20]

Governor Beveridge stated that the exposition was "in memory of the ashes, in honor of rebuilding." According to Beveridge, "Chicago inaugurated its exposition on ground which, two years ago, was blackened with fire. Now in the presence of a vast concourse, to the sound of sweet music, it is dedicated to art, commerce, and industry, that magnificent temple." "Chicago," he proclaimed, "vied with the cities of the world."[21]

In his turn, Senator Logan asserted that while there were pragmatic aspects to the event, especially for artists and artisans, the exposition demonstrated "the varied power of the human intellect, and humanity was only a little lower than the angels; not akin to the brute, but linked to a higher and more glorious order of existence." Logan, while seemingly conscious that commerce was being introduced into the park, stated that the exposition advanced the commerce and industry of the city in a selfless way that would provide benefits to society. The senator assured the crowd that the displays would profit Chicagoans' pocketbooks as well as their souls.[22]

The presence of the state's leading elected officials underlined the civic importance of the exposition. The grand building on Lake Park asserted that Chicago had indeed rebounded from the fire. For its part, the Inter-State Exposition Company had created an under-one-roof spectacle, equal parts trade show, dry-goods store, industrial showroom, fine-arts gallery, indoor garden, and fair (see fig. 2.3). Between September 25 and November 12, 1873, approximately 600,000 visitors viewed the 1,320 exhibits on display in the Industrial Palace.[23]

Figure 2.3. Interstate Industrial Exposition, Chicago, 1877. Reproduction based on an original painting by Richard Richard.

With this exposition, business leaders had fundamentally changed the role of Lake Park in the city. Chicagoans mixed moral and physical uplift with functional activity within the park. As the metropolis grew, the city allowed Lake Park to become integrated into its commercial, artistic, and civic life. The designation for the land to remain completely open was no longer a reality, but the southern portion had been left open and free from buildings.

Within approximately twenty months of the Great Chicago Fire, the city had been able to divert energy from its rebuilding efforts to create a significant event that drew national attention to the growth of Chicago, not its destruction. The city and its business leaders had asserted that Chicago was the main metropolis of the Midwest, and the exposition affirmed it.

Commerce and Culture Find a Home in Lake Park

After the success of the first year, the exposition company obtained a two-year extension for its activities from the Common Council of Chicago. The exposition ran for a few weeks in the fall with few events planned for the rest of the year, rendering the enormous structure underutilized. The men involved had invested a great deal of money and effort into the concern, including building a substantial edifice, which with minimal work could be made permanent.[24] It is unclear whether they had planned to operate it as a yearly affair, though the exposition in Cincinnati, Ohio, had become an annual event.[25]

The businessmen, convinced of the exposition's civic importance and role as a trade fair, reinvested in the project. During the ensuing years, they repeatedly modified the great building. Before the second exposition, a new machinery hall was erected on the north and a conservatory on the south of the main structure. Keeping up with the maintenance, in 1879, the exposition company paid for major renovations, overseen by Boyington.[26] The iconic structure became a useful trade hall and began to take on events year-round.

The businessmen who established the exposition operated it at a deficit until 1875, when they made a profit of $986.44. Alfred T. Andreas, a contemporary historian, asserts that the exposition became self-sustaining in 1877. In looking toward the exposition of 1878, John P. Reynolds, the exposition's secretary, wrote glowingly about the fair's ability to support whatever would "contribute to their [the business interests of Chicago's] prosperity." Reynolds continued, "[T]hey have not failed to recognize in these annually-recurring exhibitions . . . a powerful and legitimate auxiliary to their enterprise." The exposition's secretary stated that the annual event was a benefit to the city and should continue on its course.[27]

Reflecting the everything-under-one-roof nature of nineteenth-century America, the building served periodically as a convention center and the location for a range of other activities, such as dog, cat, cattle, horse, and chicken shows. Within the cavernous space, merchants displayed everything from trains to airships. In one year, there were plans for not only political conventions but also a bicycle-riding tournament and, later, the National Convocation of Knights Templar of the Masonic Fraternity. Other notable activities included the National Exposition of Railway Appliances in June 1883, described as "the largest and most complete transportation fair ever held." The organizers presented the latest in railway technology, including "the Southern Pacific's new steamer, the largest in the world." The organizers also displayed an electric railway, the first in the west, which circled inside the exposition building.[28]

Another major change within Lake Park occurred in 1875, when the Baltimore and Ohio Railroad, with the consent of the Illinois Central Railroad, obtained partial use of the exposition building. As a result, the city terminus for this line became the Exposition Building on Michigan Avenue, which also helped facilitate attendance at the exposition. The address for the Baltimore and Ohio from 1875 to 1891 was "Michigan Avenue, foot of Monroe St," the Inter-State Industrial Building.[29] Railroad companies, one of which had attempted to buy Lake Park, became another commercial interest within the park.

Further reflecting the delicate balance between being park land and commercial venture, Chicago Mayor Monroe Heath, whose focus was on balancing the city's books, asserted in his inaugural address of July 24, 1876, "I would also suggest that it might be profitable for you to inquire into the advisability of disposing of all or a portion of the unnecessary and unproductive real estate of the city, and including the block of ground known as the Lake Front, and situated between Monroe and Randolph streets, but reserving to the city, for obvious reasons, the water privileges or riparian rights."[30] The mayor's assessment recalls the Illinois Central Railroad's offer to buy that land following the fire. Heath's pronouncement demonstrates how at least a portion of Lake Park was perceived as being easily dispensed with. Part of this perception undoubtedly reflected the location of the Inter-State Industrial Building and the major industrial uses on the north end of the park.

Once the exposition company began to operate in the black, the common council wanted to charge rent for use of the property. The exposition stockholders asserted that they were interested in a successful display rather than pecuniary gain. The dispute between the two bodies remained hotly contested for a number of years. The two sides finally resolved their differences in 1885 when the Exposition Company paid $1,000 in rent, which then was to be paid annually.[31] The Inter-State Exposition, opening every autumn from 1873 to 1891, was considered a resounding success both as a spectacle and as a stimulant to trade.

Within the park, it created a significant precedent in that a temporary concern became a fixture in the park for many years. The park's overall relationship with the city evolved. It is noteworthy that it had been a partnership between a civic-minded private-interest group and the city that made the land available. Ultimately, they were able to share enough interest to make the relationship work for both parties.

Fine Arts and Music at the Exposition

The Great Chicago Fire had destroyed a number of art galleries in the city, many of which were ruined financially and unable to reopen their doors. The trade in fine arts was hampered by the scant interest of collectors, who were slow to start buying again after having lost their treasures in the inferno. The Inter-State Exposition, however, served to rally those interested by displaying many attractive items, including paintings, sculpture, wax flowers, and other craft items. The quality and merit of the items and their quality varied widely over the years.

Chicagoan Henry Chatfield-Taylor reflected on the Inter-State Industrial Building, remembering it possessed "innumerable doors and windows and three disproportionate domes, and upon its roof of glass there was a forest of poles from which fluttered the flags of all nations of the earth." Some connoisseurs were put off by art being displayed among the other goods at the exposition. At least one viewer, novelist Major Joseph Kirkland, stated that the art shows were "in [a] remote part of the building in which machines were whirling, while the Illinois Central engines were tooting just outside, and there was a scent of popcorn, and a brass band was banging brazenly from a gallery."[32] Kirkland's reaction illustrates the incongruity of the setting and the potentially unseemly juxtaposition of art alongside commercial items.

By the 1880s, the quality of artwork had risen considerably. Sara Hallowell, who managed the exposition's art exhibits and eventually became the Paris agent of the Art Institute of Chicago, was largely responsible for the improvement in quality. Through her efforts, the art exhibitions became known for their excellence. In the exhibition of 1890, Hallowell brought French Impressionist art to Chicago, and she continually transported important works to the expositions. In addition to major European works, the expositions featured American artists, such as William A. Chase, Thomas Eakins, Winslow Homer, George Inness, John Singer Sargent, James Whistler, and Alexander Wyant.[33] Collectors bought major artistic works from both Europe and the United States.

The exposition also employed William M. R. French, who came to Chicago to study engineering. French became active in the arts community, writing art reviews and becoming Secretary of the Chicago Academy of Fine Arts and, later, the Art Institute of Chicago in 1882. His brother, Daniel Chester French, was one of America's best-known sculptors, creating many great works of art, most notably the seated Lincoln in the Lincoln Memorial in Washington, D.C.

William French served as the annual art exposition's director from 1882 to 1914 and had a significant influence on the Art Institute of Chicago. He traveled a great deal to secure paintings for display at the Inter-State Exposition. As a result of their connoisseurship and hard work, Hallowell and French transformed the annual exposition into a major cultural event. The Inter-State Exposition's annual art display served as an outlet and extension of people who were also bringing their considerable expertise to Chicago's arts community. The exposition fostered fine art collecting in postfire Chicago and thus nurtured the development of a strong and long-lasting fine-arts community in Chicago.[34]

From its inauguration, the Inter-State Industrial Exposition also featured musical performances ranging from brass bands to orchestras. The music performed in the building received a great deal of attention, especially in the 1880s when fine-arts performances drew large numbers of patrons.[35] The varied musical offerings, though, were often hindered by the poor acoustics of the metal-and-glass structure.

Ferdinand W. Peck (1848–1924), a Chicago real-estate developer, music aficionado, and resident of Chicago's lakefront, brought serious musical concerts to the Inter-State Industrial building. In the mid-1880s, the developer and sometime promoter observed that the exposition building often went unused for significant periods of time. Peck, always interested in music, decided that it might be possible to establish a summer festival, which would be structured around Theodore Thomas, who was becoming America's most famous conductor.[36]

Thomas had come to Chicago in 1869, and he repeatedly performed there from 1872 to 1877. In 1877, he held his concerts in the Inter-State Exposition Building and returned there the following year. Thomas's early concerts, though successful in terms of audience attendance, were marred by the acoustical limitations of the building.[37]

Troubled by the liabilities of the structure for musical performance, Peck hired Dankmar Adler, noted architect-engineer, to modify the structure. In many ways, Adler's plan called for the construction of a figurative wooden ship within an iron-and-glass bottle. Adler altered a portion of the building into a space more conducive to serious music, designing a six-thousand-seat wooden hall within the exposition building. Situated in the north end of the building, the new auditorium was a vast improvement acoustically. In 1885, with Adler's modifications in place, Peck expanded the musical offerings by inaugurating the first Chicago Grand Opera Festival, which drew approximately 110,000 patrons during its two-week run.[38]

Peck founded the opera festival, in part, to make opera available to the populace as well as to attract excellent performers. The opening-night opera of its inaugural season was Rossini's *Semiramide* starring Adelina Patti. Remarkably, the festival staged eleven operas in just over two weeks, including Giacomo Meyerbeer's *Grand Opera l'Africaine*, Giuseppe Verdi's *Aida*, and Gaetano Donizetti's *Lucia di Lammermoor*.[39] The strain on the operatic cast to sing each of these performances must have been considerable. After these performances were completed, the city inspected Adler's modifications within the exhibition building, declared them a fire hazard, and ordered the alterations removed. Despite that setback, the success of the event had proven that there was interest in and a market for fine music in Chicago.

Thomas made such a favorable impression that in 1891, he was named the conductor of the newly founded Chicago Symphony Orchestra, but his tenure in Chicago was often tempestuous. The Chicago Symphony Orchestra was in need of a suitable permanent home, so Peck, in his continued efforts to bring music to Chicago, hired Adler and Louis Sullivan. They would plan the Auditorium Building and Peck's Chicago Stock Exchange. The massive Auditorium Building would include an expansive theater and provide, in Peck's words, a "home for opera, symphony, dance, music festivals, and large social events as well as facilities for political conventions."[40] The Auditorium Building would host some of the cultural activities, especially musical offerings, that previously had been housed in the Inter-State Industrial Building. The exposition had a significant role in promoting industry, commerce, fine arts, and other activities within the city. The exposition building, just north at Adams and the eastern side of Michigan Avenue, influenced the construction of the Auditorium Building at Congress Street and Michigan and expanded culture in postfire Chicago.

Horticultural Arts and Natural History

Again reflecting the everything-under-one-roof nature of the Inter-State Exposition Building, in 1874, workers constructed a seven-thousand-square-foot conservatory that housed trees, shrubs, and flowers. By 1876, exposition organizers reported that the conservatory was doing well thanks to the South Park Commission and "the contributions of great interest and value from a private florist whose conservatories are rich in rare plants."[41] The conservatory illuminated the interest in landscaping and the market for horticulture goods.

For its part, the conservatory presented a little bit of Eden within Lake Park's landscape, which was not known for its lush vegetation and landscaping. As the exposition's secretary reported, "[I]t is true that this region is not as yet a 'Paradise of Flowers.' Chicago's climate is not the most favorable for out-of-door floriculture; but the artificial climate of a well-constructed and well-appointed conservatory is just as effective and as genial in this city as in Cincinnati or Philadelphia."[42] With the conservatory, the Inter-State Industrial Building became a year-round operation.

The same year the conservatory was added, the exhibition organizers, in partnership with the Academy of Sciences, created a department of natural history to display objects of both scientific and general interest. Founded in 1856, the Academy of Sciences was the oldest scientific institution in Chicago and opened its own exhibit building to the public in 1869. However, as a result of an economic depression that started in 1873, it lost its property in 1876, and its collections were placed in the Inter-State Exposition Building.[43]

This arrangement between the academy and the exposition proved to be successful as the latter could now boast that the new display "as a whole, has probably not been equaled on a similar occasion in this country, except by the Smithsonian at the (Philadelphia) Centennial." The academy's secretary asserted that "the effect of such public exhibitions, their educational value, and especially their influence in popularizing these interesting studies, can hardly be over-estimated, or too generally appreciated and acknowledged."[44]

The secretary of the exposition proposed that the inclusion of these goods at the exposition was somewhat unusual in that "scientific men" tended to have an aversion to exhibiting their specimens in such locales. He noted, "[N]o other portion of the Exposition was examined by the average visitor more attentively, or made a more lasting impression upon the student of nature, than the immense collections in this department of natural wonders, admirably arranged for either scientific inquiry or for the gratification of simple curiosity. Grand as the success of this effort was, however, there is reason to believe that the interest awakened will lead to better things in the same direction hereafter."[45] The inclusion of objects that were both entertaining and educational within the exposition attracted visitors.

Once again, the exposition's support for these endeavors was striking, as the displays could not be argued to serve the needs of advertisement. Rather, these scientific presentations provided entertainment as an enticement to patrons and performed an educational function as well.

As the case of the Academy of Science makes clear, the Inter-State Industrial Exposition Building was not only a place for display but also positioned a number of institutions to remain active in Chicago as they rebuilt from the fire and depression or grew from a fledgling interest. Only with the excitement over the World's Columbian Exposition was there another climate for institutions to gain new, permanent homes within the city's parks.

The inclusion of natural sciences at the exposition, like that of the fine arts and conservatory, served to bolster and support the cause of the sciences and humanities in Chicago. The exposition's inclusiveness reflects a tendency in middle- and late-nineteenth-century America to combine aspects of what would later be termed high and low culture. But by the 1890s, the division of high and low culture would increase in and segregate Chicago.[46]

Baseball in Lake Park

While the Inter-State Exposition Building remained central to the activities in Lake Park, another conspicuous commercial presence was that of organized baseball. Starting before the Great Chicago Fire of 1871 and continuing through much of the 1880s, owners brought their professional baseball teams to compete in Lake Park. The proximity to public transportation and to the business center, as well as the availability of open ground, had again made Lake Park a good location.

In 1871, baseball entrepreneurs opened the Union baseball grounds on the north end of Lake Park. The Union baseball grounds had a capacity of seven thousand and provided a home for the "National Association Chicago White Stockings from May 8 to September 29, 1871."[47] The fire in October 1871 displaced baseball from Lake Park. Although short-lived, the baseball grounds on the lakefront demonstrated the possibilities of the site for professional sports.

Baseball returned to Lake Park with Lake Front Park I, built in 1878, and Lake Front Park II in 1883. The National League Chicago White Stockings, who played in the park from May 14, 1878, to September 30, 1882, called the wooden Lake Front Park I home. The advantage of the site remained its central location and accessibility to various forms of transportation, but the field conditions were less than ideal. As one account relates, "the infield was bumpy and uneven, and littered with stones, boulders, ashes, glass, and broken bottles."[48] This ball park served its purpose, but the later park would be more memorable.

The Chicago White Stockings played in the new ballpark, Lake Front Park II, for two seasons, from May 5, 1883, to October 11, 1884. As one contemporary source remarked, the park was "indisputably the finest in the world in respect of seating accommodations and conveniences." Imagine walking toward a ball park in which "[o]verlooking the main entrance is a handsomely ornamented pagoda, built for a band stand, and to be occupied by the First Cavalry Band, which was based out of a nearby Armory, throughout the season. Surmounting the grand stand is a row of eighteen private boxes, cozily draped with curtains to keep out wind and sun, and furnished with comfortable arm-chairs. By the use of the telephone and gong President [Albert G.] Spalding [of the White Stockings team] can conduct all the preliminary details of the game without leaving his private box." The new ball park with a capacity of ten thousand was a showplace.[49] In many ways, it must have been an impressive site, with the cool breezes on the lake combined with the bustle of the train yards on Chicago's lakefront.

The Chicago White Stockings were worthy of their new lakefront park. The team won National League pennants in 1880, 1881, 1882, 1885, and 1886. In 1880, the team had a .798 winning percentage, which is the highest in major-league history. Ned Williamson, who anchored these championship teams at third base, spent eleven years with Chicago and led the National League with twenty-seven home runs in 1884. In that year, Williamson took advantage of a change in the ground rules in his home park. The field had the shortest dimensions down the lines of any major league park in the history of the game, with left field at 180 feet and right field at 196. Williamson's numbers resulted from a change in the park's rules so that a ball hit into the left-field stands in 1884 was a home run, whereas the year before it had counted as a double.[50]

An additional benefit of the lakefront location was its proximity to the rising urban middle class. Baseball in the 1870s and 1880s was struggling for legitimacy, and one of the major figures dedicated to improving the status of baseball in these years was Albert G. Spalding. As manager, and later president, of the Chicago White Stockings from 1876 to 1891, he was greatly involved with both of the Lake Front Parks. By his considerable efforts, he made the team one of the most prosperous on the field and in the box office. He was also responsible for making baseball an acceptable leisure activity for the new rising middle class.[51]

Spalding used Lake Park to attract the middle class to baseball. For example, the White Stockings did not play on Sundays. Though Chicago at the time was brimming with immigrants, some believed that the rising middle class might turn on the team if they played on the Christian day of rest.[52] In addition, the somewhat-refined atmosphere created at Lake Front Park II with its bandstand, private boxes, and other appointments catered to the tastes of the middle class that Spalding strove to attract.

On June 24, 1884, the federal government, basing its decision on the park's original designation as free of buildings, granted an injunction banning the team from playing on the site because they were a commercial venture, and by 1885, the Chicago White Stockings had vacated the location.[53] The White Stockings moved out to the city's West Side to the Congress Street Park, even though the park was only two years old. With this move, the history of major league baseball on the lakefront came to a close.

Civic Culture in Lake Park

With the construction of the Inter-State Exposition Building, the Board of Public Works shifted the use of Lake Park for most of the last quarter of the nineteenth century. The board allowed the building to become a long-term occupant and eventually permitted other buildings to become features of the park. The use of the building for national political conventions and the construction of armories reflected an expanded civic function for Lake Park and signaled a broader civic culture and a move toward more permanent structures in the park.

Lake Park had already hosted the Democratic Convention in 1864, and the exposition building would carry on this tradition by hosting a number of other conventions. Local committees no longer needed to construct temporary structures, and national committees favored Chicago because of its geographically central location and its role as a rail hub. Conventioneers enjoyed the site, as delegates could go to a major metropolis with a range of hotels, eateries, and entertainment.

In 1880, the National Republican Party chose the exposition building for its convention. The Republicans met June 2–8, and although there was a faction of the party that wanted to run Ulysses S. Grant for a third term, the party ultimately chose a ticket with James A. Garfield as the presidential candidate and Chester Alan Arthur as the vice presidential candidate. The southern end of the exposition building was decorated for the convention, with many flags that hung from the rafters and balconies and a great number of portraits including those of George Washington, Abraham Lincoln, and other notable party leaders.[54]

The expanded purpose of the hall was noted in its annual report of 1879, in which the structure was seen as continuing to be "dedicated to public uses, and built for the very purpose of assembling large crowds of our citizens within its walls." John P. Reynolds, secretary of the exposition, commented, "[T]he very existence of such a building in this city, so admirably adapted to these [nominating conventions] and similar uses requiring immense capacity, is, of itself, a constant suggestion in favor of selecting Chicago on such occasions in preference to other cities not so fortunately provided."[55] The Inter-State Industrial Exposition's visionary leadership had provided a convention center for the city as well as a place for the city to display its wares.

Also in 1880, following the close of the Republican convention, the Greenbackers, a collection of farm and labor organizations, held their national convention in the Inter-State Building on June 9. The Greenbackers nominated James B. Weaver of Iowa for president and Barzillai J. Chambers of Texas as his running mate.[56]

In 1884, both the Republicans and Democrats held their conventions in the exposition hall. The Republicans met June 3–6 and nominated James Gillespie Blaine as the presidential nominee and Logan, Illinois' favorite son, as his running mate. Then, the Democrats met July 8–11 and nominated Grover Cleveland and Thomas Andrews Hendricks. Both conventions filled the exposition building beyond capacity.[57]

At the time that the Inter-State Industrial Building began hosting national nominating conventions, the Board of Public Works allowed the Illinois National Guard to construct armory buildings in the park.[58] Although largely disbanded after the Civil War, Illinois National Guard units were resurgent by the late 1870s and were raising money to build their own armories. The voluntary groups spent a great deal of their time "training for war, hosting balls and lectures, performing in amateur theatricals, marching in military parades, fundraising, and lobbying for larger budgets and improved militia legislation at the state and federal levels."[59] These units reflected both the increased technical training and renewed militarism in the United States.

In Chicago, the First Regiment of the Illinois National Guard was one of the most prosperous and influential units. The Board of Public Works allowed the regiment to build the First Brigade Staff and First Cavalry building on Michigan Avenue at the foot of Monroe Street in 1880. Chicagoans popularly referred to this edifice as Battery D. Then, in 1882, it built the First Regiment of Infantry at 22 to 26 Jackson Street, which had arms and other equipment used for training and provided an area for the unit to gather.[60] The regiment used its buildings for a variety of functions, including commercial ventures and firehouses. The armory buildings extended the civic message of the park and served as a reminder of order in the city center during a time that was marked by urban unrest. Units of the Illinois National Guard had been used to break strikes in this era.[61] Ultimately, the city ordered both armories demolished in March 1898, which cleared the structures from Lake Park.[62]

The commercialization of Lake Park is ironic given that Chicago had set a course that would make it a national leader in urban parks by the late nineteenth century. With the creation of the Lincoln, West, and South Park Commissions, city government leaders had been remarkably proactive in securing parkland on the city's periphery. The other park districts hired national leaders in landscape design and architecture to draft their landscaping plans. The South Park Commission hired Frederick Law Olmsted and Calvert Vaux. The West Park Commission hired William Le Baron Jenney to draft its early designs, although this district became notable later for the landscape architecture of Danish immigrant Jens Jensen. These parks became national models, but Lake Park remained largely separate from these trends in urban landscaping and park design, with a focus instead on its abilities to serve civic and entertainment purposes.

Lake Park continued for the time being to be at the center of a debate between those who wanted the park to move away from material concerns and strive for higher goals and those who wanted the park to continue to serve its mixed (and contradictory) purposes for the city. The southern end of Lake Park offered the opportunity for moral uplift, whereas the northern part of the park was occupied by buildings: the Inter-State Industrial Building, a professional baseball field, and armories.

In the late nineteenth century, many people believed that the parks, art, and music had the power to elevate individuals beyond their everyday concerns. Other Chicago city parks were designed to fully embrace this notion, but Lake Park was not. And the next undertaking for the park would use its unique role in the city.

With the successful precedent of the Inter-State Industrial Building, Chicago's business and political leaders eagerly vied with other major cities to host the World's Columbian Exposition of 1892, the celebration of the four hundredth anniversary of Columbus's voyage to "the new world." The city pulled out all of the stops to eventually beat out New York for the privilege of hosting the exposition. By doing so, the young City of Chicago could announce to the world that it had arrived. This most American of cities also demonstrated that in the midst of all of its capital accumulation, it possessed refinement and culture. Once again, Lake Park would be at the center of the swirl of activity surrounding this exposition.

3

The World's Columbian Exposition and
Chicago's Cultural Flowering

Already the Midwest's industrial giant and transportation center, Chicago came to embody the new American city during the 1890s. Although proud of their achievements in business, some of Chicago's elite resented their city's image as a sprawling, brawling, precocious youngster devoid of civilized manners and the "higher tone." Certainly, these men had amassed great fortunes, but they contended that they had also brought civilization to the prairie.[1] How better to prove Chicago's sophistication than to host the World's Columbian Exposition? And where better to hold the grand exposition than in Lake Park?

Although the White City, the popular name for the World's Columbian Exposition, ultimately rose in Jackson Park, exposition directors selected Lake Park as the site for the World's Congress Auxiliary, where an international gathering of scholars exhibited the best of the century's intellectual fare. In this way, as in many others, the exposition announced Chicago's coming-of-age and strengthened the city's development in the arts and sciences while further establishing Lake Park as the setting for the city's cultural gems.

Planning the World's Columbian Exposition

The Columbian Exposition celebrated the four hundredth anniversary of Christopher Columbus's voyage. Earlier expositions had also marked important anniversaries. In 1876, Philadelphia hosted the nation's centennial exposition. In 1889, the Great Paris Internationale drew great numbers of people to commemorate the one-hundred-year anniversary of the storming of the Bastille and the ensuing French Revolution. The Internationale had changed the game by constructing the Eiffel Tower in marking the celebration. Thereafter, any city that hosted an exposition would have to match or exceed that architectural achievement.

By the mid-1880s, a number of eastern cities, including New York and Washington, D.C., expressed interest in hosting the event, while in the Midwest, Saint Louis, Cincinnati, and Chicago all clamored for the exposition. Each city advanced its cause on the editorial pages of its local newspapers, promoting its special advantages and deprecating the pretensions of its rivals.[2]

In early 1889, the U.S. Congress began evaluating sites for the World's Columbian Exposition. By July, both New York and Chicago had gathered significant popular and financial support. As the deadline to select a site drew near, the Chicago committee pressed its case by pledging $10 million. Its financial commitment may have sealed its proposal, and the U.S. Senate awarded Chicago the World's Fair.[3] Part of what tipped the scales in Chicago's favor was its status as the second American city, with a population of a million inhabitants, and as the leading metropolis of the Midwest. What better place to celebrate the New World than in the most American of cities in the United States? The U.S. Congress, on February 25, 1890, awarded Chicago rights to host the World's Columbian Exposition of 1892–93.

A great deal of work awaited the World's Columbian Exposition board of directors, called the Directory. They assembled only three years prior to the proposed date for the opening of the fair. The Directory needed to work quickly to select a location, secure financial backing, draw up plans, and complete construction. To begin, it charged the Committee on Grounds and Buildings with the responsibility of evaluating possible locations.

As early as 1885, while Chicago was still vying for the honor of hosting the exposition, real-estate developer Telford Burnham (not related to renowned architect Daniel H. Burnham) and James F. Gookins, a former artist-correspondent for *Harper's Weekly*, advocated Lake Park as the fairgrounds.[4]

They argued that Lake Park could be the location if the park was "widened to the dock line established by the Government engineers," and the space would thus "afford ample room in the very heart of the city!" The cost of construction would be a good investment, the pair noted, because any improvements made to the park for the exposition would be of permanent benefit to the city: "The 'Lake Front' is emphatically the *people's site for the Fair*. They own it, and by its selection and permanent improvement they will derive the greatest benefits, both at the time of the Fair and for ages after." Additionally, Burnham and Gookins pointed out that the site allowed for myriad possibilities, such as a naval pageant, because of the park's proximity to Lake Michigan.[5]

To secure Chicago's bid, Burnham and Gookins presented their recommendations in a clearly articulated plan in Washington, D.C., to civic leaders. They later published their proposal again in a number of Chicago's papers on August 10, 1888, and revised and republished their plan in 1889.[6] In an effort to persuade fellow Chicagoans, the two promised that building the exposition in Lake Park would lead to "the establishment in the center of our city of a great ornamental district, made beautiful and attractive by nature and art, and devoted to public instruction, entertainment, and elevation—a district which would, with the noble structures that must gather about it, become the joy and pride of our people!"[7] To bring visitors and residents to the fairground, Burnham and Gookins additionally proposed the construction of a Grand Union Depot in Lake Park.[8]

Burnham and Gookins were not alone in the campaign for Lake Park. Other proponents also cited the proximity of the railroads and other, local means of transportation as well as the easy access provided to major hotels. In addition, advocates asserted that the site was set adjacent to Chicago's best natural feature, Lake Michigan. Although they conceded that the park's dimensions—a mere 310 feet by 5,830 feet—posed a problem, they argued that landfill could be used beyond the Illinois Central's railroad tracks to the dock line set by the U.S. Coast Survey.[9] Once the landfill was completed, approximately two hundred acres would be made available. Finally, like Burnham and Gookins, supporters of the lakefront plan touted the long-term benefits that the creation of supplementary land could bring to the city. Cultural institutions and an expansive park space near the city center would be the legacy of the Columbian Exposition.

The World's Columbian Exposition Directory realized the Lake Park site held limitations as well as promise. Time was short, and modifications would be costly, so the Directory continued to search for a more suitable site. In addition to the expense and time that would be required for the landfill project, Lake Park also threatened a complex legal tangle. The City of Chicago, the federal government, and the Illinois Central Railroad all claimed the submerged lands offshore from Lake Park. The War Department had a mandate to maintain the harbor for traffic, and it correctly noted that Chicago's harbor would no longer be navigable if the project were carried out. The Illinois Central insisted that it held the right-of-way on the lakefront and owned an extensive area of the submerged land. Accordingly, they contested the landfill plan because it would have required the relocation of tracks.[10] Furthermore, had the landfill project been feasible, Lake Park could have provided only one-half of the estimated four hundred acres required for the exposition. As a preliminary solution, the Directory voted on July 1, 1890, to use Lake Park as the primary location for the exposition and Jackson Park on the far south side of Chicago as an auxiliary site.[11]

In continuing negotiations, James W. Ellsworth, a member of the exposition's board of directors and president of the South Park Commission, lobbied hard for Jackson Park. Ellsworth apparently saw the exposition as an opportunity to landscape an undeveloped section of the South Park Commission's land. He then persuaded President Lyman Gage of the Chicago Exposition Company that Olmsted and his assistant Henry Sargent Codman should advise on the site of the exposition. Olmsted was familiar with the site, as he had visited the South Park Commission's holdings before the Great Chicago Fire. In early August 1890, Olmsted and Codman began their evaluation of Jackson Park. They concluded that with a great deal of work, Jackson Park could be the site for the exposition. The Directory asserted that a new site must accommodate the entire exposition and requested that the South Park Commissioners make Washington Park and the Midway Plaisance, which were adjacent to Jackson Park, available for the exposition as well.[12]

Although the Committee of Grounds and Buildings evaluated a number of sites, driven by financial concerns and time limitations, the Directory moved to select Jackson Park and the Midway Plaisance as the primary sites for the exposition. The committee then recommended that Olmsted and company serve as consulting landscape architects, with Abram Gottlieb as consulting engineer and Daniel Burnham and John Wellborn Root as consulting architects. Lake Park was out, until it resurfaced as the potential site of auxiliary events associated with the Columbian Exposition.

The Rise of the Art Institute on the Lakefront

With the exposition, the city had the chance to demonstrate its high level of cultural refinement as the leading American city. Since earlier expositions and fairs had set the precedent of constructing permanent structures as memorials to their events, this was an opportunity for Chicago to push forward a cultural claim that would last beyond the exposition. It had been done before by other cities. After the 1876 Centennial Fair, Philadelphians built a home for their arts museum. Inspired by Philadelphia, civic-minded New Yorkers prompted the city to construct the Metropolitan Museum of Art in Central Park.[13] Well aware of these successes, the Art Institute board members positioned themselves to benefit from the Columbian Exposition by lobbying for a new lakefront museum. The organization hoped that the new location would heighten its institutional profile in the city, attracting private and public donations to its permanent collections.

The Art Institute of Chicago enjoyed a meteoric rise from its inception on Michigan Avenue in 1882 through its relocation to Lake Park in 1893. The earliest history of the Art Institute of Chicago goes back to 1866, when instructors offered art classes in Chicago. These teachers soon organized themselves into the Chicago Academy of Design. In an attempt to put itself on better financial footing, the academy added businessmen to its board in 1878. The new board, however, was soon torn by differences related to the operation of the academy.[14]

In 1879, many of the business leaders split from the organization to form the Chicago Academy of Fine Arts, which changed its name to the Art Institute of Chicago in 1882. The old Chicago Academy of Design continued to struggle and ultimately ceased operation in 1882. The newly created Art Institute organized itself for "the founding and maintenance of schools of art and design, the formation and exhibition of collections of objects of art, and the cultivation and extension of the arts of design by any appropriate means."[15] This early mission statement has remained at the core of the Art Institute's activities to the present day.

From 1879 to 1882, the Art Institute's predecessor rented rooms on the southwest corner of State and Monroe Streets to provide art classes and space for exhibitions. In 1882, the Art Institute bought real estate, which included a three-story building, on the corner of Michigan Avenue and Van Buren Street for $45,000. The board of directors chose the lakeshore location because of its proximity to the city center in a locale deemed ideal for a museum to attract patrons and visitors. That same year, the Art Institute hired the architectural firm of Burnham and Root to design an addition to its structure. Until this new structure was built, the school's classes met in the Illinois State Armory building in Lake Park near the site of the Art Institute's ultimate destination. With this first purchase, the Art Institute of Chicago entered into a significant building program.[16] The Art Institute's leadership included banker and highly influential early president Charles Hutchinson and board members and businessmen George M. Pullman and Marshall Field. The addition was soon completed at a cost of around $22,000.

The Art Institute's new building formally opened on January 13, 1883. The space allowed for display of a more extensive collection, including paintings, marbles, and casts, which were being obtained through purchase and donation. By the mid-1880s, the Art Institute was on its way to developing a respectable permanent collection.

From its inception, the Art Institute operated an art school and museum, which provided a site to exhibit art year-round. The trustees reported in 1883–84 that the school had been in operation for four years, had 359 students, and had been self-supporting for two of those years. Thus, from the start, the organization balanced its functions as museum and instructional academy.[17]

By 1887, Burnham and Root had completed the brown Romanesque building for the Art Institute. Situated on the southwest corner of Michigan Avenue and Van Buren Street, the structure seemed suitable for the Art Institute's ever-increasing needs. In its annual report, the secretary of the Art Institute addressed the centrality of the location: "Proximity to the heart of the city is an overwhelming recommendation in the eyes of the Trustees, for no object is more distinctly entertained by them than the benefit of the great masses of the people, to whom convenience of access is essential."

The report continued, "[I]n several American cities art has, as it were, set itself apart, and the Art Museum has been placed in a remote park, where comparatively few of the people can visit it. We have preferred a central situation, although it necessitates a contracted site, where the building must be high, and deprives us of all hope of public gift of land." Even though the Art Institute was not located in Lake Park, by being adjacent to it, it did share in its central location. The Art Institute also had a large number of renters, which implies that the need for space was probably not the prime reason for the building's spectacular physical expansion in this period.[18]

In 1889, the Art Institute board, working with architects, conceived and oversaw the construction of the new structure just to the south of its existing complex. It also continued to add onto its new building. The newest structure crowned a grand decade of facility improvement, and the Art Institute now enjoyed a complex that could serve it at least through the next decade.

The Art Institute and the Exposition's Auxiliary in Lake Park

In October 1890, the Commercial Club of Chicago, an association of sixty Chicago business leaders, convened to consider the future of art galleries and museums in Chicago with an eye to the upcoming exposition and selected a committee to meet with the exposition's directors. The committee proposed a collaborative effort with the exposition to establish a permanent art gallery and museum. It stressed the benefit to the community of such an arrangement.[19]

In that same month, the executive committee of the Art Institute empowered its president to discuss a permanent art museum with the officers of the Chicago Public Library and the World's Columbian Exposition. Although they had just completed a significant building campaign, the Art Institute's board members remained ambitious. If a new structure was to be built, it would first be utilized by the exposition. Then, according to these preliminary discussions, the library and the Art Institute would share the permanent building.[20] Soon, the Directory of the exposition and the Art Institute reached a tentative agreement that excluded the library, which in the years after the exposition, built its own new structure in Dearborn Park, just west of Lake Park at Randolph Street.

Provisionally, both the exposition and the Art Institute would pay for the new structure. Because of the Directory's ultimate decision to use Jackson Park and its long-standing preference to consolidate events at a single site, it wanted to place the Arts Building there. The board of the Art Institute, located for almost a decade on Michigan Avenue, insisted that it had no intention of moving away from the city center. The two parties reached a compromise when the Directory agreed to include a supplementary program of public lectures, called the World's Congress Auxiliary, which would take place in Lake Park.[21]

Chicago lawyer Charles C. Bonney drew on the model of the World Congresses after the meetings held in Paris in 1889. "[T]he crowning glory of the World's Fair should not be the exhibit . . . of the material triumphs, industrial achievements, and mechanical victories of man, however magnificent that display may be," he argued. "Something still higher and nobler is demanded by the enlightened and progressive spirit of the present age. . . . [T]he world of government, jurisprudence, finance, science, literature, education, and religion should be represented." Although "sanctioned and approved" by the exposition, the Congresses would largely operate autonomously, under the leadership of Bonney himself. After the exposition, the board of the Art Institute would take possession of the building, securing its permanent home on the lakefront.[22]

This plan, though inspired, did not take into account the Inter-State Industrial Building, which had been in Lake Park since 1873. The industrial building's directors had improved and added to the massive structure over the years, but some argued that it had seen its best days and was impeding progress, such as the widening of Michigan Avenue. In a spirit of cooperation, the directors of the Inter-State Exposition offered their massive building for the proposed World Congresses and pledged to raise $100,000 toward the cost of a new art building. The board of the Art Institute refused a joint venture. It seemed interested in the Inter-State Exposition's location but not the building or in working with another partner.[23]

Prompted by the World's Columbian Exposition's Directory and the Art Institute's plans for expansion, the City of Chicago passed an ordinance in March 1891 permitting the construction of a permanent structure on the lakefront at Adams Street. In turn, on May 8, 1891, the World's Columbian Exposition's board of directors passed an act supporting the construction of a permanent structure on the lakefront for use of, first, the World's Congresses and then the Art Institute. From this, the World's Columbian Exposition, the World's Congresses, and the Art Institute of Chicago would all benefit. This plan, however, did not include any tangible benefit for the Inter-State Industrial Exposition, which still owned and operated its building in Lake Park.[24]

In July 1891, the city ordered the demolition of the Inter-State Building, but the exposition company obtained an injunction preserving it. Again, in September 1891, the City Council of Chicago, at the bidding of Alderman Thomas Gahan, chairman of the Committee on Wharves and Public Grounds, advanced a resolution calling for the demolition of the old exposition building. This time, the exposition company stated that it would comply with the resolution. This decision provided a prime location for the World's Columbian Exposition and the Art Institute to collaborate on the construction of a new, permanent structure.[25]

Moving quickly to secure the lakefront location, the Art Institute employed the New York architectural firm of Shepley, Rutan, and Coolidge to design its new structure, which would also serve as a memorial to the World's Columbian Exposition. The building committee of the Art Institute and the Committee on Grounds and Buildings of the World's Fair accepted the neoclassical design. The Art Institute board selected Hutchinson and M. A. Ryerson to secure funding for the project, which the sale of the Art Institute's Michigan Avenue property to the Chicago Club for $425,000 would partially fund.[26]

Once again, the Art Institute met opposition, this time in the form of disagreement over the acceptability of permanent construction in Lake Park. Although the Inter-State Industrial Building at Adams Street and Michigan Avenue was conceived as a temporary structure, it had remained standing from 1873 until 1892. Consequently, some individuals had challenged the construction of structures in Lake Park. In August 1889, for example, Warren F. Leland and Sarah E. Daggett, adjoining property owners to Lake Park, voiced their opposition to the proposed erection of an electric powerhouse south of the Inter-State Industrial Building (see fig.

Figure 3.1. The Leland Hotel and Lake Park, 1880s. (ICHi-04450) Chicago History Museum.

3.1, which shows the Leland Hotel and a small part of the park). The two filed a bill for the purpose of enjoining the city and the exposition company from allowing the addition. Judge Murray Floyd Tuley delivered a broad injunction against the powerhouse. Leland and Daggett renewed their opposition when they learned of plans for the construction of the permanent Art Institute building and that "an ordinance had been passed for the occupation of 400 feet opposite Adams Street for the permanent Art Institute building."[27]

Leland and Daggett were not the only ones to file court cases against activities in the park. In 1887, Aaron Montgomery Ward had become a property owner on Michigan Avenue facing Lake Park. Ward would file the first of his court cases in 1890. His first case pressed the city to stop construction of structures in the park and to uphold the land's original designation.[28] This first case was eventually decided in his favor in 1896.

On May 31, 1892, Leland and Daggett, who now wanted to bar all structures on the lakefront, obtained an injunction to halt construction of the new Art Institute building, which was already behind schedule. Workers had only partially demolished the old Inter-State Exposition Building and were starting to dig the foundation for the new edifice. For a time, the World's Congresses in Lake Park seemed in jeopardy because it would have proven difficult to find an alternate location at such a late date. The situation was direr for the Art Institute, as it stood to lose the money promised by the World's Columbian Exposition for the construction, and it had already sold its former building. The outraged editors of the *Chicago Tribune* accused Leland and Daggett of trying to preserve Lake Park as "a tramps' paradise rather than the site of a stately art building. There is no accounting for tastes."[29]

After Leland and Daggett halted construction, Lake Park quickly became the very eyesore they had tried to prevent. Water filling the excavation site stagnated and created a "sickening stench," which some feared could engender disease. In addition, "the landscape was sadly marred by a high board fence over the surface of which glaring advertisements of beer, tobacco, patent medicines, theaters, circuses, corner lots, and vaudeville companies have been spread."[30] The appalling state of Lake Park made a mockery of those who sought to elevate the city through a stately building dedicated to high cultural pursuits. Others, however, wanted to keep the park free of buildings.

On June 23, 1892, the court dismissed the injunction. The judge ruled that the Illinois legislature in 1890 had granted Chicago the right to erect structures associated with the Columbian exposition on the lakefront and to preserve some of them. The Congresses and the Art Institute could continue with their original plans. Construction resumed immediately.[31]

While controversy on the lakefront raged, planners diligently pushed forward with the World's Congress program. The U.S. Senate recognized the World's Congress Auxiliary on May 25, 1892, just as it had earlier acknowledged the World's Columbian Exposition. In June, the Department of State called on the diplomatic and consular officers of the United States to solicit foreign governments to join in the congresses. Finally, with the dedication of the World's Columbian Exposition in the Chicago Auditorium building, on October 21, 1892, the World's Congress was instated as well.[32] Given all of the site discussion, it seems ironic that the dedication occurred directly across from Lake Park.

The 1892 Democratic National Convention

In the summer of 1892, in the midst of preparations for the World's Columbian Exposition, the Democratic National Committee chose Chicago as the site of its convention, anticipating the use of the auditorium where the 1888 Republican National Convention had been held. The managers of the auditorium, however, notified the convention organizers that the state-of-the-art structure would not be available. As the convention was already slated for Chicago, local Democrats struggled to come up with suitable alternative sites.[33]

Past conventions had been held in the Inter-State Industrial Building, but demolition had removed that choice. As a result, the Democratic National Committee pressed Lake Park into service and returned to the old practice of constructing a "Wigwam" for its meeting, building a temporary structure in Lake Park at Michigan Avenue between Madison and Washington Streets. The Democratic Committee, which had utilized a temporary structure in Lake Park for the 1864 convention, erected another such building for an approximate cost of $30,000.[34]

The Wigwam was a large rectangular pine shed with a canvas roof, a design that allowed for circulation of air and some natural light. Unfortunately, on June 13, a storm, which one account described as a "squall, or hurricane rather, swept over the city."[35] The strong winds pulled the canvas from the top of the structure and shredded it, but the rest of the wooden structure stood up against the tempest.

Workers had just a week to repair the damage, and they fixed the structure by installing a flat roof with skylights. Although not as aesthetically pleasing as the original structure, the refurbished building was practical. More important, the Wigwam was ready for the convening of the Sixteenth Democratic National Convention on June 21, 1892. Hempstead Washburne, the Republican mayor of Chicago, welcomed the Democratic delegates to the city. While the citizens did all they could to accommodate the delegates and other interested parties, the weather did not cooperate. Usually, the lakefront is cooler than the inland areas during the summer, but in June 1892, this advantage did not make much difference. Just as bad weather had hampered construction, during the convention, "rain, humidity, and rain was the lot of the delegates in Chicago, with a short day of very hot sun."[36] As it turned out, the roofing, which had been hurriedly applied, did not keep the elements out.

One reporter described the interior during the convention: "[T]he Wigwam was like the hot room of a Turkish bath that day [Wednesday]; in the night the parallel was continued, and the unruly mob of spectators and the helpless delegates were drenched by the shower-bath from the roof. Umbrellas were even necessary inside the building, and the pilgrims to the National Democratic convention of 1892 blessed the genius who devised the skeleton rain-protector. But beyond the umbrella, there were very few blessings wasted during that exciting session."[37] The experienced delegates must have longed for the comforts offered by the auditorium. Despite the lack of physical comfort, those in attendance carried on with the work of selecting a presidential nominee.

The convention also received criticism for the way Chicago's ward bosses packed the hall with party faithful, which had long been a tactic at conventions. One journalist disapprovingly wrote: "[P]acked conventions have repeatedly done things of which the party had reason to be ashamed. Candidates have been nominated against the expressed wishes of State conventions and even the delegates themselves. The boisterous applause and vindictive hisses of thousands exert an influence on men which must not be regarded too lightly." The journalist had hoped that the Wigwam could point the way toward future reform. In the end, however, the convention "mob" nominated former president Grover Cleveland of New York for president and Adlai Ewing Stevenson of Illinois, a favorite son, for vice president to run against President Benjamin Harrison.[38]

With the 1892 convention, some of the nineteenth-century uses of Lake Park continued, even while Chicagoans were discussing future possibilities for the park. The park's most important attribute remained its existence as open space bordering the city center. In a political context, the park provided an area for formal and informal interaction, a place for democracy. The area also served as overflow space for the central city. If permanent structures located elsewhere could not accommodate a civic event, then the lakefront could be imposed upon. Consequently, Lake Park continued to be a significant part of the Chicago experience for many visitors.

Gateway to the World's Columbian Exposition

In addition to the World's Congresses, Lake Park served as an official gateway to the World's Columbian Exposition in Jackson Park. In keeping with the theme of the exposition, Chicago's Board of Public Works erected a sculpture of Christopher Columbus by Howard Kretchmar in Lake Park. Approximately two thousand people gathered on April 25, 1893, to watch Mayor Carter Harrison; George R. Davis, director-general of the exposition; and Ferdinand W. Peck, president of the exposition, along with other officials, unveil the twenty-foot figure set on a thirty-foot granite pedestal, draped with the flags of Spain and the United States. "[T]he discoverer stands in an attitude of expectancy and strength, a half smile on his face as if of triumph and hope, long deferred, realized," one journalist reported. "There is no suggestion of the sailor about him, but the artist meant to typify not only Columbus the man, but the abstract ideas of discovery as well, an idealized Eureka, in bronze."[39] The icon of discovery seemed appropriate for Lake Park, the intended site of the World Congresses where scholars would gather to discuss the latest advances in their respective fields.

Lake Park also served as a gateway to the main exposition, thanks to the Illinois Central (IC) Railroad's new depot at Park Row at Michigan Avenue. Once Jackson Park, near the IC's right of way, had been chosen as the site for the exposition, the company initiated a number of improvements in Chicago. One of these was the multi-million-dollar passenger depot near Lake Park to replace the fifty-year-old South Water Street Station (see fig. 3.2). Designed by Bradford L. Gilbert of New York, the monumental station featured a clock tower and grand arches and doubled as the railroad's corporate headquarters. The IC managed to complete construction of the mammoth depot by the spring of 1893, just in time to transport the first visitors to the World's Columbian Exposition.[40]

Another set of improvements the railroad initiated was the construction of additional tracks, both on the street surface and elevated, between downtown and the fairground. The railroad also bought more than forty engines and three hundred passenger cars to accommodate the anticipated increase in rail traffic. The IC recouped its investment with the 40,116 special trains it ran during the fair, which carried 8,780,616 passengers.[41] Thus visitors and residents were welcomed to the city and to the exposition through Lake Park.

Within Lake Park, visitors could view the newly installed and impressive Rosenberg Fountain. In 1893, the Board of Public works had the elaborate drinking fountain positioned near Michigan Avenue and Eleventh Street, close to the new train station. Joseph Rosenberg had grown up south of the park at Michigan Avenue and Sixteenth Street and, in 1891, left a bequest in his will of $10,000 to erect a water fountain. He wanted it "to provide the thirsty with a drink." Rosenberg was the son of Jacob Rosenberg, an influential Chicagoan, and relation to the heir to the Rosenberg fortune. In Chicago, this remarkable family founded Michael Reese Hospital and Chicago's KAM Temple. As a young man, Rosenberg left Chicago and lived in San Francisco, but at the end of his life, he felt some sentiment for the city of his youth and left money for the fountain.[42]

As stipulated in Rosenberg's bequest, Franz Machtl of Munich received the fountain commission. The fountain is set on a circular base upon which stands a small Greek temple, topped with a statue of the Greek goddess Hebe offering a cup (see fig. 3.3). Originally designed to be nude, the statue is cast draped in a clinging diaphanous gown, reflecting the story of her dismissal after exposing herself while serving nectar to the guests at an Olympian festival; Greek vases often depict Hebe in a sleeveless gown. Hebe had been both the cupbearer to the gods and the goddess of youth, with the power to rejuvenate the aged. The memorial to Rosenberg was constructed near his childhood home; the classical image was fitting to his wishes.[43]

ILLINOIS CENTRAL DEPOT, CHICAGO

Figure 3.2. Illinois Central depot, Chicago, ca. 1919. The Rosenberg Fountain is in the foreground. Postcard no. 1311, V. O. Hammon, Chicago.

Figure 3.3. Rosenberg Fountain, featuring Hebe the cupbearer. Chicago Park District Special Collections.

Culture and Learning at Lake Park: The World's Congresses

With the World's Congresses set to begin in May 1893, workers built a stately new structure in Lake Park that would later become the Art Institute of Chicago. The architectural firm of Shepley, Rutan, and Coolidge designed the white, neoclassical building with Ionic and Corinthian columns incorporated into the façade, which harked back to the Grecian roots of Western civilization and coordinated with the neoclassical theme of the exposition's White City. Between the north and south wings stood two expansive audience rooms, each with seating for approximately three thousand persons with additional room for another thousand. The north side room, called "The Hall of Columbus," honored the inspiration for the exposition while the south side room, "The Hall of Washington," honored the first U.S. president. The architect's plan included another thirty-three smaller meeting rooms, each with a capacity of one hundred to seven hundred persons.

As a result of the delay imposed by Leland and Daggett's injunction, the building was not yet complete when the World's Congress Auxiliary moved in on May 1, 1893. Nonetheless, the scholarly meetings commenced on May 15 as planned in the midst of scurrying workers. Completed on July 1, the large structure met most of the demands of the Congresses, although it failed to offer sufficient space for the numbers who wished to attend the Women's Congresses, the Educational Congresses, and the Religious Congresses.[44]

Bonney officiated at the opening of the World's Congress Auxiliary. Bonney, who had proposed the idea of the congresses and served as its president, spoke of the promise of the endeavor that he believed would promote harmony and understanding among people. In his opening remarks, he alluded to the historical statues in the hall, referring to "Demosthenes and young Augustus, who shared the platform with them and spoke effectively in marble. Zeus, too, looked down from an advantageous position on the wall back of them, lending his countenance to the affair." Bonney expressed his hopes for the auxiliary: "A single week of years stands between us and the twentieth century. If the causes now in operation shall go on unchecked the world will witness in these seven years the crowning glories of more than seven centuries of human progress. With this hope I proclaim the formal opening of the World's Congresses of 1893."[45]

Bonney planned an extremely busy meeting schedule and had difficulty accommodating everyone who desired to take part. The congresses brought together a vast number of experts in a wide array of fields. During the summer and into the fall of 1893, approximately six thousand individuals delivered addresses to audiences totaling over seven hundred thousand attendees. The conferences and symposia dealt with issues of importance to 1890s society, with the guiding principles of the programs being in line with those of the whole exposition, "to promote understanding, intelligence and industry."[46]

Gathering experts in numerous fields, the congresses created an arena for an informed exchange of ideas on the most pressing topics of the era: women, medicine, surgery, temperance, commerce and finance, literature, education, religions, art, philosophy, and evolution. A number of notable speakers lectured including John Dewey, who presented "Reconciliation of Science and Philosophy," and historian Frederick Jackson Turner, who presented a paper entitled "The Significance of the Frontier in American History." Other noteworthy lecturers included Samuel Gompers, the first president of the American Federation of Labor, and Clarence Darrow, the noted lawyer. Among the many luminaries who frequented the meetings, the congresses accorded honorary status to King Oscar of Sweden and Norway, Lord Chief Justice Coleridge of England, Alfred Lord Tennyson, Professor Max Muller, and Dr. George Ebers of Germany.[47] These world leaders brought a stateliness to the proceedings, giving them credibility.

The congresses' executive committee controlled the meetings, asking speakers to address the audience only in their area of expertise in order to illuminate their field. The executive committee also insisted that orators limit themselves to their statements. Debating, making of resolutions, or other activities that could cause controversy would not be tolerated. In this way, the organizers sought to forestall unpleasant or potentially explosive confrontations over emotionally charged subjects.[48]

In addition to these general prescriptions, the congresses also circumscribed the role of women at the meetings. For example, the executive committee determined which sessions would be suitable for women to attend. The executive committee, however, did permit the creation of the Women's Branch of the World's Congress Auxiliary, for which Bertha Palmer served as president and, as vice president, Ellen Martin Henrotin, wife of Charles Henrotin and president of the General Federation of Women's Clubs of the United States.[49]

The women's auxiliary could act independently or in accord with the men's. In the context of the 1890s, relative to their time, the women at the Congresses enjoyed a fair degree of freedom, independence, and equality, which the executive board thought impossible without its safeguards. Despite these restrictions, women and issues of concern to them were given prominence, as the World's Congress of Representative Women was the first to be called to order. Lucy Stone, Susan B. Anthony, and Julia Ward Howe attended the first sessions, and they were joined by women from a wide range of classes, races, and ethnicities.[50] Within the limitation of action imposed on them, the concerns of many women were advanced at the meeting.

These meetings were open to all free of charge and maintained decorum despite the large numbers who thronged to the buildings. The congresses followed a protocol in which the invited participants and delegates were seated first.[51] Then the public, as space allowed, filled in the remaining seats. On the whole, those in attendance adhered to the rules of the congresses' organizers.

The congresses embodied the motto "Not Things, but Men," which put them in stark contrast to the material concerns of the activities in Jackson Park and especially the Midway Plaisance. The directors of the congresses viewed the meetings as a chance "to establish fraternal relations among the leaders of mankind; review the progress already achieved; state the living problems now awaiting solution, and suggest the means of further progress." In this light, the congresses engendered a spirit of purpose in the participants and attendees, and both groups were seemingly ennobled as a result of the affiliation.[52]

The best-attended congresses were those on women, but according to contemporary observers, the final month, devoted to the "World's Parliament of Religions," was the high point. Daniel Burnham, director of Works of the World's Columbian Exposition, for one, asserted that the Parliament of Religions would be the only thing remembered of the exposition in a thousand years. Harlow N. Higinbotham, who had become president of the World's Columbian Exposition Company in 1892, believed it to be the finest work of the whole exposition. So the two major organizers of the exposition, upon reflection, both asserted that the congresses were the most significant enterprise of the spectacle created in Chicago in 1893. In all, the parliament seemed to show that diverse Christian denominations could come together in peace.[53]

In his farewell address, Bonney emphasized the harmony that prevailed during the congresses: "The spirit of order, decorum, dignity, and peace has been sovereign during the sessions of these Congresses. This ruling spirit has so promptly rebuked any attempt to overstep the limits of propriety as to leave little occasion for presiding officers to exercise their authority; little occasion to guard seats reserved for delegates, or to insist upon tickets or badges of admissions."[54] Bonney commented that the congresses reflected civilized humanity.

The World Congresses served a transitional purpose in Lake Park. The new building served to elevate the park, which still lacked any significant landscaping. In contrast to the Democratic Convention's poorly constructed Wigwam, the massive neoclassical structure, future home of the Art Institute, both reflected the White City and designated the park as a space for high culture. Ultimately, the park would become connected with ideas and art rather than with the business and commerce that thrived on the other side of Michigan Avenue.

Chicago's Cultural Flowering

The World's Columbian Exposition marked a cultural turning point in Chicago. Prior to the exposition, the city could still be described as an emerging metropolis in America's hinterland. When it was chosen as the site of the exposition, many—particularly, resentful New Yorkers—doubted the "Windy City" could deliver a world-class event. Determined to silence all skeptics, Chicagoans showcased their city's industrial, commercial, and cultural achievements. As one contemporary journalist noted, "[I]t is pleasant that this epoch will date from Chicago—a city struggling up out of its material necessities and commercial and mercantile demands to those higher standards which make for light and beauty, the development of art and the increase of knowledge."[55] Implicit in this statement are the ideas that the exposition would increase the economic and cultural prosperity of the city and that Chicago stood to benefit greatly from the ensuing cultural awakening.

Simultaneously, the exposition brought Chicago's artists, scholars, and musicians into the greater national community. Not only did artists gather in Chicago but they also met local patrons who commissioned works. In this way, the new industrial elite, caught up in the spirit of the exposition, promoted cultural pursuits in Chicago. Artifacts from the exposition, for example, formed the basis of the Field Museum of Natural History and generated donations to the Art Institute of Chicago.[56] As a result, Chicago, long associated with meatpacking, commercial structures, and grain elevators, became known for its art museum, natural-history museum, and public libraries as well as the Chicago Symphony Orchestra (1890), the Chicago Historical Society (1892), and the Chicago Academy of Sciences (1893).

It is noteworthy that many of these institutions arose near or within Lake Park or the city's other parks. As the exposition's White City provided a model for what might be possible for a modern city, Lake Park demonstrated the natural link between urban parks and cultural institutions. Much has been made of the divide between the White City of the World's Columbian Exposition and the industrial city of Chicago. Parts of this idealized city would find a permanent place within the city, paving the way for the future of Lake Park and transforming Chicago's lakefront.

4

Making the White City Permanent

As John Coleman Adams, Protestant pastor and book author, observes in "What a Great City Might Be—A Lesson from the White City," the World's Columbian Exposition offered a model for the modern city on the eve of the twentieth century. Chicagoans set about envisioning their Midwestern industrial metropolis, drawing upon the expertise of urban planners, landscape designers, and architects who embraced the concept of the City Beautiful. Exemplified by the work of Frederick Law Olmsted, Daniel H. Burnham, and Edward H. Bennett, the City Beautiful featured large landscapes punctuated by imposing civic structures, glorifying the nation and suggesting social order.[1] These two ideals—the White City and the City Beautiful—merged in the proposals for the development of Lake Park and ultimately set out a plan for Chicago.

Why was there this focus on the lakefront, instead of on Chicago's downtown or City Hall? Plans for the World's Columbian Exposition had drawn attention to Lake Park's potential, and the agreement to build a structure in the park in which the world congresses would meet during the exposition and that the Art Institute would occupy afterward, represented a first step toward realizing that potential. Not only did Lake Park already belong to the city but it also was fresh ground as an ambitious landfill project had created much of its acreage. Here, the semblance of natural, open space would contrast with overcrowded tenements, dirty streets, and noisy packinghouses. This tumultuous urban environment had produced the Haymarket Square uprising of 1886, but, in contrast, a well-groomed park would provide a disciplined, healthful environment, symbolic of the social order, or so hoped the capitalist elite.[2] Equally important, Chicagoans envisioned Lake Park as their communal front yard, a space to put their values and achievements on display. As architect Burnham, who had been the director of works at the World's Columbian Exposition, declared, "Our self-respect before our neighbors and all nations and the world must be maintained and to this end we must . . . make inviting our front door yard."[3] To the casual observer, it looked as if it would be just a matter of time before a number of neoclassical buildings would be added to Lake Park. As a consensus grew within Chicago, Burnham set out an increasingly larger vision that soon included a boulevard to connect Lake Park and Jackson Park and expanded his vision into the Plan of Chicago (1909), which encompassed the entire city and, in the process, transformed its lakefront.

In the sweep of progress, one man vociferously opposed the seemingly inevitable development of the park. Aaron Montgomery Ward, Michigan Avenue property owner and mail-order magnate, opposed the development of Lake Park. In keeping Lake Park free of structures, Ward was both protecting his rights as a property owner and promoting his vision of the proper use and appearance of the park by maintaining its original designation as free and open land. From 1890 through 1910, Ward filed four court cases that derailed the grand plans for the park. In spite of Ward, advocates for the development of Lake Park carried forward with their efforts to build a new "White City" in Lake Park.

Constructing Cultural Icons

The World's Columbian Exposition had already left its stamp on Lake Park with the World's Congresses Auxiliary Building. As planned, at the close of the exposition the directors of the Art Institute of Chicago renovated and redecorated the building to create a massive museum. The new neoclassical facade facing Adams Street provided a fitting structure for conspicuous cultural display while its low, horizontal orientation contrasted with the skyscrapers of the Loop. Architects separated the building from the commercial center by placing a margin of eighty feet between the Art Institute and

Figure 4.1. Art Institute. Postcard no. 1478, V. O. Hammon, Chicago.

Michigan Avenue (see fig. 4.1). Visitors were required to ascend the building's formal stairs and move into the space of the building inside the park.

Remaining true to its original charter, the Art Institute provided for both the display of art and for education. As part of its mission, it also offered free admission on certain days of the week. By moving into Lake Park, the museum became a far more public and recognizable institution. At the same time, the Art Institute's board of trustees welcomed Chicago's mayor and comptroller as ex-officio members while the city agreed to excuse the Art Institute from property taxes on its new building.[4] These provisions served as a guide for the city's future relationships with other cultural institutions in its parks.

Eager to display their own beneficence in the impressive new building, many Chicagoans who had spent large sums of money on artwork in the late nineteenth century donated treasured pieces to the Art Institute. These donations equaled almost half of the cost of constructing the building itself. Although the Art Institute did not have a notable collection when it started to build its new edifice, it attracted one soon after it opened its doors on December 8, 1893.[5]

Mrs. Henry Field, wife of the brother of retail magnate Marshall Field, made one of the largest donations in memory of her husband. The Henry Field Memorial Collection composed of forty paintings was valued at $300,000. She also commissioned Edward Kemeys (1843–1907) to sculpt two bronze lions (see fig. 4.2). Seizing an opportunity for publicity, the Art

Institute placed the sculptures in front of the new building and staged an unveiling on May 10, 1894. According to one newspaper account of the ceremony, "the bronze lions that have for several days stood swathed in covers of dirty canvas were stripped of these unsightly coverings. Calcium lights had been turned on the two lords of the animal kingdom and these unusual sights attracted a good sized crowd. When all was ready a couple of institute employees seized the covers and quickly pulled them off the lions. The lights were then turned on and the magnificent works of art were shown up splendidly." The lions stand in two different poses, one on the prowl and the other in a defiant attitude. Chicagoans today treat them as symbols of the city.[6] Together, the city, the Art Institute, and Mrs. Field built a rich, permanent cultural institution in Lake Park. This spectacular new building also served to commemorate and conjure up some of the magic of the World's Columbian Exposition.

As the Art Institute was renovating its new building in November 1893, the city's civic leaders broke ground for a second cultural institution, the Chicago Public Library (CPL), at Michigan Avenue and Randolph Street. As with the Art Institute, the architectural firm of Shepley, Rutan, and Coolidge designed the neoclassical-styled library. The CPL agreed to share this massive building with the Grand Army of the Republic (GAR), the leading veterans' organization after the Civil War. The new structure would occupy the whole of Dearborn Park, another site set aside by the Illinois and Michigan Canal Commissioners as public land in the 1830s. As Daniel L. Shorey, ex-president of the library board, stated at the groundbreaking ceremony, "The founding of this library was the first of the great acts . . . to make our city a place attractive to people of taste, intelligence, and character." Together, the Art Institute of Chicago and the Chicago Public Library provided the cornerstones of what would become a stately park, punctuated with impressive cultural institutions.[7]

Proposals for the Development of Lake Park

With the close of the World's Columbian Exposition, a wide range of individuals put forth plans for the development of Lake Park. During the exposition in June 1893, Alderman Martin B. Madden introduced a preamble and order to the city council that called for the improvement of Lake Park. Noting that the Illinois Central Railroad divided the park, he recommended lowering the railroad tracks and filling the lake to 750 feet west of the government breakwater in order to increase the park's size. In November 1894, Madden repeated his call for the mayor and commissioner of public works to work closely with the Illinois Central and the drainage-canal contractors. In addition, Madden contended that the park should connect to the city's

Figure 4.2. Kemeys' lions at the Art Institute, ca. 1905. Joliet Area Historical Museum, Joliet, Illinois.

boulevard system. He predicted the eventual construction of "the great Lake Shore drive" along the waterfront linking Lake Park with Jackson Park and Jackson Boulevard. As the centerpiece of Lake Park, Madden advocated the "reproduction of the Court of Honor, which was the great feature of the World's Fair, and said to be the most enchanting dream any artist has ever conceived." Ferdinand W. Peck, the leading force behind the auditorium building, and James W. Ellsworth, president of the South Park District Board and a proponent of the World's Columbian Exposition, offered their support for Madden's proposal.[8]

Initially, local government bureaucrats entertaining Madden's proposal envisioned the park as a lakefront site for their own offices. In October 1894, Cook County proposed a new courthouse in Lake Park that at least one newspaper encouraged. The *Inland Architect* offered its prediction that Lake Park would soon provide additional land for governmental offices adjacent to the Loop.[9]

In addition to politicians, civic-minded businessmen in the Commercial Club of Chicago also envisioned Lake Park as a setting for the display of the city's cultural institutions. The club, which hosted monthly programs, wielded considerable influence because its members served as presidents of a number of business and cultural bodies. The club's interest in Lake Park dated to at least early 1890 when members discussed making the site a permanent home for the Art Institute. Following the World's Columbian Exposition, the Commercial Club devoted itself to creating a comprehensive plan for the improvement of the entire lakefront. At a meeting in December 1894, George C. Walker, business leader and company president, addressed the central theme of the evening, "What Shall Be Done with the Lake-Front." Walker argued that the city should oversee a plan for the lakefront that would minimize the role of the Illinois Central Railroad and make additional land from the railroad's right-of-way toward the lake.[10]

At the same meeting, John H. Hamline, a noted Chicago lawyer and expert on the lakefront, highlighted the complicated legal history of the park, which included cases involving the Illinois Central Railroad and its claim of riparian rights to land the railroad had already made by filling in the lakeshore. Hamline stressed that it would soon be possible to start filling in the submerged land of the inner harbor at little cost with material provided by drainage-canal contractors. In order to assuage concerns over the loss of moorage in the harbor, Hamline assured his fellow businessmen that the filling would not interfere with the city's waterborne traffic, which was beginning to use the Calumet River more than the Chicago River.[11]

With the landfill, Hamline declared, "a magnificent park, grander than Lincoln Park, could be constructed." A fellow club member, the hardware merchant Adolphus Clay Bartlett agreed, "I think a park of this kind would be unique. There is not another city in the world that could have in its immediate vicinity a park, a garden, fronting upon a body of water as we could have fronting on Michigan Avenue." The Commercial Club's plans for Lake Park called for a post office and a new city hall, both designed by a notable architect, "so that with the park surroundings they would form the grandest water approach of any city in the world." To further impress visitors, Hamline suggested that "a gigantic figure of Chicago" could be erected "at the mouth of the harbor."[12]

As the discussion about the future development of Lake Park gained momentum, Ellsworth encouraged Charles B. Atwood, an architect of several buildings at the exposition, and Burnham to develop a plan for Lake Park.[13] Given their successes with the exposition and professional contacts, Atwood and Burnham were well positioned to forward the plans for Lake Park. The pair presented a draft plan to the subcommittee of the Council Committee on Wharves and Public Grounds in June 1895.[14]

Using the White City's Court of Honor as a point of departure, Burnham and Atwood presented their vision for a park with fountains, playgrounds, flower beds, graveled walks, macadamized driveways, grass patches, statuary, trees, vine-covered walls, and a copy of the MacMonnies fountain from the World's Columbian Exposition, with a bronze statue of Columbus nearby. They recommended the construction of the Crerar Library, a collection that railroad supplier John Crerar would endow; a music hall; a National Guard armory; and an exposition building. Reflecting the neoclassical style of the Art Institute and the Chicago Public Library, these new structures were depicted with long, horizontal lines.[15]

Confident that the Illinois Central would support plans for developing Lake Park, Burnham urged his audience to move forward with the plan. Equally sure about winning the cooperation of the Michigan Avenue property owners, Charles L. Hutchinson, president of the board of the Art Institute of Chicago, declared the board "would raise no objection to building east of the tracks." They had, in fact, shown support for re-creating the park during preliminary planning for the World's Columbian Exposition. A number of prominent individuals, including Charles T. Yerkes, the industrialist famous for his handling of Chicago's street railway operations, and George M. Pullman, the manufacturer of the Pullman Palace Car, agreed that the landfill program should go forward. The supporters of Atwood and Burnham's proposal stressed the necessity of constructing the retaining wall so that the construction and filling of the basin could begin.[16]

Reflecting the general consensus in Chicago that something should be done to improve Lake Park in the wake of the World's Columbian Exposition, other groups, such as the Chicago Municipal Improvement League, advocated their own plan for Lake Park as an area for civic architecture. The league was "formed for the express purpose, first of securing the Lake Front to the city, and then for the proper improvement of the site."[17] Additionally, at the league's urging, the committee consulted with Olmsted, landscape architect for the World's Columbian Exposition in Jackson Park.[18]

With his typical zeal, Burnham was already working tirelessly on his own plans for Lake Park. He held several meetings at his office through 1896 with Chicago Mayor George Bell Swift, Ellsworth, and the other members of the South Park Commission.[19] Chicago's city council moved forward with efforts in line with the agenda Ellsworth and Burnham set out and in July 1896 transferred authority for Lake Park from the Board of Public Works to the South Park Commission.

The South Park Commissioners had demonstrated their land-management skills during the World's Columbian Exposition by hosting the fair in their domain: Jackson Park. So the city granted them the power to extend the lakeshore and create space for a permanent armory, a parade ground for the Illinois National Guard, and a site for the Field Columbian Museum.

In taking control of Lake Park, the commission did not initially take possession of the area north of Jackson Street, which included the Art Institute at Adams Street, the two armories located between Monroe and Madison, and a temporary post office at Washington Street.[20] Historically, the park had been the result of two land plats. It may also have been a protective measure as the commission may have been wary of the undecided court case Ward filed in 1890 concerning the city's right to grant permission to build structures in Lake Park.

When the South Park Commission took control of part of Lake Park in 1896, it believed that it had gained the right from the Illinois General Assembly or the governor to build structures in the park. With these rights, the commissioners contacted Field, who had indicated his desire to build and endow a museum of natural history based on the collection gathered during the World's Columbian Exposition.[21]

With the southern part of Lake Park controlled by the South Park Commission, Ellsworth invited Burnham, department-store owner Field, industrialist Pullman, and others to his home for dinner on October 10, 1896. The gathering received considerable newspaper coverage of Burnham's post-dinner presentation of his evolving vision for Lake Park.[22]

The World's Columbian Exposition, Burnham began, demonstrated that the people of Chicago were not obsessed with "mere money gaining and laying up of goods." Just as the exposition had served as a rallying point and a source of pride, the lakefront could do the same for the city. "The next great work of the people and for the people must go on, and it is already here," Burnham continued. Calling Lake Park "our front door yard," he urged his fellow citizens to take action in order to earn "self-respect before our neighbors and all nations and the world."[23]

The development of Lake Park would benefit the city itself, Burnham asserted, by making "the rich content to learn to live and spend their money among their own people. If the rich will stay on our shore the poor will be benefited by it, and to keep them here there is nothing so efficacious as the building up of delightful surroundings." Burnham advocated making the city more livable for all its residents, and his ambitious goals pointed toward a higher purpose for Chicago. The newly created park would represent a new Chicago, a city at once industrial and cultural.[24]

In case people weren't already persuaded of the need to clean up the park, Burnham recounted the following anecdote: "A visitor to the city looked out from the Auditorium Building and asked 'Can one shoot snipe in that marsh down there? It looks loke [sic] a good place for it.' The visitor was quite in earnest. He was not surprised that we should have a slough bordering Michigan boulevard."[25] Burnham, who had visited many of Europe's finest cities, expressed chagrin that someone would accept such conditions in Chicago. He described the current view as "a disgusting ash-heap, fringed with rotten piers and unsightly fishermen's derricks." His ambition was that, "The front of our city should be very beautiful, and it can be made so." The time had come, he insisted, for Chicagoans to do something grand with the lakefront, and he advocated a beautiful park that would connect with the city's other parks. "Let us take the margin of the lake for the people to whom it properly belongs. This move will contribute to their health and happiness more than anything which is in the power of the city to do."[26]

Ellsworth took measures to ensure citizens' support. "I do not like to propose a project which would impose an extra tax," he declared, "but the expense would be light compared with the great advantages." The group then viewed Burnham's architectural sketch of a boulevard extending along the shore and connecting Lake Park with Jackson Park.[27]

Burnham's vision had expanded beyond Lake Park to include a boulevard system that could at last connect Lake and Jackson Parks, and Burnham, through his advocacy, was already working with the South Park Commission to realize that vision. It looked as though the park might well be developed in line with the World's Columbian Exposition. But before the park could be improved, the city first had to get around to filling in the lakeshore.

Prior to the World's Columbian Exposition, the Army Corps of Engineers had opposed the lake-fill project. In July 1895, however, the city received authorization from the Secretary of War to build "a bulkhead along the dockline and for filling the area behind it except for a small yacht harbor at the southern end." This interference was a bit overreaching as the Chicago River—not the Outer Harbor on Lake Michigan—had always served as the harbor of Chicago, and since the1880s, the Calumet River had been accommodating more water traffic. As a result, arguments against filling in this area were cleared away. In 1896, the City of Chicago passed "an ordinance directing the area shoreward of the dock line established by the Corps of Engineers in 1871 to be filled in for use as a public park."[28]

The Illinois Central Railroad had argued in court, beginning in the 1870s, that it owned the riparian rights off of Lake Park, which it had gained when it had attempted to buy the park. The U.S. Circuit Court upheld in 1888 the city's and the state's ownership of the submerged lands against the claims of the railroad.[29] In 1896, the U.S. Supreme Court affirmed this ruling and granted title to the city for the land. Perhaps, building on the good relations the World's Columbian Exposition engendered, the Illinois Central Railroad lowered and modified its tracks so that filling in the lake could be facilitated (see fig. 4.3).

Figure 4.3. Lowering of modified Illinois Central Railroad tracks on lakefront, August 19, 1896. Chicago Park District Special Collections.

With these significant hurdles out of the way, the South Park Commission could move ahead with the expansion of the park. The commission was well positioned to take a small park and transform it into Chicago's premier cultural hub. Even with a number of competing visions, the overwhelming message was for the development of Lake Park along the lines of the World's Columbian Exposition. This vision would take considerable time and financial resources to realize, but the work was begun with great expectations for the future.

Ward Contests the Plans for Lake Park

Popular support for an enlarged Lake Park seemed high, and the South Park Commission assumed that the property owners along Michigan Avenue would also support a grand park. Since the 1860s, the Michigan Avenue property owners had held some oversight over Lake Park. Given the support of Chicago's city council, business leaders, and others, it seemed to be just a matter of time before a new White City would emerge in the park. Ward disrupted this vision.

Over its history, Lake Park had been the focus of a great deal of litigation. The best-known court cases involving the park, however, were those Ward filed. Born February 17, 1844, in Chatham, New Jersey, Ward was one of a long line of Yankees who made their fortunes in Chicago. As a young child, he moved with his parents to Niles, Michigan, and attended school there until the age of fourteen. In 1865, he was hired by Chicago's retail leaders Field, Palmer, and Leiter. After a couple of years, he took a job as a traveling salesman for a firm in Saint Louis. Through this experience, he learned a great deal about the needs of rural farmers and developed a new approach to sales, which was building a mail-order sales company, thereby making his fortune.

As a wealthy man in 1887, he bought two lots on Michigan Avenue fronting Lake Park. At that time, the massive Inter-State Industrial Building dominated the park's landscape. Ward presumably paid a premium for his property on Michigan Avenue that fronted a park with an unobstructed view of the lake. Over the years, the city had permitted a number of structures and activities in and around the park. In 1890, Ward filed a suit against the City of Chicago for violating the original designation of the site.[30] In this court case, Ward contested the city's right to grant permits to certain parties, such as the North Chicago Street Railway Company, which had "erect[ed] wooden buildings in which an asphalt street paving substance is prepared." He not only requested "an injunction against the city, the street railroad company, and the Baltimore and Ohio and Illinois

Central railroads, restraining them from further adding to the land's un-sightliness," but also sought to have the lakefront cleared and returned to the public. As a finishing touch, he demanded compensation "for the inconvenience suffered."[31]

Ward's case had solid legal standing. In the 1830s, "the canal commis-sioners platted the land east of State Street between Madison and Park Row, and sold lots along Michigan Avenue on representation [that] the land eastward would always remain 'forever open, clear and free' of building and any obstructions whatsoever. This position was reaffirmed in 1839."[32] While Ward's case made its way through the courts, building in Lake Park continued with the construction of a temporary hall for the Democratic National Convention of 1892 and a temporary post office. As he witnessed these additions rising from the park, Ward must have believed that it would be only a matter of time before more buildings were erected. Even osten-sibly ephemeral structures seemed impossible to uproot. The Inter-State Industrial Building had stood as a "temporary" structure in Lake Park for almost twenty years before it was torn down.

In 1896, the Illinois Supreme Court ruled in favor of Ward in the court case he had filed in 1890. The court prohibited further construction and called for the removal of the post office, the armories, the Lake Front police station, and the engine house. Ward allowed the Art Institute to remain in the park, however.[33]

After the ruling in his first case, Ward filed a second suit in 1896 to counter the unfolding plans for the development of Lake Park. As they had in the first case, Ward's lawyers centered their arguments on the original platting of the site and its two additions. They contended that "the reso-lution of April 29, 1844, and the designation of the ground by the city as Lake Park by an ordinance of August 10, 1847" demonstrated that the city had accepted and understood the restrictions on the use of the land. Con-sequently, Ward desired "a permanent injunction against the construction of buildings thereon and diverting the park from the purposes for which it was dedicated."[34] To those who envisioned a glorious park reflecting the Columbian Exposition's Court of Honor, it was inconceivable that Ward would fight these evolving plans in court.

As if to underline his influence, while his second case was being argued in 1898, Montgomery Ward and Company built the city's tallest building and operated the premier mail-order business in the world from his property at 6 North Michigan Avenue (see fig. 4.4).[35] As a property owner, Ward may have wanted to preserve his right to a lot with a clear view of the lakefront. Ward's second court case would not be decided until 1902, but at its core, it challenged the city's right to grant permission for the construction of a

Figure 4.4. View north on Michigan Avenue, featuring the A. Montgomery Ward building, ca. 1903. Chicago Park District Special Collections.

lakefront armory and parade grounds in the park. Ultimately, the courts upheld the earlier ruling that Lake Park should remain free of buildings.[36] During the years around the turn of the century, however, it was unclear how this situation would be resolved. Confident that its bold vision for the park would eventually win the day, the South Park Commission moved ahead with its ambitious plans for Lake Park.

The South Park Commission Expands and Improves Lake Park

Taking control of Lake Park in 1896, the South Park Commission drew on the experience it had gained during the World's Columbian Exposition and dedicated itself to advancing the civic vision that had emerged in the wake of the exposition. Between 1896 and 1907, the commission tripled the size of Lake Park by filling in the outer harbor beyond the Illinois Central tracks. During previous decades, a number of landfill projects had been carried out on Chicago's lakefront. Before the Great Chicago Fire of 1871, the Illinois Central filled in land north of the park, and the Board of Public Works had begun filling in a small lagoon to expand the park. After the fire, the city used fire debris to fill in the area between the shoreline and the Illinois Central tracks offshore. Noting the success of this project, Chicago's Board of Public Works called for additional fill, yet it made only limited improvements or alterations to the park.[37]

This landfill project called for an enormous volume of fill because some of the offshore areas were twenty feet deep. To reduce costs, park commissioners invited the city's street-cleaning department to discard all variety of material in the offshore area and entered into arrangements with dredging companies to deposit material in the Lake Park basin. As the Illinois Telephone Company dug underground tunnels throughout the city in 1905 and 1906, it also hauled unwanted fill to the site. But waiting for free landfill strained the commission's patience, so at times they paid a nominal fee for fill. By 1907, the South Park Commission had begun bringing the entire park to uniform grade. The state legislature had legally secured the park commissioners' clear title to the area created by landfill, and the commission had expanded the park to 186 acres (see fig. 4.5).[38]

The commission began to improve and landscape the southern section of the area between the Illinois Central Railroad tracks and Michigan Avenue. Workers brought a twenty-five-acre section of the park to a uniform grade, covered it with soil, and seeded it. They also started to build gravel walkways and lined the paths with knee-high chain fences. At the same time, the park district planted a large number of trees and shrubs on the eastern end of the park and reported that 25.13 of Lake Park's 186.43 acres were improved.[39]

Figure 4.5. Site of Grant Park, 1902. Chicago Park District Special Collections.

The South Park Commission also made a change that might be considered an improvement by subtraction, as on June 12, 1897, the commission removed Howard Kretchmar's Columbus statue, which had been erected for the World's Columbian Exposition, and deposited it in the storage yard at Washington Park. The district claimed it had to take down the statue because the landfill program had begun on the lakefront. A journalist for the *Chicago Tribune* offered another reason, the statue's unsightliness: "[P]erhaps, down in his secret heart, Mr. Peck is aware that this rampant and unpleasantly assertive piece of bronze is a failure. . . . Perhaps he is greatly relieved now that Christopher is to be moved to the junk shop."[40]

Hutchinson of the Art Institute probably requested to have the colossus melted down, but the South Park Commission demurred. Then, after the ten-ton statue had been in storage for six years, the commission finally permitted it to be melted down for a new statue of President William McKinley.[41] Chicago had already participated in the national trend of commemorating Civil War heroes in its parks, and they had more than McKinley's statue in their plans.

Shortly after Abraham Lincoln's assassination, the city created Lincoln Park as a memorial to the war and its martyred president. The Lincoln Park commissioners secured the services of American sculptor Augustus Saint-Gaudens to create a figure, known as Abraham Lincoln, the Man (the Standing Lincoln). The unveiling of the statue in 1887 generated a great outpouring of popular support. Chicago's civic leaders hoped that "[t]he figure of the president from Illinois, martyred on behalf of union, might command popular loyalty and evoke feelings of nationalism." Illinois Civil War hero and U.S. president General Ulysses S. Grant is also commemorated in a Lincoln Park statue. The equestrian statue, designed by Louis T. Rebisso and dedicated in 1891, was placed atop a sizable structure, incorporating stairs and an arched pedestrian throughway at the base.[42]

Honoring General John A. Logan

In Lake Park, the South Park District Commissioners decided to honor Civil War General John A. Logan, a native son, with a monument (see fig. 4.6). Given the timing, the individual, and the location, the dedication of this monument became an event of national importance. The commissioners decided that the monument should be placed in Lake Park near the intersection of Ninth Street and Michigan Avenue in the area that had recently been landscaped. Lake Park seemed an especially appropriate place for the memorial because during his political career following the war, Logan had made several official appearances in the park. In 1873, he spoke at the opening of

Figure 4.6. Logan monument, ca. 1905. Joliet Area Historical Museum, Joliet, Illinois.

the Inter-State Industrial Exposition, and in 1884, he received the Republican vice-presidential nomination in that same building. Shortly after Logan's death in 1886, the State of Illinois set aside funds for his monument, and once it was completed, the South Park Commissioners expended $13,943.40 for the construction of the foundation, mound, approaching steps, and walk.[43]

The commissioners desired an equestrian sculpture standing on a mound two stories high. They commissioned Alexander Phimister Proctor to design the horse and the nationally prominent Saint-Gaudens to create the sculpture. The monument depicts the moment in which Logan audaciously took lead of the Army of the Tennessee.[44]

When Logan's wife was asked what date she would like for the unveiling, she chose July 22, 1897, the date of the Battle of Atlanta, in which Logan played a role. The Grand Army of the Republic also expressed an interest in taking part in the ceremony because Logan had been a founding member of the GAR and served as its first commander in chief. Logan had been eager to recognize comrades-in-arms, and so he had inaugurated the observance of Memorial Day (also known as Decoration Day) on May 30 when he directed GAR members to place flowers on soldiers' graves.[45] Because Logan had been a volunteer, the veterans held him in special esteem, and some veterans believed the dedication of the Logan memorial would be their last opportunity to honor a national hero of Logan's stature. For the dedication, members of the GAR arranged an opening ceremony for the new hall at the corner of Michigan Avenue and Randolph Street that they were sharing with the Chicago Public Library.

At one o'clock that afternoon, with a large crowd gathered on the lakefront, Phinney's U.S. Band played "The Assembly," and the festivities began. The highlight of the day was the unveiling of the statue by General Logan's grandson, five-year-old John A. Logan III, known as "Little Jack." According to a reporter, "[i]nvoluntarily every one in the stand rose to his feet, and the boom of the cannon in the immediate rear of the monument was followed by prolonged and enthusiastic cheering, starting from the stand and sweeping back and forth over the thousands collected in the streets and on housetops for blocks around. Hats were swung, handkerchiefs waved, and for several moments the scene was one of a soul-stirring character." A number of speakers addressed the crowd. After Illinois Governor John R. Tanner accepted the monument, George R. Peck, Civil War veteran and noted railroad attorney, spoke at length on Logan's commitment, bravery, and patriotism. "How can we ever forget, while this brave figure guards the City's front, that art is the true minister of life?" Peck asked. "Its noblest conceptions rise from events which have moral grandeur in them; from illumined moments, when some soul has reached its highest exaltation. Seeing that they are beautiful, it keeps them so forevermore."[46] In his address, Peck confronted the larger meaning of the monument within the park: "Here we make a sacred place. Here we consecrate a name already consecrated in our bravest annals." The orator also looked to the future: "[I]n coming years, the throngs that crowd the avenue will see a silent figure always on duty. They will know,—and all the world will know,—it is Logan."[47]

The dedication of the monument was an event of national importance, so much so that President McKinley, out of respect for the hero, had originally planned to attend the dedication. Speaking on the president's behalf, General Russell A. Alger, secretary of war, read the president's words of praise for Logan as a man and soldier.[48] Those in attendance celebrated Logan's life as well as what it meant to be an American hero.

Following the dedication speeches, the Logan Day parade commenced. On that warm summer day, approximately a third of the soldiers of the U.S. Army gathered along with roughly seven thousand members of the National Guardsmen of Illinois. Beyond this impressive martial display were choruses, bands, civic leaders, and politicians, all of whom had gathered to pay their respects to John A. Logan with patriotic songs, orations, and a parade. On Lake Michigan, military ships moved in formation and provided a conspicuous display for those on shore.[49] The dedication of the Logan monument demonstrated the increasing national importance of Chicago, and the centrality of Lake Park allowed for an event of national magnitude. The city demonstrated that the park could draw crowds for a full-scale event without the benefit of a fair.

Changing the Park's Name

This process of commemorating the Civil War continued in 1901 when the State of Illinois transferred the entire park east of Michigan Avenue between Randolph Street and Park Row to the South Park District Commissioners. On October 9, the commissioners rededicated the area as Grant Park.[50] Although Ulysses S. Grant had died in 1885, his importance as a symbol of service to the Republic continued to grow. For the populace of Illinois, Lincoln, Grant, and Logan represented a nearly holy triumvirate of sacrifice and bravery that embodied Illinois' lasting contribution to the nation.

Plans for Grant Park and the Field Museum

Despite the legal wrangling involving the newly named Grant Park, the South Park Commission continued to move forward with its grand plans for the park. But in 1902, the Illinois Supreme Court again decided in favor of Ward in the case he filed in 1896. The court based its findings on his earlier case, filed in 1890. On this occasion, it found that the city and the state had no right to allow the Illinois National Guard to build "an armory on land to be filled east of the Illinois Central and north of Monroe Street."[51] In the winning argument, Ward's lawyers argued that the area created from landfill should be subject to the same rules as the original park. During the complicated case, Ward had lost in the Illinois Superior Court, but the decision was overturned in the Illinois Supreme Court, "which decided that the owners of property abutting on Grant Park were entitled to have the park kept open to the lake line wherever it might be."[52] The Illinois Supreme Court refused the city's request for a rehearing of the suits and in 1902 compelled compliance with the earlier suits sustaining Ward. This court decision stopped the construction of the armories, and each side had expended considerable resources in time and money.[53]

Undaunted by this latest turn of events, the South Park Commission decided to gain the power it needed to create the kind of park it had envisioned. This time, the commission attempted to bring cultural institutions into the landscape as "park facilities," which were well within their rights to build and maintain. In 1903, the state legislature gave the commission the right to build in the park by "enabling the park districts to construct and care for 'museums and libraries'" and consider them as "'park facilities.'" By this logic, park districts could build anything they wanted by designating it a "park facility." In preparation for legal challenges, the commission "sent experts to Europe to prepare documents showing that in Europe great parks included cultural buildings."[54]

In paving the way for museums in Grant Park, in 1903, the South Park Commission lobbied for an act that would allow it to maintain museums in its parks by raising tax monies for their support. The park commissioners were assuring their ability to support the Art Institute, Field Columbian Museum, and the Crerar Library. They argued that by funding these institutions, they would be better able to serve more of Chicago's burgeoning population.[55] As a result, in 1903, the city granted the right for several buildings and monuments to be built in the park, including a city hall.[56]

The South Park Commission focused its attention on securing the central feature of Grant Park. Since 1896, the commission had been in discussions with Field, who had expressed strong interest in building and endowing a museum.[57] In the summer of 1903, Field wrote to the park commissioners, "I am ready to go forward with the building whenever materials and labor are at reasonable figures, which probably will be as soon as the ground is ready for building. Regarding exact location, I think that can be safely left to your Board, Messrs. Olmsted Brothers, Messrs. D. H. Burnham & Co., and Trustees of the Museum."[58]

At this point, Lake Michigan off Grant Park had been filled with material for over seven years, and the end of the massive landfill project was in sight, but the commission still needed a plan for the park that included the entire area. The World's Columbian Exposition had established Burnham as one of the best-known architects in the nation. Although his firm had high-profile commissions nationally, Burnham himself maintained a special interest in planning activities in Chicago.

The commission consulted with Burnham as it proceeded with the landfill project and made plans for Grant Park as a cultural center. In addition to Grant Park plans, Burnham's architectural firm, D. H. Burnham and Company, made a number of the plans for the district's smaller parks. Bennett, one of Burnham's ablest architects, drafted many of these plans, which included field houses and other facilities for community use. In an arrangement reflecting the World's Columbian Exposition, the commission provided the park land, but Burnham would have considerable oversight of the project, and Olmsted's successor firm would be in charge of the landscape. One of the preeminent landscape architecture firms in the United States, the Olmsted Brothers, a firm founded by Olmsted's sons, received the commission for landscaping Grant Park. In 1903, the firm presented its plan for the park. Working with the existing Art Institute of Chicago on the north end of the park, the plan featured the Field Museum at the center of the park beyond the Illinois Central tracks. The plan also included the John Crerar Library.[59] In an action that must have provided the South Park Commissioners with supreme confidence in their endeavors, the citizens of Chicago voted in 1903 to support a tax levy to fund the museums in the park.[60]

To counter this expanded vision of what would be in the park, Ward filed the third of his court cases in 1903. Ward's case targeted the Field Museum, for which excavation had already started in the park.[61] As the last case had, this case would take a number of years to be decided, so in the meantime the commission pressed on.

As President Henry G. Foreman of the South Park Commission explained, "[I]t was our intention to make this a beautiful front yard for the city, . . . and to remove for all time the stigma of having a rubbish pile between Michigan avenue and the waters of the lake, but certain property owners seem determined to balk [at] the creation of a beautiful park in that location. . . . The committee on new parks, facing the complication, believes it best to cancel contracts for filling in and improving the lake front and to abandon the work in every way. If this committee, at the regular December meeting of the park commissioners, should report in favor of such a course and the report should be concurred in, the work will come to a standstill and no one can tell when it will be resumed."[62] Although upset, the district continued with its work and gathered support from the state, the city, and the citizens of Chicago.

Although Ward made no public statement on his case, he allowed his attorney, George P. Merrick, to explain his opposition to the commission's plans. Merrick stated that more than the Field Museum was included in the park's plan.[63] The commissioners also planned for the John Crerar Technical Library and a monument to Dr. Samuel Guthrie, the inventor of chloroform.[64] Ward also believed that the commission would not stop with these institutions and monuments in the park. Ordinary Chicagoans, however, feared that Ward's opposition might cost the city the opportunity to have the $4 million Field Museum on the lakefront.

In 1904, the city formally transferred the deed for the Art Institute building and the landfill area west of the Illinois Railroad tracks to the commission.[65] By 1905, the landfill reached the target level—twenty-nine feet above the city datum—and the park commissioners could begin the work of leveling and planting. Landscapers first blanketed the newly created land with soil and planted a variety of trees, including elm, poplar, willow, ash, linden, catalpa, birch, maple, and hackberry, as well as a variety of shrubs, including barberry, dogwood, weigelia, pearl sweet, snowberry, and button bush—a total of five thousand plants—which they fertilized with manure from the stockyards.[66]

The commissioners put the construction of Crerar Library in Grant Park to a popular vote, and citizens expressed their approval. The commissioners advanced an ordinance that allowed the Crerar trustees to build the library "between Madison and Monroe streets projected, and west of the Illinois Central tracks, a building of classical design to cost $1,000,000."[67] The library's board then submitted an application on February 15, 1905, allowing the library to be placed in the park "north of and in line with the Art Institute Building. This ordinance was passed in accordance with the provisions of an Act concerning free public libraries in public parks, approved May 14th, 1903, and in force July 1st, 1903."[68] To keep the public informed, the South Park Commission displayed a model of the Olmsted Brothers' 1903 plan in the Art Institute (see fig. 4.7).[69]

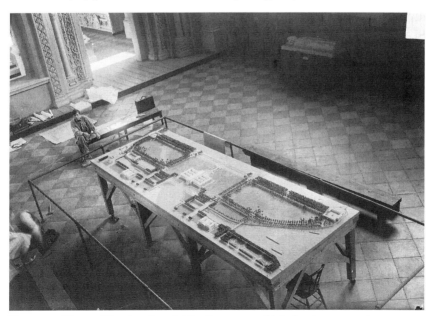

Figure 4.7. Olmsted Brothers' model for the proposed lakefront, ca. 1905. (DN-0006213) Chicago History Museum.

The funding for the Crerar Library included financial resources to construct the library building, an endowment for its operation, and $100,000 for a statue of Lincoln. The library's trustees gave the commission for the statue to Saint-Gaudens, who had already created the figure of Logan in Grant Park and a statue of Lincoln for Lincoln Park. Saint-Gaudens wanted to make this Lincoln commission his most magnificent work and spent more than a decade on it. Once completed, it was displayed in the Metropolitan Museum of Art in New York.[70]

In 1905, the South Park Commission shored up support for the new museum with encouragement from the "administrators of [the] Field estate and the trustees of the Field Museum of Natural History for the location and construction of the building." Two years later, the commissioners signed a contract with the "trustees of the Field Museum of Natural History for the erection of a museum building in Grant Park at a total estimated cost of $4,000,000."[71] Burnham had already begun to design the neoclassical Field Museum, which was slated to begin construction by 1908. The contract further specified that the museum would be ready for occupants in four and a half years from the signing of the contract in 1907.[72]

In another setback, Ward filed a petition in 1907 to keep the city from allowing the construction of the Crerar Library and the Field Museum in Grant Park.[73] In the face of the tremendous gift these two institutions represented, the press vilified Ward. The pressure on him was so great that his business partners and friends were enlisted in an attempt to get him to relent.[74] Ward made it clear that he was not against the Field Museum but, rather, its proposed location. In 1908, Ward considered allowing the Field Museum but only if all other structures would be excluded. He stated again that he was only upholding the area's original designation as open and free.[75] In this case, Ward asserted that he was not interested in just his private property but also in maintaining Grant Park as a green ward.

The commissioners continued to have the Olmsted Brothers draft and revise designs for the park. From 1903 to 1908, the Olmsted Brothers delineated a formal, verdant setting in which to place the Field Museum and Crerar Library, both of which would be in harmony with the Art Institute. All of their plans were predicated on the park serving as the site for the Field and the Crerar.[76] With all of its governmental and popular support, the South Park Commission must have felt confident that it would win the case.

Burnham and Bennett and the 1909 Plan of Chicago

After nearly a generation, the World's Columbian Exposition still exerted considerable influence on the minds of those planning for the future of America's burgeoning urban centers. In Chicago, the South Park

Commission had engineered an expansive park out of Lake Michigan to expand Grant Park. In the nineteenth century, Chicago's lakeshore was dominated by private property and railroad right-of-ways. If the landfill program for Grant Park could be replicated and expanded, Chicagoans could reclaim the shoreline for an extensive series of parks.

City business leaders, especially those involved with the Commercial Club of Chicago, directed their attention to these areas of city and park planning. In an unprecedented act for the club, which generally sponsored papers or discussions, it "advanced $25,000 for a Plan of Chicago."[77] With this financial support, Burnham and Bennett formally began working in 1906; in 1909, they published their Plan of Chicago, communicated by the exquisite drawings of Jules Guerin.[78] The city adopted the plan as the general blueprint for the city's development in 1910. Though city planning had existed before the 1909 plan and had even preceded the World's Columbian Exposition, the exposition and the Plan of Chicago serve as milestones in the history of city planning. Burnham and Bennett developed a comprehensive plan focusing on the city center and its transportation system, providing for the future growth and progress of the metropolis.[79] In addition to practical concerns, Burnham and Bennett delineated an elegant metropolitan area. The pair would devote a considerable amount of the remainder of their careers to promoting and helping to realize aspects of their Plan of Chicago.[80]

The plan expanded on Burnham's idea for an offshore boulevard to link Grant Park and Jackson Park. In the new concept, Burnham and Bennett placed Grant Park at the center of the lakefront stretching the length of Chicago's entire shore, from Evanston to the Indiana state line, punctuated by a series of lagoons and park areas. These man-made features would culminate at Grant Park, where a large yacht harbor would serve to unify the whole design. At Grant Park, the plan called for "passenger docks and slips for cargo vessels" on the north and "a scenic drive" and "lighthouse and pavilion" on the south. The lakefront would be an integral part of the city, reserved for recreational and cultural purposes except for areas near the Chicago and Calumet Rivers.[81]

Sweeping, panoramic views of the lakeshore at Grant Park featuring the yacht harbor were incorporated into Guerin's depictions, where the harbor appears almost to reach out to embrace the boaters as they sail into the refuge of its harbor, which evokes the colonnades of Saint Peter's Square in Rome (see fig. 4.8). In fact, figure CXXXVI in the plan, depicts "Rome. St. Peter's Cathedral, showing the approach."[82] The illustrations demonstrate the artistic inspirations of the designers and their grounding in Western design.

While the Plan of Chicago looked to the architectural past, especially to the Baroque urban plans of Paris and Rome, Burnham and Bennett also

Figure 4.8. Plan of Chicago (1909), proposed development in the center of the city, from Twenty-Second Street to Chicago Avenue. (ICHi-03549) Chicago History Museum.

looked toward the future, anticipating the needs of twentieth-century Chicago. The architects believed that Chicago would continue to swell in size and population. Some of their most innovative work centered on providing ample areas for recreational use, especially on the lakefront. As Burnham and Bennett noted in their plan, "[I]n 1899 the Chicago City Council created the Special Park Commission, at the same time adopting resolutions recognizing the value of parks in preventing crime, promoting cleanliness, and diminishing disease."[83]

So important to the whole plan were the lakefront and its development as an area for recreation that when Burnham and Bennett enumerated what must be done to realize their plan, they stated that first would be "the improvement of the Lake front."[84] More than a place for recreation, within the plan, Grant Park would become both a major focus of the city and its cultural center.

Burnham and Bennett's drawings for Grant Park reflected those of the Olmsted Brothers, with the Field Museum planned to be built in the middle of the landfill section of the park in line with Congress Street. Increasing the structure's impact, the architects made Congress Street the central axis of the city. Thus, the Field Museum, for physical as well as aesthetic reasons and by virtue of its planned location, would have been the most important cultural building in the city as well as one of the foci of the plan.[85]

At the time the Commercial Club published the Plan of Chicago, it was not clear whether the Field Museum would be allowed to be built in the park. Undeterred by the continuing court cases, Burnham and Bennett included the Field Museum in the 1909 Plan: "To create a great cross avenue without utilizing the element of symmetry which this noble building stands ready to furnish would be to set at defiance every law of civic order, and to perpetrate a crime against good taste that could never be atoned for. It is inconceivable that in the present state of public taste any people would permit such a barbarism."[86] Their statement appears to be aimed at Ward or any other Michigan Avenue property owner who would voice opposition to the construction of the Field Museum in Grant Park.

Court Decisions and Compromise Landscape

Although much of the Plan of Chicago had been drafted by 1908, the final document was not distributed until July 4, 1909.[87] A few months later on October 26, 1909, the Illinois Supreme Court again found in Ward's favor in his third case, which was to block the construction of the Field Museum.[88] Despite the South Park Commissioners' best efforts, Ward had once again kept Grant Park free of permanent structures. With this victory, Ward gave an interview in which he maintained that he prosecuted these cases for the benefit of the people of Chicago.[89] To some, this must have seemed strange, as Chicago's voters had approved a number of bonds for the building and maintenance of cultural institutions in the park. His litigation stalled the efforts of the South Park Commission and the vision put forth by the Olmsted Brothers and others for the park. Only time would tell if Ward's actions would simply delay or completely dash the commissioners' grand plans for Grant Park. Many in the city perceived Ward as an obstructionist, and he received a great deal of negative press at the time.[90]

In the short term, Ward's court cases delayed the commission's plans to develop Grant Park along its City Beautiful proposal, which would have furthered the park's transformation into a cultural center. Although Burnham and Bennett had written about the importance of the Field Museum being a central feature of Grant Park, because of the court's decision, the museum was not built at the center of the expansive park in line with Congress Street. Rather, it was located on additional recovered lake land south of Twelfth Street provided by the Illinois Central Railroad. Workers began construction on the Field Museum in 1909. The massive structure took eleven years to build and was finally completed in 1920.[91]

Burnham received the commission for designing the Field Museum. Most of the work was completed after his death in 1912 by his successor firm. In addition to the Field Museum, Burnham and his firm had a significant impact on the appearance of the area around Grant Park. Burnham's firm had designed Orchestra Hall, the Railway Exchange Building, and the Peoples Gas, Light, and Coke Company building, which served to define the skyline as seen from Grant Park for the next century.[92]

Despite the decision in the third case filed by Ward, the South Park Commission was not ready to give up the fight. The commission filed a fourth court case against Ward in which they tried to push through their park plans by "condemning the easement rights of Mr. Ward."[93] This would have allowed the commissioners to make plans for Grant Park without the approval of the surrounding property owners. The courts were not swayed by this high-handed approach, and the Illinois Supreme Court quickly decided in Ward's favor once again in 1910.[94]

Ward's court cases dissipated much of the momentum for the development of the park in the years following the World's Columbian Exposition. Although the South Park Commission had moved forward with a monumental effort to fill in the lakebed to create additional land, it was unable to build the cultural landscape that Burnham and others had envisioned and promoted. By holding fast to his position, Ward altered Grant Park's history at a crucial moment. As a result of his action, a new White City would not arise in quite the way that many had assumed it would. In fact, the park would continue as a compromise landscape, especially with the Field Museum shunted off to the south end of the park. Even Ward's victory was a compromise, as the museum was built on the lakefront on landfill just outside of the park's historical boundaries.

In retrospect, Ward counted his efforts to keep Lake Park open and free of permanent building his greatest achievement after his retail business. It has been estimated that the court battles cost him $150,000, which he declared he spent "for the poor people of Chicago—not the millionaires."[95] The court cases clearly informed the debate surrounding Lake Park and those surrounding the entire lakefront.

Both Burnham and Ward greatly influenced the appearance of Grant Park. Ward had his sizable office building on Michigan Avenue, and Burnham had his office built on the top of the Railway Exchange Building, 224 South Michigan Avenue, which was built in 1903 4. The two powerful men, undoubtedly, looked down on the open land and had the power and ego to test their wills over the landscape. Daniel Burnham died in 1912, and the litigious Aaron Montgomery Ward died the following year. It would be for the next generation to decide how Grant Park would look. Most of this work would fall to Bennett, Burnham's coauthor of the 1909 plan, who would design Grant Park as a cultural center within the constraints of Ward's legal decisions.

5

The New Design

Between the end of the nineteenth century and 1909, the South Park Commission made extensive plans for Grant Park. In addition, Daniel H. Burnham and Edward H. Bennett published their 1909 Plan of Chicago, which envisioned Grant Park as a primary focus of the city and provided an ambitious vision for the entire lakefront. Meanwhile, Aaron Montgomery Ward's sustained and successful opposition to the park's development and litigation dashed aspects of these visionary plans. With the Illinois Supreme Court's decision in 1911 in *South Park Commissioners v. Montgomery Ward and Co.*, the South Park Commission clearly would need to discern a new course of action.

Between 1914 and 1930, the South Park Commission moved forward with modified plans for Grant Park. The court had made it clear that the Field Museum could not be built in the middle of the park as proposed. The South Park Commission confronted the challenges of creating and landscaping the new land on the lakefront and mitigating the impact of the railroad tracks on the park's landscape. The commissioners would also struggle in this period to accommodate the automobile, which required new roadways and parking areas. After Burnham's death in 1912, Bennett (1874–1954) and his architectural firm would go on to exert the greatest influence on the design and appearance of Grant Park during the early part of the twentieth century.

The Olmsted Brothers' Plan

The South Park District Commissioners had hired the Olmsted brothers' firm in 1903 to create a comprehensive design for the vast park. It was a unique park because of its centrality and would require a unique design. New York's Central Park was built far from the business center as was the land set aside for Los Angeles's Griffith Park. While other cities, such as Boston, had commons or smaller parks near the city center, its scale and formal design made Grant Park singular.

From 1903 through 1908, the brothers revised their plans and made large cultural institutions the primary foci of the park. To gather public support, the commissioners displayed the design model in the Art Institute. The Olmsted brothers' plan divided the park into three large segments. After almost a century of flux, this segmentation would dictate the division of the park moving forward.

The center of the park ran from Jackson Street to Hubbard Place (later renamed Balbo). This section featured a grand approach at Michigan Avenue that emphasized the magnificent façade of the proposed Field Museum. The northern segment extended from Randolph Street to Jackson Boulevard and featured the Art Institute, along Michigan Avenue. This section was to include the North Meadow on the east and featured tree-lined promenades. The architects balanced their design with a South Meadow, which mirrored that of the north, and incorporated the Crerar Library on the south. In a slight variation from the 1909 plan, yacht clubs were to be placed on the southern extent of the park in line with Park Place (Eleventh Street) and a yacht harbor south of the park.[1] The Olmsteds' design placed the Field Columbian Museum east of the Illinois Central Railroad's right-of-way.

The Olmsted design addressed many of the site's limitations. First, the railroad from above Van Buren Street to below Harrison Street would be deemphasized by lowering the railroad tracks and creating a tunnel that would be covered with landscaping. Although some of the details, such as a playing field, gymnasium, and swimming basin, changed over time, on the whole, the Olmsted brothers kept to their tripartite division of the park, which provided the point of departure for future designs.[2]

In addition to the formal plans for Grant Park, the South Park Commission wished to move forward with its boulevard system to connect Grant Park to Jackson Park and to connect the South Park system with grand boulevards to the Lincoln and West Park Districts. In the 1890s, Burnham had conceptualized a plan to connect Lake Park with Jackson Park, and the idea stuck with the commissioners. In 1908, with the process of reclaiming the submerged lands for Grant Park almost completed, the district moved ahead with an extensive plan to join Grant and Jackson Parks, including planning for the newly created land extending a thousand or more feet out into Lake Michigan for the approximately eight miles between Grant Park and Jackson Park.[3]

On May 2, 1907, the Illinois state legislature approved a shoreline boulevard to run between the two parks, "authorizing the Commissioners to acquire the riparian rights and take possession of submerged land in Lake Michigan." The Commercial Club of Chicago supported these efforts to gain rights to the submerged land. To further assure that it was on solid legal ground, the commission had the land titles and riparian rights investigated, made lake-bed soundings, and plotted the information on maps. In addition to connecting the two large parks south of the Chicago River, the South Park Commissioners broached the idea of building a bridge over the Chicago River to extend Michigan Avenue and connect Grant Park to Lincoln Park on the north side of the city. By 1908, the State of Illinois, the City of Chicago, and the Lincoln and South Park Boards of Commissioners had moved to approve the link.[4]

Other changes in the city's design were affecting Grant Park as well. In 1910, the South Park Commission designated Michigan Avenue as a boulevard, widened the road from Randolph to Twelfth Streets, and installed electric streetlights. The larger thoroughfare along the entire western length of the park created a more definitive boundary to the park. In 1911, the South Park Commission's superintendent, J. F. Foster, reported that work was progressing with the selection of lamps to line the street; by 1913, the boulevard was fully lit and boasted a twenty-five-foot-wide sidewalk.[5] Unlike the streets of the adjacent Loop, the boulevard accommodated both street traffic and provided ample room for people to stretch their legs.

Surprising Uses of the Newly Created Park Land

In 1911, the decision of the court in *South Park Commissioners v. Montgomery Ward and Co.* scuttled significant aspects of the early plans of the South Park Commission. In the last of the Ward decisions, the judge ruled that buildings could not be erected on the original area of Grant Park. In the short term, this meant that the Olmsted brothers' park plans featuring the Field Museum and the Crerar Library needed revision. The ruling was a major setback for the South Park Commission, which remained, nevertheless, committed to the project.

In the meantime, the South Park Commission allowed Grant Park east of the Illinois Central right-of-way to be used in innovative and even startling ways. Burnham probably did not envision the lakefront being used for such popular events as martial Fourth of July celebrations, aviation meets, and even international sports competitions. Yet, at a unique moment when the eastern part of the park was not landscaped, it could be used for staging large events. As in the past, Grant Park's proximity to public transportation and its central location made it an attractive area for these activities.

One of the earliest and most noteworthy examples came with the Fourth of July celebrations. Since 1908, the Sane Fourth Association had pushed for ordinances to restrict fireworks and explosives. In July 1909, the South Park Commissioners permitted the Sane Fourth Association to occupy part of Grant Park for two weeks for an observance centered on a military encampment and military tournament that were open to the public (see fig. 5.1).[6] During these encampments, U.S. Army soldiers took up residence in Grant Park. Before sizable crowds, they trained on horseback, marched, fired weapons, raised the flag, and carried out other activities that emphasized the holiday as a patriotic observance. The tournament brought people out of their neighborhoods, where fireworks and fires had often led to injury and destruction, and is a forerunner of the Grant Park Fourth of July celebrations that ran for many years and featured large fireworks displays.

The 1910 display stressed safety and American values. John R. Young, tournament secretary, reported that the U.S. Army Tournament in Grant Park, from July 4–14, 1910, drew 1,700,000 people to its performances and that "over 600,000 persons visited the camp June 28, 29 and 30 and July 1, 2, 3, 10 and 12—days upon which no performances were given." Despite the numbers of people in attendance, the tournament occurred without major incident or injury.[7]

Young concluded, "[T]hat the Tournament was a stimulus to patriotism [was] plain enough, when one recall[ed] the respect shown the flag by the audiences—how eager they were to pay their tribute to the colors. That it was of value as an example of law and order was demonstrated by the magnificent behavior of the crowd at all times: for example, on the night of July 4, the arena light went out ten minutes after the performance began, and for fifty-seven minutes 100,000 men, women and children sat or stood quietly and without complaint, waiting. There is nothing in the history of amusements in this country [that could] be compared to this situation."[8] Apparently, the organizers had found the blend of patriotic ceremonies and a military parade that held the audience's attention.

The success of the Sane Fourth Association elicited interest from other municipalities, and the association in Grant Park inspired other tournaments. Almost forty other cities made requests to the War Department for tournaments for the following year.[9] As a result of the summer celebrations,

Figure 5.1. U.S. Army tournament, 1910. Photograph by Charles R. Clark. (CRC-180B) Chicago History Museum.

Grant Park had taken on a significant civic function as the central gathering place to mark Independence Day and provided a national model that encouraged other communities to celebrate the occasion in a similar fashion.

In addition to the large scale events in Grant Park, the Sane Fourth Association in 1911 held a number of events at other sites across the city, including "moving pictures, band concerts, and patriotic talks most of which were appropriate for children." The organization also staged a parade that ran from "26th and Michigan; north to Randolph; west to State; south to Van Buren."[10] The staging of spectacles, designed to foster Americanism, was a function that the park provided in varying degrees through World War I.

The Sane Fourth Association continued to achieve its goal to create a way to celebrate the nation's independence with minimal bodily injury or fire damage. The group had enough success that it could report on July 4, 1912, it "achieved a day practically free from accident, and the fire loss on that day [according to Chief Charles F. Seyferlich] was next to nothing."[11]

In addition to events related to the Fourth of July celebrations, other spectacles made use of the unlandscaped eastern part of the park. Perhaps the most stunning use was the early aviation tournaments. The first such event was the International Aviation Meet from August 11 to 20, 1911 (see fig. 5.2). As the Wright brothers had first flown successfully just the year before, flight was truly in its infancy, and this would be the first chance almost any of the citizens of Chicago had to see an airplane in flight. The event attracted around two hundred thousand people each day. Aviators from around the

globe flew their planes but also attempted, with considerable difficulty and physical risk, to set new records, such as maximum time aloft. Unfortunately, a number of accidents marred the meet, which also proved to be a financial disaster.[12] In spite of this failure, the following year, the district allowed the Aero Club of Illinois an aviation meet from September 16 to 21, 1912.

In a related event, the park served as an unofficial touchdown point for the first flight across Lake Michigan in July 1913. Aviator "Jack" Vilas, with William Bastear, flew from Saint Joseph, Michigan, to Grant Park, passing over the crowds in Grant Park at four o'clock. The crowd, already gathered to attend athletic meets in the park, greeted the pilots' feat with enthusiasm.[13] These aviation spectacles were ideal for the lakefront park because its open spaces, which flying required, could still easily draw large crowds.

In addition to flight, Grant Park became a site for sporting contests. In 1912, the South Park Commission built five tennis courts and four baseball fields in the park. Although most of Chicago's parks featured athletic contests, Grant Park served as the location for the higher-profile competitions, which included local or regional contests. For example, the park hosted the International Games, which featured Olympic sporting events for athletes primarily from the United States and Canada. In order to better serve the participants of these events, the South Park Commission constructed underground restrooms.[14] This is the first documented set of restrooms in the park. Earlier visitors might have used facilities in businesses along Michigan Avenue, or they may have used those at the Art Institute of Chicago.

Figure 5.2. International Aviation Meet, Chicago, 1911. Chicago Park District Special Collections.

Bennett and Grant Park's Final Design

With the deaths of Burnham in 1912 and Ward the following year, it was time for new players to take center stage. Bennett and his architectural firm emerged as the force primarily responsible for the design of Grant Park. For the South Park Commission, Bennett was the natural choice, as he had worked closely with park commissioners in the past and was a close associate of Burnham. As coauthor of the 1909 Plan of Chicago, he was uniquely positioned to provide a design for Grant Park and leadership for the improvement of the lakefront. Perhaps still feeling the sting from the protracted litigation in the court cases with Ward and desiring a fresh start, the South Park Commission shelved the Olmsted brothers' comprehensive plans and went forward with projects that improved discrete aspects of the park. The architectural firm of Bennett, Parsons, and Frost drafted plans that would ultimately provide the definitive design for the park.

Before his work on Grant Park, Bennett created designs for the South Park Commission's smaller parks. In his lifetime, Bennett garnered a reputation as a premier architect, city planner, and central figure in the City Beautiful movement. Born in England, Bennett received training in architecture from 1895 to 1902 at the École des Beaux-Arts in Paris. He then traveled to New York where he worked with architect George B. Post. His life changed when he took a position with Daniel Burnham, who had Bennett draft a plan for the military academy at West Point and then employed Bennett's skills in realizing a plan for San Francisco, which was interrupted by the earthquake and resultant fire that devastated the city in 1906.[15] With these high-profile projects for background, Bennett set to work with Burnham on the 1909 Plan of Chicago.

In his professional career, Bennett developed zoning and comprehensive plans that included regional concerns, especially transportation. Bennett, drawing on his training in France, used neoclassically designed structures to define the landscape. His work incorporated the progressive era's desire for efficiency in urban areas, which called for improved governmental services.

Given the considerable demands of his work in Chicago, Burnham began to scale back his professional involvement and tended to refer projects to Bennett and his partners William E. Parsons (1872–1939) and Harry T. Frost (1886–1943). Bennett quickly gained a reputation for himself and took on a number of major projects. During his career, he drafted plans for other cities, including Minneapolis, Detroit, and Portland, Oregon.[16]

Bennett served from 1913 to 1930 as the consulting architect for the Chicago Plan Commission, which architectural historian Joan E. Draper calls "a semi-official, quasi-public organization, created not by ordinance, but only by councilmanic resolution."[17] The plan commission advised the city, but its recommendations did not carry the weight of law, so Bennett, who during these years founded Bennett, Parsons, and Frost, was a guiding force in the design of Grant Park but did not have the final say in matters related to its design.[18] Bennett's first efforts in Grant Park involved designing decorative work along Michigan Avenue. Bennett and his architectural firm would go on to create a series of plans for Grant Park between 1917 and 1929.[19]

The design and installation of an ornamental concrete balustrade, a blocks-long work featuring walkways, colonnades, fountains, and pylons, was the first part of Bennett's work for Grant Park. Between 1914 and 1916, Bennett worked on his park design's cornerstone on the northwest corner of Michigan Avenue and Randolph Street. The Olmsted brothers' 1908 plan had proposed covering over a section of the railroad tracks, but Bennett decided to obscure the view of the tracks instead with an elegant elevated promenade evocative in design of the World's Columbian Exposition, which brought the added benefit of screening out some of the noise and smoke from the engines. Visitors could stroll along the new embankment.

H. Eilenberger and Company was the general contractor for the project. The Architectural Decorations Company completed all of the concrete casting in a temporary plant near Randolph Street, with workers transporting elements for the balustrade over industrial tracks set up in the park (see fig. 5.3).

Figure 5.3. Early balustrade along North Michigan Avenue, between Washington and Madison Streets, 1914. (ICHi-32192) Chicago History Museum.

The South Park Commission also hired contractors to construct ornamental concrete west of the Illinois Central's right-of-way, beginning between Randolph Street and the Art Institute and running south to Ninth Street.[20]

Bennett and the South Park Commission used the balustrades and the design elements of columns and fountains to delineate a formal space, keeping in line with the tenets of the Plan of Chicago and reflecting Bennett's interest and training in academic classicism. This section was landscaped with trees and other greenery.[21] Some of the project's difficulties and costs were connected to bringing electricity and water to the area, but the area could be used for strolling both during the day and, when it was lighted, at night.[22]

The Art Institute of Chicago carried forward with its own plans to improve its building and grounds. The institute was the great exception to Ward's court cases that barred permanent structures from the park's landscape. Because limited frontage was available on Michigan Avenue, in 1917, the Art Institute expanded by building an extension over the Illinois Central right-of-way. Shepley, Rutan, and Coolidge, in essence, designed a unique, two-story, covered bridge (see fig. 5.4). This long and relatively narrow hall was a bridge over the tracks and allowed for larger and more elaborate

Figure 5.4. The lakefront, ca. 1917. The Art Institute is in foreground, with Gunsaulus Hall and Navy Pier on the horizon. Photograph by Kaufmann and Fabry Co. (ICHi-38981) Chicago History Museum.

expansions in the future. In their design, the architects took into consideration the vibrations the railroad passing underneath caused. This engineering solution demonstrated the innovative nature of the Art Institute's leadership when faced with an obstacle to its growth.

With this new structure, the Art Institute not only expanded its physical complex but also made significant improvements to the nearby landscape by installing a fountain, which was the first gift to the city of Chicago from the lumber merchant Benjamin F. Ferguson (1837–1905). Inspired by works of public art that he saw during his travels in Europe, Ferguson left the Art Institute a bequest of $1 million for the construction of monuments and statues "along the boulevards or in other public places in Chicago."[23] From the fund's earnings, in 1907, the trustees of the Art Institute commissioned Lorado Taft, notable sculptor and teacher at the School of the Art Institute, to design and build a bronze fountain. As proposed, Taft's project cost under $60,000.[24]

Six years later, on September 9, 1913, the district unveiled Taft's Spirit of the Great Lakes on the south wall of the Art Institute. Taft's sculpture took the form of five female figures symbolizing the Great Lakes. Water flowed from the top figure, representing Lake Superior, on to Michigan, Huron, Erie, and finally Ontario. The fountain, dedicated to Ferguson, was the first of many works by Taft in Chicago.[25]

The Art Institute next dispersed monies from the Ferguson monument fund for a bronze statue of George Washington. Perhaps reflecting the patriotic spirit engendered by the Great War, the Art Institute in 1917 installed the statue by the main entrance on Michigan Avenue. Based on a well-known marble original by Jean Antoine Houdon (1741–1828) that stands in the Virginia State Capitol at Richmond, the Art Institute's bronze Washington was one of twenty-two copies the Gorham Company cast. Serving as both a work of art and a symbol of American democracy, Washington is portrayed in the uniform of a continental soldier. The statue became a popular feature of the Art Institute and the focus of flag ceremonies and other patriotic activities.[26]

The following year, the South Park Commission placed a statue of Washington's compatriot Alexander Hamilton just north of the Art Institute. Bela Pratt sculpted the statue, which is set in the balustrade in a decorative niche along Michigan Avenue between Madison and Monroe Streets. Dedicated on September 28, 1918, Hamilton, holding an open scroll, complements the neoclassical balustrade. The Ferguson fund paid for the statue of Hamilton, one of three works that marked the Illinois Centennial of 1918.[27] The statues of Washington and Hamilton stand as civic lessons in bronze and aptly reflect a theme of national sacrifice.

During World War I, the South Park Commission provided sites for a number of fundraisers and civic events related to the conflict. H. S.

Richards, South Park Commission member, wrote that "various street-dances and entertainments in connection with Liberty Loans, Red Cross affairs or other war activities were given by local organizations at which the park forces assisted in providing facilities." Like many Chicagoans, their chief park was pressed into patriotic service. In Grant Park, specifically, in 1918, the district allowed for a military demonstration, which occupied the park for two weeks. Also in 1918, following the exhibition, the district permitted a circus to operate in Grant Park "under the auspices of the Stage Women's War Relief organization for the benefit largely of the soldiers' and sailors' clubs."[28]

The war economy did not have an immediate effect on the physical development of Grant Park, although, in 1918, the South Park Commission was briefly restrained from large-scale changes because of the high cost of wartime construction. The district did, however, carry on with projects that had already begun, had been contracted, or were deemed mandatory. This work included laying down sod, which required some land movement, and planting near the Logan monument.[29]

Concerts in Grant Park

The South Park Commission made a significant addition to its programming in Grant Park when the Chicago Band Association (CBA) built a small, wooden bandstand in 1915 (see fig. 5.5). It is likely that the commission paid for this structure to be erected at Michigan Avenue and Congress Street.[30] It appears that the band shell remained in the park until 1921, and its story is closely linked with William Weil, the association's director.

Weil, who had served as the music director at the Louisiana Purchase Exposition of 1904 in Saint Louis, founded and conducted the band. Under his baton, the CBA held its inaugural concert at the Chicago Board of Trade on January 2, 1911. As one journalist wrote, the band planned to "furnish a refreshing treat for home folks and visitors during the summer in the center of the city. Nightly concerts [were performed] at Grant Park on the Lake Front."[31] Between 1911 and 1915, the CBA also played at a number of sites around the city and set the precedent for free public concerts in the park.

In 1915, the CBA performed in the band shell in Grant Park, inaugurating its schedule of biweekly summer concerts on Wednesday and Saturday nights from early July through the middle of August. These uniformed performers played popular music and became a regular feature of the park through 1921. The band was also requested to perform in other venues, such as the New Year's Day concert at the Art Institute in 1917, Jackson Park, Washington Park, Lincoln Park, and many other locations.[32] The district probably sponsored most of the early concerts, but, in 1920, business groups

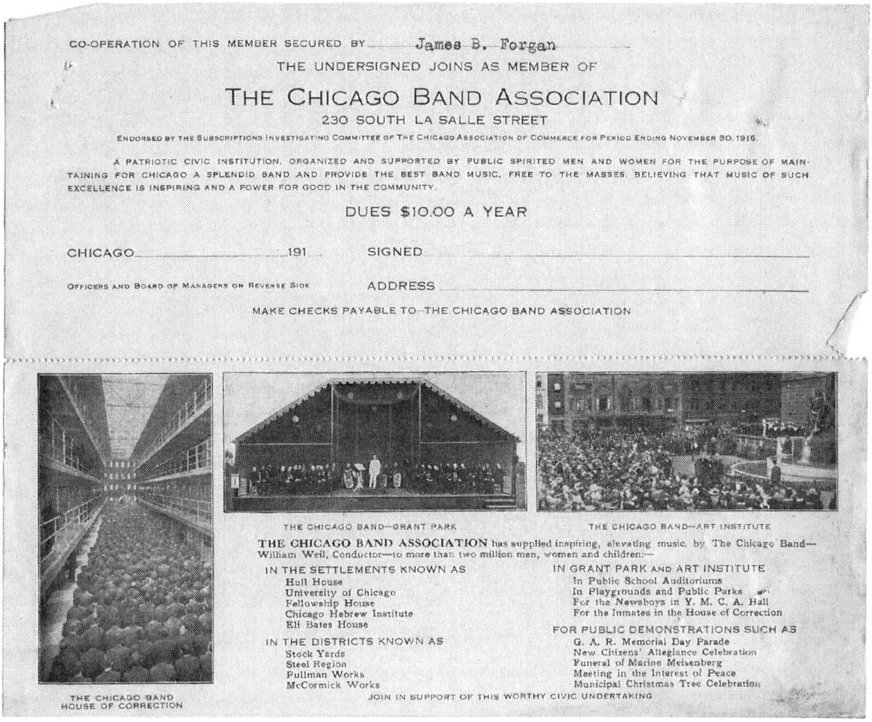

CO-OPERATION OF THIS MEMBER SECURED BY James B. Forgan

THE UNDERSIGNED JOINS AS MEMBER OF

THE CHICAGO BAND ASSOCIATION

230 SOUTH LA SALLE STREET

ENDORSED BY THE SUBSCRIPTIONS INVESTIGATING COMMITTEE OF THE CHICAGO ASSOCIATION OF COMMERCE FOR PERIOD ENDING NOVEMBER 30, 1916.

A PATRIOTIC CIVIC INSTITUTION, ORGANIZED AND SUPPORTED BY PUBLIC SPIRITED MEN AND WOMEN FOR THE PURPOSE OF MAINTAINING FOR CHICAGO A SPLENDID BAND AND PROVIDE THE BEST BAND MUSIC, FREE TO THE MASSES; BELIEVING THAT MUSIC OF SUCH EXCELLENCE IS INSPIRING AND A POWER FOR GOOD IN THE COMMUNITY.

DUES $10.00 A YEAR

CHICAGO .... 191 ... SIGNED ....

OFFICERS AND BOARD OF MANAGERS ON REVERSE SIDE ADDRESS ....

MAKE CHECKS PAYABLE TO THE CHICAGO BAND ASSOCIATION

THE CHICAGO BAND HOUSE OF CORRECTION

THE CHICAGO BAND—GRANT PARK

THE CHICAGO BAND—ART INSTITUTE

THE CHICAGO BAND ASSOCIATION has supplied inspiring, elevating music, by The Chicago Band—William Weil, Conductor—to more than two million men, women and children:—

IN THE SETTLEMENTS KNOWN AS
Hull House
University of Chicago
Fellowship House
Chicago Hebrew Institute
Eli Bates House

IN THE DISTRICTS KNOWN AS
Stock Yards
Steel Region
Pullman Works
McCormick Works

IN GRANT PARK AND ART INSTITUTE
In Public School Auditoriums
In Playgrounds and Public Parks
For the Newsboys in Y. M. C. A. Hall
For the Inmates in the House of Correction

FOR PUBLIC DEMONSTRATIONS SUCH AS
G. A. R. Memorial Day Parade
New Citizens' Allegiance Celebration
Funeral of Marine Meisenberg
Meeting in the Interest of Peace
Municipal Christmas Tree Celebration

JOIN IN SUPPORT OF THIS WORTHY CIVIC UNDERTAKING

Figure 5.5. Chicago Band Association membership form, ca. 1916. (ICHi-38983) Chicago History Museum.

paid for the Chicago Band to play in Grant Park, while the commission paid for concerts in other parks.[33]

The CBA created a unique niche for itself as the civic band of Chicago by drumming up support for local charities. During World War I, the band marched and performed for a number of war-related causes. For example, in 1918, the band performed in support of the Red Cross, the YMCA, the U.S. War Library, Smokes for Sammy (collecting money to buy tobacco for servicemen), Northwestern University Settlement, Eli Bates Settlement, and Hull House–Henry Booth House settlements. The band played at many of the South Park Commission's fifty band concerts held in July and August.[34]

Partially to recognize the role of the CBA within the city, the association gave one of its most important performances on Wednesday, August 17, 1921. On that evening, the association held the Chicago Association of Commerce Night, Rotary Club of Chicago Night, and the Chicago Band Association Night on the bandstand at Michigan Avenue at Congress Street. The concert celebrated Weil's tenth year as director and conductor of the band association.[35]

After 1921, the CBA began to decline along with the health of its director, who died in 1926. The demise of the orchestra was gradual, making it unclear when the CBA finally officially disbanded or when the bandstand was removed, but after Weil's death, free public concerts in Grant Park came to an end for a time.[36] With the Chicago Band Association, music had become a feature in the park.

The Field Museum

The Olmsted brothers had envisioned in their 1908 Plan for Grant Park that the Field Museum and the Crerar Library would be central features of park. When the court ruled in favor of Ward in 1911, it forbade construction within the historical designation of Grant Park. Determined to build these two long-anticipated cultural institutions on the lakefront, the South Park Commission creatively modified its plans. The Illinois Central Railroad offered an area of land it was reclaiming from the lake to the south of Twelfth Street as a site for the museum. The court ruling didn't apply to this site because it lay just outside the original designation of public land on the park's southern boundary.[37] As part of the land-transfer agreement, the Illinois Central obtained permission for a new central depot complementing the architectural style of the Field Museum. Although the railroad ultimately chose not to build this station, the Illinois Central increased its right-of-way along the lakefront from three hundred to six hundred feet.[38]

In 1913, the South Park Commission moved quickly to create land and enclose an area to be filled with a breakwater. It then directed contractors to deposit landfill south of Grant Park between Eleventh and Sixteenth Streets. After considerable discussion, in 1915, the South Park Commission and Field Museum trustees reached an accord on the construction of the museum on landfill south of Grant Park at Twelfth Street, east of the Illinois Central's right-of-way.[39] An undisputed site for the museum was finally established. But the physical challenges of building the museum would be no less problematic than locating the building had been.

Burnham created the early design for the museum, with the architectural firm of Graham, Anderson, Probst, and White overseeing its completion.[40] After the landfill operation was completed in 1915, the Thompson Starrett Company began construction of the Field Museum on July 26, 1915, pushing ahead with the work foundations and construction south of Grant Park in 1916 and 1917. The South Park Commissioners reported in 1917 that they hoped the Field Museum of Natural History would be finished by June 1918.[41]

This was not to be. Problems with construction of the Field Museum varied from wartime material shortages to the difficulties of constructing a building on newly created landfill. The frame and exterior of the vast building took another two years to complete. Half of the Field was buried underground, making it proportionate in height to the Art Institute, and the distinctive columns and pediments of Field's neoclassical façade were in keeping with the Art Institute's design. Situated just outside of Grant Park, the magnificent edifice of the Field Museum was decidedly removed from the center of activity in the park (see fig. 5.6).

By early 1920, with only interior work remaining, the museum's trustees made plans to transport the exhibits from the Field Museum of Natural History, in the former Palace of Fine Arts Building (now the Museum of Science and Industry), in Jackson Park to the new site, and the commission began to improve its landscape. On October 20, 1920, the South Park Commissioners passed an ordinance that extended Grant Park "to include the area from Randolph Street to 13th street, a total area of 205.14 acres."[42] The Field Museum ultimately opened within Grant Park, although the commission had to expand the park to make that happen.

The other major structural feature of the Olmsted brothers' 1908 plan had been the Crerar Library. Since 1897, the library had been operating on two floors of the Marshall Field Annex building at Wabash and Washington Streets. However, both the library's trustees and South Park Commissioners

Figure 5.6. Field Museum of Natural History, 1921. Chicago Park District Special Collections.

had set their sights on a location in Grant Park. Unlike the Field Museum, the library's funding did not depend on its location. In 1912, after the Ward ruling, the Crerar Library's trustees secured a site on the northwest corner of Randolph Street and Michigan Avenue, north of the Chicago Public Library. Wartime shortages delayed the completion of the library until 1920, and readers entered the neoclassically inspired skyscraper early the next year.

The Lake Front Ordinances of 1919 and Grant Park's Boundaries

The South Park Commission had plans, surveys, and drawings made for a comprehensive design of the newly created land on the lakefront, but the commission could not act without the cooperation of city authorities, particularly the City of Chicago, and railroad executives to recover riparian rights lost in the mid-nineteenth century to the Illinois Central Railroad. In exchange for these rights, the Illinois Central wanted the city to permit the railroad to enlarge its right-of-way.[43] In order to set out the "rights, privileges and obligations of each of the parties" and work toward realizing the Burnham Plan of Chicago, the City of Chicago, the Illinois Central Railroad, and the Secretary of War, who had long been involved in the Chicago Harbor's riparian rights, agreed to the Lake Front Ordinances of 1919.[44]

In addition to making the development of the lakefront possible, the ordinances provided for some tangible improvements in and around Grant Park. The Illinois Central agreed to "depress its tracks from 9 to 14 feet below ground level, construct 12 viaducts and new freight facilities, electrify 405 miles of its tracks, and tear down its old station at 11th Street and build a new one at 12th Street that would be similar in design to the Field Museum."[45]

The South Park Commission allowed the Illinois Central Railroad to build a pedestrian subway under Michigan Avenue at Randolph Street. Approved by a city ordinance dated July 21, 1919, this passageway led to the existing passenger station.[46] In this way, the city facilitated safer foot traffic across the widened Michigan Avenue, which would soon have considerably more traffic with the opening of the Michigan Avenue bridge. One of the aims of the ordinances was to permit automobiles and foot traffic beyond the railroad tracks.

In a further show of support, Chicagoans, in the February 24, 1920, general election, passed the first bonds that made a great number of projects possible related to the ordinances. The South Park District now had $3,700,000 to spend on Grant Park alone.[47] The Chicago Plan Commission, with Bennett as its consulting architect, had been instrumental in gathering support for these measures. Over the years, other bond issues would raise hundreds of millions of dollars to go to projects outlined in the plan.[48]

The city and South Park Commission undertook work on an enormous scale. Workers filled in Chicago's lakeshore for approximately six miles. Contractors had already filled the area at Twelfth Street and continued to the south of the Field Museum. To facilitate the fill project, in 1920, General Superintendent Foster reported that contractors had built a breakwater that stretched "from 12th Street to 24th Street. The contractors continued the project and ultimately reached 57th Street."[49] This made it possible for the lakefront park to complete Burnham's vision that the lakefront should connect between Grant Park and Jackson Park.

Despite the optimism and cooperation expressed in the Lake Front Ordinances, each of the parties would fall short in fulfilling its obligations. Although the railroad did make a number of modifications according to the ordinances, the Illinois Central did not build a new train station and lagged in the electrification of its engines. The South Park Commission did not complete all of the landfill projects that it had outlined in the Plan of Chicago, such as the string of "islands" that Burnham and Bennett had planned. The Lake Front Ordinances, however, demonstrated a cooperative spirit among such diverse entities as the city, the park commission, and the railroad, whereas conflict had typified many of the previous dealings among these groups.

1920s Chicago: Grant Park and the Automobile

In 1920, the U.S. Census reported that more than half of the nation's population lived in cities, marking a significant transition from the country's agrarian past. The Roaring Twenties introduced major social changes, including women's suffrage and the prohibition of the sale of alcohol. In the broadest sense, the United States experienced a profound cultural shift during the decade that marked a major change in technology, including the increasing use of the automobile and the radio. American society became known for its culture of consumption. In Chicago, the 1920s marked one of the greatest building booms in the city's history. This era gave the city such iconic structures as the Wrigley Building and Buckingham Fountain. The city also gained a reputation for organized crime, symbolized by figures like Al Capone, and a vibrant jazz culture, featuring Louis Armstrong.

The automobile transformed the American landscape, particularly city centers. In 1909, Chicago had three hundred licensed vehicles, although this underrepresented the actual number of cars, since many were unlicensed. By the 1920s, the automobile had become a regular feature of Chicago's urban landscape. The number of automobiles increased annually, driving the City of Chicago's need to add, expand, and improve its roadways.

Along Michigan Avenue, Grant Park received more traffic as a result of the opening of the Michigan Avenue bridge, an innovative double-deck bridge (see fig. 5.7). Engineers Hugh Young and Thomas Pihlfeldt built a drawbridge divided in half at the center of the river; each half weighed around 3,340 tons. The bridge had wide pedestrian walkways on both the east and west sides of the bridge and accommodated four lanes of traffic.

Figure 5.7. New Michigan Avenue bridge, Chicago. Postcard.

Bennett, who had designed the balustrades on Grant Park's western edge, received the high-profile commission to create the neoclassical decorations that would obscure the mechanical workings of the state-of-the-art span. Bennett's efforts were later joined by bas-reliefs by sculptor Henry Hering, depicting historical subjects, such as Chicago pioneers and the Battle of Chicago from the War of 1812.[50]

Opened to the public on May 20, 1920, the bridge, wide for that time, formed a plaza of sorts over the Chicago River. The bridge increased the desirability of the real estate along the river at Michigan Avenue. Within ten years, the bridge was bordered by some of Chicago's most recognizable buildings of the decade, including the Wrigley Building (1921–24), the Stone Container Building (1923), the Tribune Tower (1925), and the Medinah Athletic Club (1929). These structures and the bridge served as an anchor for the commercial development of North Michigan Avenue and for the movement of people, especially in automobiles, to and from the Loop, south of the river.[51]

In a significant decision for future park usage, the South Park Commission built a surface parking lot in Grant Park at Monroe Street in 1921. With space for eleven thousand automobiles, this lot supplied parking near the Loop accessible from Michigan Avenue.[52] With the success of this lot, the commission further considered the need for parking in the city. A number of automobile clubs and the Association of Commerce had weighed the possibility of building an underground garage in Grant Park. This underground parking plan would have the dual advantage of providing parking and allowing for the continued development of the surface of the park for recreation. The district hoped that income from the garage would offset its cost, which had been calculated at around $10,000,000. Although not acted on at that time, this idea lingered as a possibility for the park.[53]

In order to further accommodate the automobile on the eastern edge of the park, in 1921, the South Park Commission formally proposed building an outer drive (later, renamed Lake Shore Drive) along the lakefront and outlined means of securing funding for the project, which would realize the dream of a boulevard connecting Grant and Jackson Parks along the lake shore. The commissioners would also extend Grant Park's boundaries to the harbor line. The City Plan Commission provided direction for this project and advocated enlarging the park with landfill into the harbor. The commission filed a request for the extension, and on August 17, 1921, the Secretary of War permitted the change to the harbor line, and preparations began for the park expansion.[54]

The commission immediately started construction on a bulkhead for the extension. Once this was in place, contractors deposited fill into the area. By now, the contractors had become expert at filling in Lake Michigan's shoreline, and as a result, by 1923, they had almost finished the harbor extension.[55] The commission had enlarged the park by three hundred feet to the east and began work on the roadway that terminated at Randolph Street.

Because of the increased traffic along Michigan Avenue and the peril it held for people on foot, the South Park Commissioners advocated that the Illinois Central build a pedestrian subway at Van Buren Street under Michigan Avenue in 1924. Pedestrians now could safely cross under the multilane boulevard, and automobiles could more easily make their way along Michigan Avenue. In 1925, the district provided some of the funds and allowed the Illinois Central to build another pedestrian subway at Roosevelt Road.[56] The South Park Commission then repaved Michigan Avenue between Randolph Street and Jackson Boulevard and added a lane on Michigan's east side between Randolph and Monroe to facilitate the movement of traffic. These changes aided motorists exiting the parking lot within Grant Park at Monroe. The district also added a lane on Michigan's east side between Washington and Randolph Streets.

One of the unintended results of the Outer Drive was that it cut off access to the lake for the Chicago Yacht Club, the Columbia Yacht Club, and the Illinois Naval Reserve. The yacht clubs reached an accord with the South Park Commissioners in 1924 when the secretary of war and State of Illinois granted the clubs the right to create a little offshore island and connect it to the park.[57] In 1925, the Chicago Yacht Club relocated to an area of additional fill deposited beyond the Outer Drive at Monroe Street.[58] The Columbia Yacht Club, however, moved north to the foot of Washington Street and moored a ship off the lakefront that served as its clubhouse. For its part, the Illinois Naval Reserve relocated north near Randolph Street on the lakefront.[59]

Another complication was that the Outer Drive ended at Randolph Street. Addressing this limitation, Hugh E. Young, chief engineer for the Chicago Plan Commission, began in 1926 to make preparations for a span over the Chicago River from Randolph Street north to Ohio Street. Because of delays caused in part by the Great Depression that began in 1929, it would be more than a decade before this bridge was completed.

As a result of construction along Michigan Avenue and the creation of the Outer Drive, Grant Park was bounded on the west and east by significant roadways and a large parking lot on the north. Visitors to the park now could use the Outer Drive to drive along the east side of the park or get to the Field Museum, but it made Grant Park an island bounded by busy roads. The commission didn't completely neglect pedestrians, however, and had constructed under-the-road passageways and walkways and placed stop-and-go signals and stop signs along its boulevard system to ensure visitors could still get to the park in safety.[60]

South of Grant Park and Soldier Field

South of Grant Park, the South Park Commission worked with the city and the Chicago Plan Commission on the "Lake Front Park Development." Charles Wacker, chair of the Chicago Plan Commission, outlined in 1921 the goals of the project: "[W]hile the Chicago Plan is a practical and commercial one, there is another and deeper motive in planning for the future greatness of our city than its splendid material upbuilding. This is the social, intellectual, and moral upbuilding of the people. City building means man building."[61] This kind of project would make an environment in which people could thrive, not just live. Chicago's citizens concurred and approved $20,000,000 in bonds.

The plan called for another landfill project, which would add 1,138 acres between Sixteenth and Thirty-Ninth Streets. The expansion provided the land for the extension of Grand Boulevard as well as lagoons, bathing beaches, and areas for sports, such as baseball, tennis, and golf. These ambitious projects would consume the energies of the Chicago Plan Commission and the South Park Commission for a number of years.[62] The groundwork for this project had been set in place by agreements reached in the Lake Front Ordinances of 1919.

In 1921, the commission called for architects to draft designs for a stadium south of the Field Museum. The first architectural proposals proved too costly so the commissioners requested revisions to be submitted by the middle of 1922. Once again, the district collected bids and this time hired the architecture firm of Holabird and Roche to build the stadium in a fine neoclassical style that would complement the Field Museum and recall the World's Columbian Exposition.[63]

Construction of the Municipal Grant Park Stadium began in 1923 and was completed the following year. The city used the site for the City Police Field Meet on September 8 and 9, 1924.[64] On October 9, 1924, the city and the district held the first official event at the stadium in observance of Chicago Day, with the mayor and others addressing a crowd of around forty thousand people who then watched a polo game with sides captained by Frank Bering and Colonel R. R. McCormick. During the first year, the commission used the stadium for football games, festivals, circuses, concerts, and civic demonstrations.

The success of the first year convinced the district to expand the complex. Voters eventually approved the South Park Commission referendum for $3,000,000 in South Side developments, which included expansion of the stadium in keeping with the architects' original designs. In the meantime, the city rededicated the stadium as Soldier Field on Veterans Day, November

11, 1925, in honor, as former Governor Frank O. Lowden declared, of "all the fallen heroes of all the wars we ever fought."[65] In 1926, with architectural modifications complete, Vice President Charles Gates Dawes dedicated the structure to the war dead during the Army-Navy football game. Over the years, Soldier Field would be used for a wide array of activities, including boxing, football, and car races.[66]

Within the historic boundaries of Grant Park, the South Park Commission continued to offer a variety of activities that ranged from baseball and trap shooting to civic gatherings. Following the precedent of earlier Fourth of July military encampments, the district permitted the Hopi Indians as well as a group of Boy Scouts to camp in the park in 1924. The next year, Saint John's Military Academy bivouacked in the eastern part of the park.[67]

After filling in the lakeshore and constructing the Outer Drive, the commission continued to bring other areas east of the railroad right-of-way to uniform grade, completing the last section of land, between Roosevelt Road and Congress Street, in 1924. The commission also hired contractors to lay the remaining sewer and water system in the park. This new area, featuring "an elevated central garden, a large athletic field . . . , a broad lake shore driveway, and ample walks and cross drive," opened to public in 1923.[68]

Improvement at the Art Institute of Chicago

The Art Institute of Chicago continued to influence the landscape in Grant Park. Just south of the Art Institute in 1924, the memorial Spirit of Music was dedicated to Theodore Thomas, founder of the Chicago Symphony Orchestra and musical director of the World's Columbian Exposition. The monument lauded Thomas's life and career and underlined the close relationship between Grant Park and classical music in Chicago.[69] It was fitting that Thomas's monument was set in the park, as he had conducted symphonic music in the Inter-State Industrial Building in the 1880s.

With a commission paid from the Ferguson monument fund, Albin Polasek, who directed the sculpture department of the School of the Art Institute of Chicago from 1917 to 1943, created the fifteen-foot-tall, bronze figure of a heroic woman holding a lyre. Polasek designed the main figure to stand on a round base decorated, as described in a popular guide to public sculpture, "with low relief figures of Orpheus playing his lyre, Chibiabos, from Longfellow's 'Song of Hiawatha' singing, and a group of animals listening." The whole display was framed by a granite wall with a seating area architect Howard Van Doren Shaw designed that featured a profile bas-relief of Thomas flanked by orchestra members with their instruments.[70] If viewers had difficulty discerning the allegorical statue, they would have no problem with the bas-relief. The dedication ceremony included a program in

Orchestra Hall with the unveiling of the sculptural work.[71] While previous monuments had commemorated military or political heroes, Spirit of Music was among the first to celebrate Chicago's cultural leaders.

In 1924, the Art Institute also began construction of the Goodman Art Theater as an extension of the building, set beyond the Illinois Central's right-of-way. Shaw created some innovative solutions in response to the Montgomery Ward decisions setting the building limitation in the park. To be compliant with the court rulings, Shaw's design situated the building underground with the back of the stage bordering the Illinois Central tracks and only the entrance above ground. The theater also was to serve as the center for the School of the Art Institute's drama department.[72] Completed in 1925, the theater was named for Kenneth Sawyer Goodman, a playwright who died at the age of thirty-five in the influenza epidemic of 1918.

Toward a Final Design for Grant Park

In 1925, the firm of Bennett, Parsons, Frost, and Thomas proposed the Revised Plan for Grant Park.[73] While Bennett kept the three-part division of the park first set out by the Olmsted brothers, he drew inspiration from the gardens of Versailles. He created a park of multiple uses with a balance of formal spaces, such as an architecturally significant entrance at Congress Street, and areas of more active use, such as the playing fields. In keeping with the precepts of the City Beautiful, he unified his design with neoclassical features, such as colonnades and a central fountain. As Louis XIV's garden had demonstrated order and a clear understanding of the power between the king and his people, Grant Park came to embody the orderly city of the twentieth century. As a result, the park design reflected the tastes of the cultural and economic elite.

With the needs of the twentieth-century city in mind, Bennett and his partners planned for the extensive use of the automobile and the Outer Drive. With the anticipated increased activity beyond the Illinois Central's right-of-way, the South Park Commission knew it eventually would need to construct a number of bridges over the lowered rail lines between Jackson Boulevard and Roosevelt Road. In 1925, the district began building bridges at Jackson Boulevard and Seventh Street, budgeting $225,000 for each of these spans. After tearing down the old viaduct at Van Buren, the commission erected a new pedestrian bridge from the supports up and then started construction of bridges at Jackson, Congress, and Harrison.[74] The bridges also necessitated roadways, some of which would connect to the Outer Drive.

Where the earlier design by the Olmsted brothers had placed the Field Museum at the center of Grant Park, Bennett proposed a magnificent fountain at the park's center, which would be allowed according to the court rulings that had banned buildings within the park's boundaries (see fig. 5.8). With enthusiasm the South Park Commission promised, "[T]his fountain will surpass anything of the kind that has yet been attempted."[75] Kate S. Buckingham (1858–1937) donated $750,000 for the fountain as a gift to the city and a monument to her brother Clarence (1854–1913), a former trustee of the Art Institute. She also provided $300,000 for the fountain's ongoing maintenance and operation.[76] The South Park Commission demonstrated considerable foresight in having Buckingham provide for the maintenance, as it has truly made the fountain a lasting monument.

Bennett and his architectural firm positioned the fountain at the center of the park, east of the Illinois Central Railroad tracks and in line with Congress Street, where it would serve as a visual intermediary between Lake Michigan and the city. Bennett drew inspiration from the Latona Basin, a fountain at Versailles. The base of Buckingham Fountain, 280 feet

Figure 5.8. Buckingham Fountain. Chicago Park District Special Collections.

in diameter, represents Lake Michigan. Bennett then divided the basin with four pairs of highly stylized, bronze sea horses. Each pair was placed in a quarter of the basin, depicting the four states bordering Lake Michigan.[77]

Beyond its spectacularly impressive geyser, which shoots three hundred feet into the air, the fountain is also a notable work of art. Bennett assembled a team of skilled artists to create aspects of the work. For the specific sculptural details, Bennett selected French sculptor Marcel Loyau to design and cast the long, bronze sea horses, which won the Prix National in the 1927 Paris Salon. Bennett invited Jacques Lamber of Paris to sculpt the fountain's dolphin motif and baroque decorative elements. The engineering staff of Chicago's Water Department installed the water jets to create a night spectacle, with much of the spray illuminated with lights. The formal construction and assembling of the parts of the fountain took place in 1926 and 1927. On August 26, 1927, fifty thousand people gathered in the park for the dedication. John Philip Sousa performed, and the South Park Commissioners dedicated the work to the City of Chicago.[78] By 1925, Bennett, Parson, Frost, and Thomas devised a formal entrance and plaza to Congress Street that took advantage of the sight line the fountain provided (see fig. 5.9). Dating back to Burnham and Bennett's 1909 Plan of Chicago, when Congress Plaza was conceived of as a primary focus of the city's design, the entrance coordinated with the balustrades along Michigan Avenue and larger rostral columns to designate this area as the park entrance. The plaza incorporated architectural decorations, statues, a bridge over the Illinois Central right-of-way, and small fountains to create a unified landscape at Congress and Michigan Avenue.[79] Work began in 1927 on the entrance, which was completed in 1931.

Beyond Congress Plaza, Bennett, Parsons, and Frost (Thomas was a partner only until 1924) planned for a wide bridge to span the Illinois Central's railroad tracks. In 1927, the commission started construction on three bridges, one at Congress Street and the others at Harrison and Van Buren. Given the central location, the double bridge at Congress Street would be the grandest of those built in the 1920s in Grant Park. Most of the structural work of the bridge, plaza, and approach was completed in 1928. The following year, the district repaved all of Congress Parkway and the plazas at Van Buren and Harrison Streets. At this point, the commission assumed the responsibility to maintain the viaducts over the Illinois Central's tracks.[80]

In 1929, the design for Congress Street was crowned with sculptor Ivan Mestrovic's statues known as the Indian Bowman and the Indian Spearman. The two large, muscular figures are depicted in action but without their weapons. As with other notable public sculptures within the park, the Ferguson fund paid for the massive statues.[81]

Figure 5.9. Congress Plaza, ca. 1931. Chicago Park District Special Collections.

Although some aspects of the 1925 Revised Plan for Grant Park were implemented, others were only partially realized, and some not at all. For example, the plan called for a Court of the Presidents, but the South Park Commission installed only a statue of Abraham Lincoln, originally commissioned by the Crerar Library at a time when the library anticipated building within Grant Park. The sculptor Augustus Saint-Gaudens had completed the statue of Lincoln in 1887 for the Lincoln Park District in Chicago. The South Park Commission finally placed the Lincoln statue in Grant Park in 1926 to join another statue that Saint-Gaudens had executed of Civil War hero John A. Logan, placed in the park in 1897.[82] With its installation, the Lincoln statue completed the park's triumvirate of memorials to Illinois' Civil War heroes: Logan, Grant, and Lincoln.

On August 21, 1930, the Chicago Park District dedicated two open spaces to civic leaders. It named the northern open field for Edward B. Butler, who had served as president of the Commercial Club of Chicago at the time of the Plan of Chicago and played a significant role in the passage of the Enabling Act, making it possible for the city to improve the lakefront. Butler Field is bounded by Columbus Drive on the west, Monroe Street on the north, Lake Shore Drive on the east, and Jackson Boulevard on the south. The South Park Commission named the southern open field for Charles L. Hutchinson, former president of the Art Institute of Chicago. This area is bounded by Columbus Drive on the west, Balbo Avenue on the north, Lake Shore Drive on the east, and Roosevelt Road (Twelfth Street) on the south.[83]

The fields as created did not exactly correspond with the 1925 Revised Plan for Grant Park. Butler and Hutchinson Fields had been drafted as symmetrical sections of land. The South Park Commission had extended Monroe Drive, though, and, as a result, Hutchinson Field occupied three blocks, but Butler was only two blocks north to south.[84]

In addition to statues, a grand entrance, and a monumental fountain, Bennett's design for Grant Park incorporated some aspects of Progressive Era neighborhood parks. He included open space for baseball fields and, instead of a formal field house, he set out bathrooms, referred to as comfort stations, that flanked the playing fields.[85] Bennett and his partners organized the massive expanse into a series of smaller spaces that took into account a variety of uses people had for the park. Yet, despite the division and different landscapes within Grant Park, the overall impression was one of formality and stateliness within the city.

A Site for Cultural and Civic Institutions

The building boom of the 1920s had a significant impact on the southern end of Grant Park. The South Park Commission built a peninsula that bounded the Chicago Harbor and continued to make a long, narrow spit of land toward the south that would eventually be called Northerly Island. This was the first of a number of planned "islands" that would run to the south toward Jackson Park. In time, the commissioners completed Northerly Island, and the area behind it was designated as Burnham Harbor.[86]

On the landfill east of the Field Museum, the South Park Commission built two more cultural institutions: Shedd Aquarium and Adler Planetarium. With a bequest of $3 million from John G. Shedd (1850–1926), the former president of Marshall Field and Company, the architectural firm of Graham, Anderson, Probst, and White designed the new aquarium with Magnus Gunderson providing engineering assistance. The aquarium officially opened in 1929.[87]

That same year, workers began construction on the Adler Planetarium. Whereas Bennett's 1925 Revised Plan for Grant Park had included the aquarium, it did not include the Adler, which demonstrates how rapidly the 1920s building boom progressed. The architect, Ernest Grunsfeld Jr., a graduate of the Massachusetts Institute of Technology and the École des Beaux-Arts, won the American Institute of Architects gold medal in 1931 for his design. Standing at the end of a narrow peninsula forming the harbor's south boundary, the planetarium marks a departure from the neoclassical style that had been at the center of the park's design. Ernest L. Lieberman and Peter L. Hein founded one of the premier engineering service companies, Lieberman and Hein, which provided engineering services for the innovative twelve-sided, art-deco public building.[88] Indeed, the planetarium expressed the pride of its benefactor, Sears & Roebuck executive Max Adler, who had sponsored the project because, he said, "I wanted to give some evidence of my feeling for Chicago—my pride in the city which had made it possible for me to accumulate my modest fortune."[89]

Together, the Field, Shedd, and Adler served to interpret the earth, sea, and sky, which give a visitor a comprehensive approach to natural history. It is ironic that a generation after the final decision in the much-vaunted Ward court cases banning structures from the park, three structures graced the lakefront just south of the historical boundaries of Grant Park. This demonstrates the significant energy the South Park Commission put into keeping to its vision of the park.

And, yet, one property owner on Michigan Avenue continued to protest construction in the park. In 1927, the Chicago Yacht Club started plans to build a new clubhouse on the landfill east of the Outer Drive at Monroe Street, and the Illinois General Assembly granted the club the right to erect the structure. The Stevens Hotel, however, filed an injunction in 1929 to halt the yacht club's efforts, taking up Ward's cause to keep Grant Park free of buildings. The courts eventually ruled that the new structure, built on pilings in the harbor, was technically outside of Grant Park's boundaries and not bound by the park's original designation.[90]

The Chicago Yacht Club conducted a groundbreaking ceremony on Saturday, November 30, 1929. Unfortunately, as the Great Depression affected the country over the next few years, the club's membership rapidly declined, and it lacked the funds to continue construction. Without a structure at Grant Park, the club used the yachting facilities at Belmont Harbor to the north. Eventually, the club acquired the "House of Tomorrow" from the Century of Progress Exposition of 1933–34, which the club moved to the foot of Monroe Street. Ultimately, in 1946, the club commissioned plans for a new building for its site at Monroe Street, which was completed in 1951.[91]

In a case similar to the Chicago Yacht Club, the Illinois Naval Armory added a structure just outside of Grant Park. In 1928, workers began construction north of Randolph Street, beyond the Outer Drive.[92] C. Herrick Hammond, state supervising architect, and architect Zachary T. Davis designed the massive three-story building. As one contemporary wrote, "the building is in what is to be one of the most beautiful parks in the world and must not only harmonize with the park surroundings but must harmonize also with the Shedd Aquarium, the Field Museum, Soldier's Field Stadium [sic], and the Art Institute."[93] The state situated the new three-story armory "at the foot of Randolph Street on the outer drive near where the new outer drive bridge is to be built." This structure provided a site that helped foster military preparedness for many years, but it was demolished in 1982 in order to straighten Lake Shore Drive.

Meanwhile, the Art Institute continued to expand beyond the railroads with the addition of the Alan C. Mather wing in 1926 and later the Agnes Alerton wing. Once again, the owners of the Stevens Hotel on Michigan Avenue protested that their right of "easement of light, air, and view, over Grant Park to the lake unobstructed by any buildings" had been infringed upon. The hotel hired George P. Merrick, the attorney who had argued Ward's cases, to file a suit against the Art Institute and the South Park Commission in 1930. Circuit Court Judge Hugo A. Friend granted an injunction that temporarily halted construction. But when the case went to the court of appeals, the justice ruled that on the basis of an exemption to the Ward decision allowing the original building to stand in the park, the Art Institute's expansion was permissible. After the Stevens case was settled, the Art Institute faced few challenges in building further additions.[94]

Capping this impressive era of expansion and improvements, the Art Institute added an outdoor sculptural fountain. Paid for through the Ferguson fund, the trustees placed the Triton Fountain in the Alexander McKinlock Memorial Court in 1931. The sculptor, Carl Milles (1875–1955), who lived in Lidingoan island near Stockholm, Sweden, made the fountain to celebrate Swedish Americans, especially John Ericsson, who constructed the USS *Monitor*, one of the nation's first iron-clad ships, which saw service during the Civil War.[95] With its modernist style, the fountain, composed of a number of half-human, half-fish forms, is a point of departure from earlier neoclassical works in the park.

Realizing the Vision

Between 1914 and 1930, the South Park Commission gave Grant Park its definitive form. Drawing on the model of the 1893 World's Columbian Exposition and propelled by the city's commitment to the 1909 Plan of Chicago, Grant Park became the centerpiece of a recreational lakefront. The commission also provided infrastructure—water, electricity, and roads—for the park and the lakefront. As the 1920s drew to a close, Chicagoans could finally see and celebrate their sustained efforts to create the city's "front yard."

Bennett was the figure most responsible for the final design of Grant Park. He and his architectural firm designed the balustrades along Michigan Avenue, the formal entrance at Congress Street, and Buckingham Fountain. In addition to Bennett, a number of interested parties influenced the park and its features, most notably, the trustees of the Art Institute, who expanded their space with new additions.

Within the history of Grant Park and Chicago's lakefront, much has been made of the role of Ward. Heralded as the "Savior of the Lakefront," his legal battles to keep the historical boundaries of the park "forever open, clear and free" continued to shape the development of the park. With the South Park Commission's commitment to building the Field Museum on the lakefront near the center of the city, the park's landscape and design work were delayed by a generation. From a design standpoint, rather than being the central feature of the park, the Field Museum was shunted off to the south, which limited its visual impact from the city. In its place, the commission and Bennett positioned the impressive Buckingham Fountain. In spite of Ward's efforts and his legacy of litigation, by 1930, the Field Museum, Soldier Field, Shedd Aquarium, and Adler Planetarium had all been built prominently on Chicago's lakefront. Nevertheless, Ward had a significant influence within the historical boundaries of Grant Park and informed the development of the entire lakefront.

Ward's sustained litigation also delayed the final design of the park and may have significantly influenced how visitors experience the park. It is likely that had the Field Museum been built at the center of Grant Park, the park would have been more pedestrian friendly. Coupled with this was that when the Field Museum was finally designed, the city was scrambling to accommodate private automobiles. The park, which already included a surface parking garage, also became the proposed site for underground garages, and the South Park Commission extended the park for the construction of the Outer Drive. Because of the pressure to accommodate automobiles within the park's landscape, the commission largely incorporated the park into the city's grid. Workers constructed a large, surface parking lot and a number of bridges for roads over the railroad tracks and connected these streets to the Outer Drive.

Of the two men who had a great influence on the design of Grant Park, Ward has gained greater renown for his park battles, as opposed to Bennett's role, which seems to have been diminished over the years. Bennett's designs, though in line with the City Beautiful, stood in marked contrast to more celebrated Chicago architects, such as Louis Sullivan and Jens Jenson. By comparison, Bennett appeared too steeped in European traditions to receive much acclaim in Chicago, the most American of cities. Furthermore, the plans for Grant Park did not reflect one set vision by Bennett and his architectural firm. As had been the case throughout its history, a great number of groups and individuals influenced the final design of Grant Park. Bennett served as consulting architect to the Chicago Plan Commission, and the South Park Commission hired Bennett and his firm to design significant aspects of Grant Park. Over the course of his long and distinguished career,

Bennett also created a number of designs for Chicago's Century of Progress World's Fair (1933–34). He retired from architecture in 1944, and a new generation of architects rapidly put their mark on the city.

Given the grand dreams of the turn of the century, the ultimate design of Grant Park was a compromise. And yet, without Bennett's steadfast approach, vision, and tenacity over decades of legal wrangling and numerous design changes, Grant Park would not have the enduring appeal coupled with functionality that it has today. Bennett helped to fashion a distinctive and enduring cultural landscape.

Gateway and Cultural Center: From a Century of Progress to Postwar Park

The prosperity and significant building boom that typified the 1920s began to come to an end in October 1929 with the start of the Great Depression. Despite the economic climate, Chicagoans proposed another fair for 1933 during which the city would celebrate its first hundred years. Even with the severe economic downturn, the fair's organizers pressed forward with preparations, which would require additional work in and around Grant Park.

A Century of Progress International Exposition

Much has been written about the great fair that raised people's spirits during the Great Depression. Since the early 1920s, a number of Chicagoans had been discussing the idea of the city hosting another world's fair. The 1920s were an ambitious time for Chicago to consider organizing an event of this magnitude, as it had been little more than a generation since

Chicago gained renown for hosting the World's Columbian Exposition of 1893. Yet, major business and civic leaders lobbied to use this fair to celebrate Chicago's centennial.[1]

By 1925, this idea had a considerable following, and in 1928, the city shored up support by gaining a state charter to operate the "Chicago Second World's Fair Centennial Celebration."[2] As with the World's Columbian Exposition, organizers initially suggested that Grant Park should be the site for the fair.[3] Advocates would again cite all the attributes of this location, including its proximity to the central business districts and hotels, the multitude of transportation links, and its picturesque location on the lake. Due to the design and landscape work completed in Grant Park in the 1920s, the fair's directors decided to place the fair just south of the park. The exposition planners worked with municipal representatives with an eye toward the long-term benefits the fair could bring. The South Park Commission had already moved temporary events, such as circuses, from the eastern end of Grant Park toward Soldier Field. The park land south of Grant Park with the additional acreage acquired through landfill could logically be the location for the temporary grounds of the exposition. The South Park Commission could also use the exposition as a spur to encourage the completion of the park's landscaping.

Charles Wacker, the chairman of the Chicago Plan Commission, also wanted to use the 1933 fair as an impetus to push forward aspects of Daniel H. Burnham and Edward H. Bennett's 1909 Plan of Chicago. For example, the creation of Northerly Island had been proposed in the 1909 plan and could serve as part of the site of the exposition.[4] Grant Park had already repeatedly demonstrated the long-term benefit of landfill programs. The fair's organizers decided that the grounds would extend from "the Shedd Aquarium and Adler Planetarium at 12th Street south along the lakefront to 39th Street. This site included Northerly Island, which extended south from the Adler Planetarium to 23rd Street and created a lagoon between it and the mainland." In June 1929, the state legislature authorized the use of this land for the exposition, and on April 16, 1930, the park commission gave its permission to build an exposition that would "open a new era in the exposition projects of the world."[5] Once the site had been selected, workers rapidly built on the newly created landfill. The exposition authority planned to use a bit of Grant Park for the festivities. The plan was that after the fair, the grounds would be returned to the South Park Commission. In 1930, the first building completed for the fair was the administration building, situated between Soldier Field and the Field Museum.[6]

The deepening economic downturn called plans for the fair into question. The fair's commissioners, however, pushed forward. While some have reasonably argued that the Great Depression kept labor and material costs low, it may also have lowered the expectations for the fair, which had been built up to the point that many anticipated a fair twice as grand as the one of 1893.[7]

Preparations included improvements to Grant Park, as the southeastern end of the park served as an entry to the fairgrounds. This work included planting trees along the park's wide boulevards of Monroe, Jackson, Congress, and Balbo, Twelfth Street, and the major north-to-south right-of-ways of West Drive (Columbus Drive) and East Drive (Field Drive/Outer Drive). In many ways, the South Park Commission conceived an expansive approach to the fair and eventually built a small-gauge railway to transport fairgoers to the grounds. Visitors to Grant Park had spectacular views of the fair, especially at night when the grounds were lit up.

In spite of the Great Depression, some lesser projects moved forward in the park, including the addition in 1931 of Frederick Cleveland Hibbard's (1881–1955) two bronze eagles to the Congress Street plaza. Hibbard, a Chicago resident, had studied sculpture at the School of the Art Institute and lived in Hyde Park. The South Park Commission made Hibbard's eagles, depicted in mid-flight clutching fish, the focus of two reflecting pools with small fountains serving to frame the formal entrance.[8] These two eagles joined the other impressive Congress Street elements Bennett designed and the statues of the Spearman and the Bowman Ivan Mestrovic created.

As plans for the fairground emerged in the early 1930s, the exposition authority named an architectural commission to oversee the work, which included some well-known names in Chicago, including Bennett and Daniel Burnham Jr., but also some young and newly influential figures, such as John A. Holabird and Raymond Hood. These architects conceived their work with the modernist aesthetic of art deco and that style's exuberant colors. The fanciful color palette and design concept set the fair apart from the white monochrome of the earlier World's Columbian Exposition and existing structures within Grant Park.[9]

Situated upon recently created land, the fairgrounds comprised 424 acres, including part of Grant Park, Burnham Park, and all of Northerly Island. The Field Museum, Shedd Aquarium, and Soldier Field would be featured components of the exposition but were located outside of the fairgrounds. However, the organizers included the recently built Adler Planetarium inside the official grounds. Its art-deco style blended nicely with the fair's architecture.[10]

The fair A Century of Progress opened in May 1933 under inauspicious circumstances (see fig. 6.1). The Great Depression continued to ravage the economy with a great number of people out of work. Earlier in the year, Chicagoans were shocked by the assassination of their mayor, Anton Cermak, during a purported attempt on the life of President Franklin D. Roosevelt.

Yet, not all the news from Chicago was bad, as federal prosecutors successfully tried and convicted Al Capone and sent him to prison. Within Chicago's parks, the South Park Commission opened the Museum of Science and Industry in Jackson Park in the renovated Fine Arts building that previously had been part of the World's Columbian Exposition. A Century of Progress served to temporarily transport visitors from their daily cares toward a promised brighter future.

Figure 6.1. A Century of Progress, 1933–34, aerial view. Chicago Park District Special Collections.

The fair organizers had created a magical landscape with theatrical lighting, bright colors, and a modern design. The "rainbow city," as it was popularly known, served as a metaphor for Chicago's rise from muddy morass into urban metropolis. The organizers took the unofficial motto "Science Finds, Industry Applies, Man Conforms."[11] Grant Park provided an entry to the fair and a vantage point from which to view its architectural splendor. It also offered an orderly landscape that presented Chicago in its best light to visitors. On opening day, Martha S. McGrew, an assistant to the fair's general manager Lenox R. Lohr, said, "The morning of the fair . . . we went up on the roof and looked over at the 12th Street bridge. It looked like the lines were all the way over to the Art Institute. It was the biggest thrill of all. People coming to the fair."[12] Many visiting the fair traversed Grant Park by foot and taxi, used the small-gauge railroad, or even arrived by boats that landed at the Twelfth Street dock, northwest of the Shedd Aquarium.[13]

Visitors enjoyed the exhibits and the many entertainments offered, including the high-flying Skyride, which carried fairgoers high above in "rockets," while children, particularly, enjoyed the Enchanted Isle. Sally Rand garnered perhaps the most salacious press coverage for her famous fan dance, which was part of the Streets of Paris concession.[14] In addition to the attractions, the directors fostered patriotic sentiment with the Avenue of Flags, the States Building, and the building of the U.S. government.

The exhibition featured a number of displays from foreign countries, one of the most spectacular being the Italian exhibition. With Benito Mussolini's rise to power in 1922, Italy wanted to assert its place in world affairs. The Italian government used the fair as an opportunity to garner good press and assert its claim of reviving the glories of its Roman past. Many Italians lived in Chicago, and some took pride in the new Italian government.

The fair's pageantry and spectacle included one of the great events of early aviation history. Italo Balbo, Italian Fascist and aviator, flew to the fair with his squadron on July 15, 1933. Balbo, a regional Italian political leader who allied himself with Mussolini, conducted this goodwill flight of twenty-four Savoia-Marchetti SM.55X flying boats from Italy to Chicago. The trip, which included a stop in New York, remains one of the great early exploits in the annals of aviation. Flying in formation, the Italian pilots made their way around the globe before splashing down on Lake Michigan. The flight captured the imagination of a great number of people around the world.

Italian citizens of Chicago also had a part in one of the most interesting chapters in the fair. The Columbus Monument Committee raised funds for a statue of Christopher Columbus in Grant Park. During the World's Columbian Exposition of 1893, a Columbus monument had served as both a celebration of Columbus and a commemoration.[15] For the 1933 world's fair, the committee paid for another statue and organized the dedication of the monument in the southern part of Grant Park at Columbus Drive and Roosevelt Road.

On August 3, 1933, Italian Day at A Century of Progress, a crowd of twenty-five thousand including dignitaries gathered for the dedication of the new Columbus statue. The event included the unveiling of a larger-than-life Columbus, which stands on a pedestal featuring fasces that are bound elm rods with ax heads symbolizing Roman imperial power. The Fascist Party had appropriated this symbol as its own in the twentieth century as a way of linking itself with the imperial past. Columbus, being from Genoa, provided a potent symbol of one who embodied the exploring spirit, the spread of Christianity, and the glory of Italy's past. Representatives read messages from Premier Mussolini and President Roosevelt at the event. Judge Francis J. Borelli, chairman of the monument committee, also read a telegram General Balbo sent from Newfoundland. The day's festivities ended with a performance of *Aida* in the court of the Hall of Sciences.[16]

The Columbus monument evoked the glories of the past. By extension, Balbo, in leading his air squadron around the globe, could be viewed as a new Columbus. The city further honored the achievement of the Italian with the dedication of Balbo Avenue, which runs through Grant Park.[17] Another extant remnant of the fair is the Balbo column, a Roman column that stood in front of the Italian exhibit at the fair. It remains east of Soldier Field as a reminder of Balbo, the Fascist era, and A Century of Progress itself.[18]

Enmeshed in the spectacular setting and views, entertained by music and roller coaster alike, the fair served as a tonic for those beset by severe economic reversal. The exposition seemed to argue for Americans to maintain faith in progress and technology towards a brighter future. General Rufus Dawes, president of A Century of Progress and brother of Charles Gates Dawes, vice president of the United States, said, "Here are gathered the evidences of man's achievements in the realm of physical science—proofs of his power to prevail over all the perils that beset him. Here in the presence of such victories men may gather courage to face their unsolved problems."[19]

Because of the Great Depression, some people questioned the exposition's rosy forecast for the future of the nation's capitalistic system. The exposition, however, promoted the role of corporate America and featured a number of displays corporations sponsored, including General Motors, Firestone, and International Harvester. Grant Park already had many architectural testaments to Chicago businessmen, including the Art Institute of Chicago and the aptly named Field Museum, both receiving significant financial support from Marshall Field. The Shedd Aquarium and the Adler Planetarium also received significant support from their central benefactors. The park and

A Century of Progress together served to reinforce the importance of big business in America.

President Roosevelt paid a visit to the fair late in its first season, during which he and the exposition organizers discussed a one-year extension.[20] The fair's leadership decided to remain open for a second season, despite the temporary nature of the structures. Although not quite as triumphant or as grand as the inaugural year, the second season enjoyed considerable economic and popular success. During the two seasons of the event, over thirty-nine million people visited the grounds.[21] The exposition authority ran the fair from May 27, 1933, to November 12, 1933, and then from May 26, 1934, through October 31, 1934.

Visitors to A Century of Progress left with a variety of memories. Some would recall the astounding technological marvels, such as the television or the spectacular Skyride. Others would reflect on the beautiful lakefront setting, the concerts, and its attractions. Chicago's lakefront provided a portal to a transitory world.

In 1936, the board of A Century of Progress returned the fairgrounds to the Chicago Park District as planned. The profits from the fair were turned over to organizations involved in the exhibition's production, including those charged with the preservation of its artifacts. Based upon proportions agreed to prior to the fair's opening, "the Park District and the Museum of Science and Industry each received 25 per cent; the Art Institute received 20 percent; the Chicago Regional Plan received 4 per cent; and the Yerkes Observatory and the Smithsonian Institution each received 3 per cent." In all, the organizations shared a surplus of $160,000.[22]

The Band Shell and the Roots of a New Institution

While A Century of Progress was the focus of much time and attention of many people in the early 1930s, another attraction also influenced Grant Park. In 1931, the South Park Commission built a band shell on the southern end of Grant Park in Hutchinson Field. The preparations for A Century of Progress may have influenced its design, as it reflected the art-deco style. Despite increased financial hardships the failing economy caused, the commission constructed the band shell, as Mayor Cermak explained, "to raise the spirits of depression ridden Chicagoans with free band concerts." The commission attracted $25,000 for the structure, and the mayor and other dignitaries broke ground on July 10, 1931. The district put on four concerts a week during its ten-week season.[23] These performances harkened back to the William Weil–led concerts of the Chicago Band Association.

While musical concerts were not new to Chicago's parks, James C. Petrillo, president of the Chicago Federation of Musicians from 1922 to

1962, championed the idea of free performances in Grant Park for the people of Chicago. Beyond the civic spirit exhibited in organizing the concerts, Petrillo also realized that the concerts could provide an opportunity for his musicians, who had been particularly hard hit by both the Depression and the advent of the new "talking" films, which largely eliminated the need for musicians in movie theaters. In Chicago, talking films had meant a reduction from 2,000 theater musicians to 125. The musicians also faced a threat from recorded, or "canned" music, as Petrillo called it. Increasingly, musicians were not needed to perform live music for radio. This new festival was seen as a prime opportunity to secure employment for union musicians.[24]

But Petrillo had a hard time getting the concerts off the ground, explaining in an interview, "[T]he first time I mentioned park concerts, they laughed in my face. The park employees hadn't been paid for 21 months. Where are you going to get money for park concerts when the policemen aren't being paid?" Yet, Petrillo, who had been on the West Park Board in 1933, lobbied Mayor Edward J. Kelly to appoint him to the Chicago Park District. Eventually, Petrillo won over Robert Dunham, chairman of the new district, with his concert idea. Dunham, however, wanted proof that the concerts would draw crowds. He allowed Petrillo to pursue the idea with the understanding that if the concerts caught on, they would be put into the budget. With a band shell, seats, security, parking spaces, and $100,000 raised from the public, Petrillo inaugurated the symphonic series.[25]

On July 1, 1935, commencing with the march from Wagner's *Tannhauser*, the Grant Park concerts made their debut (see fig. 6.2). The Chicago

Figure 6.2. Grant Park concert at night, ca. 1930s. Postcard.

Symphony Orchestra presented the first concert under the direction of Eric DeLamarter, who had conducted the orchestra at the Swift Bridge during A Century of Progress. These daily concerts may have contributed to Petrillo's belief in the viability of a summer concert series.[26] The first season of summer concerts in Grant Park consisted of sixty-six evening concerts, with twenty-six symphonic programs and forty band concerts. Dr. Frederick Stock, who succeeded Theodore Thomas as conductor of the Chicago Symphony Orchestra in 1905 and who held that prestigious post until 1942, conducted two of the symphony concerts. The first year, the cost of the series was borne in large part by the Chicago Federation of Musicians, with the Chicago Park District providing maintenance, lighting, and policing.[27]

Petrillo threw all his energy behind the festival, securing the biggest stars of the day. From 1936 through 1943, the Chicago Park District and the Musician's Union were joint sponsors, despite the fact that the Chicago Park District assumed the financing of the concerts. NBC and CBS broadcast the concerts, which further increased the listenership. During the early years of the festival, Petrillo and the union continued to be instrumental in programming the concert series. Featured performers included classical violinist Jascha Heifetz, conductor Andre Kostelanetz, and soprano Lily Pons. Later, other groups became involved, including the Chicago Board of Education, which in 1940 sponsored a contest for public and parochial school bands and orchestras. In that summer, there were 101 concerts in Grant Park, the largest number ever to be held there in a single summer season.

During warm summer nights, Petrillo made Grant Park the place to be. The park's central location and open air appealed to concertgoers, especially in an era with little air conditioning. In addition to the cool lakefront breezes, the Grant Park band shell attracted its audience, in part, through star power. In the 1930s, the festival attracted a number of big-name stars in popular music, such as big-band leader Benny Goodman, to grace the art deco–styled band shell (see fig. 6.3).

World War II took its toll on the concerts. The 1943 season featured thirty-six concerts, many fewer than in previous years. That same year, the musicians' union ended its sponsorship of Petrillo's project, perhaps a result of the improvement in the economy after the Depression. In addition, Petrillo directed his considerable organizational skills elsewhere, assuming the presidency of the national American Federation of Musicians in 1940, a position he held until 1948.

With this transition, the Chicago Park District initiated a program featuring the newly formed Grant Park Symphony Orchestra, a replacement

Figure 6.3. Benny Goodman performing at the Grant Park band shell, 1941. Chicago Park District Special Collections.

of the various symphonic orchestras and bands that had previously been used. The new orchestra had the advantages of a permanent resident conductor, long-term continuity, and coordination of programming. The park district also continued to include other musical groups in the series, such as the armed-services bands and the Chicago Symphony Orchestra. In

1945, with Nicolai Malko as permanent conductor, the festival's concept of programming "serious" music on weekdays and more "popular" music on weekends took shape.[28] After World War II, attendance at the music festivals started to decline, with the trend continuing throughout the 1950s and 1960s.[29] Although a new shell had been discussed and plans drafted numerous times, the realization of these plans was still a few years away. The band shell constructed in the 1930s, originally meant to be a temporary structure, remained on site until 1975.

The WPA, World War II, and the Postwar Park

While the "rainbow city" of A Century of Progress was a temporary dream city, the fair did leave some lasting contributions to the lakefront and Grant Park's landscape. In 1934, the State of Illinois combined the city's twenty-two park commissions into one centralized entity, the Chicago Park District, creating a single organization charged with managing all the parks, including Grant Park (see fig. 6.4). On the lakefront, this organization would eventually transform the former fair lands into Burnham Park,

Figure 6.4. Tennis instruction in Grant Park, May 22, 1935. Chicago Park District Special Collections.

132

which is 555 acres. By 1939, the Chicago Park District had constructed its main administration building on 425 East McFetridge Drive, between the Field Museum and Soldier Field. Holabird and Root designed the structure that interrupted the architectural relationship between the two enormous neoclassical structures.

Managing the influx of people and cars was critical to keeping the park active and vibrant. The Art Institute of Chicago had approximately one million visitors annually. South of Twelfth Street, the Field Museum, John G. Shedd Aquarium, and Adler Planetarium grew into their expansive complexes, although they were still less than a decade old in the 1930s. At the north end of the park, the Illinois Naval Reserve Armory featured an active training vessel. The Chicago Yacht Club took up residency on the lakefront just off of Grant Park at Monroe Street. Housing itself for a time in a structure left over from A Century of Progress, the club built a substantial new building in 1947.

The Chicago Park District tapped into the largest and most popular of the New Deal federal programs, such as the Works Progress Administration (WPA), for construction of transportation routes in and around the park. The federal government had established the WPA under the Emergency Relief Appropriation Act of April 1935 to create public jobs for the unemployed. Harry L. Hopkins, friend and political adviser to President Roosevelt, directed the program that had an average enrollment of two million workers during its seven-year run.

The WPA played a major role in providing funding and laborers to improve the flow of traffic through the park with the completion of the Outer Drive bridge over the Chicago River. The bridge extended the Outer Drive, the major north-south roadway along Chicago's lakefront, to provide relief of the traffic in the congested city center and improve park access. The project, which required a significant landfill and engineering of land within and adjacent to the park, included an elevated roadway for Randolph Street, which was extended to the lakefront. The WPA engineered the roadway as a bridge that spanned the Illinois Central's right-of-way.

President Roosevelt dedicated the Outer Drive bridge on October 5, 1937. His visit to the city became particularly notable because he gave his quarantine-the-aggressors speech, making clear that although the United States remained neutral, he recognized the aggressive tendencies of Germany, Italy, and Japan.[30] The Outer Drive was rechristened Lake Shore Drive in 1946.

While federal programs improved Chicago's roadways, they also created one of the city's most famous traffic engineering problems. North of Randolph, the WPA engineers created the problematic Lake Shore Drive

"S" curve that drivers encountered between Grant Park and the bridge over the Chicago River. Further south, engineers of the Outer Drive isolated the Field Museum by wrapping the northbound traffic lanes on the east side and southbound traffic lanes on the west side around the museum. This effectively cut off the Field Museum from its neighboring institutions, the Shedd Aquarium and the Adler Planetarium, and posed a hazard for pedestrians trying to get to the Field from either side. It also created a barrier between Lake Michigan and Grant Park as the Outer Drive became a multilane, highly traveled thoroughfare. Just as the Illinois Central's right-of-way had cut Chicagoans off from the lake in the nineteenth and early twentieth centuries, the new drive separated pedestrians from the lakeshore.

The Chicago Park District had already developed part of Grant Park for surface parking, intending to alleviate some of the pressure people who drove downtown created. The largest lot at Monroe Street, south of Randolph Street near the Outer Drive, was an area of reclaimed land adjacent to the expansive Illinois Central train yards. The loss of land to surface parking would eventually force the district to consider both landscape concerns and parking in future designs.[31]

When the Japanese attacked Pearl Harbor on December 7, 1941, the city rallied to the war cause, and Grant Park served as a backdrop for the drama of the war. During World War II, Chicago became a major center for industry, training, and home-front activities. Historian Perry Duis notes, "[T]ens of thousands of other military personnel who were passing through the city by rail enjoyed the hospitality of the USO, as well as the Chicago Servicemen's Centers at 176 W. Washington and in the Auditorium Building, the latter serving twenty-four million meals by the end of the war."[32] These military service centers were steps away from Grant Park.

During this time, the Chicago Park District continued its operations, and the institutions within Grant Park remained popular attractions. Significantly for the lakefront, the commissioners of the Chicago Park District leased Northerly Island to the City of Chicago's Department of Public Works in 1946 for use as an airfield at a rate of $1 per year for fifty years (see fig. 6.5). Merrill C. Meigs, Chicago aviation pioneer, had encouraged the city to locate an airfield on the site after A Century of Progress. Work began on June 20, 1946, with plane service beginning the following year.[33] Park users thrilled at the sight of airplanes and helicopters landing and taking off. Business leaders favored the site for its convenience to the Loop. While the airport enlivened the lake views with small aircraft gliding onto or up from its tarmac, it also gave more of the parkland over to the transportation needs of the city.

Figure 6.5. View taken from Stevens Hotel showing band shell, Field Museum, Shedd Aquarium, Adler Planetarium, Soldier Field, Northerly Island, Chicago 1941, aerial view. Postcard. Curt Teich.

After World War II, Grant Park remained a symbol of culture and stability in the city. The Chicago Park District offered a full array of organized league sports, such as sixteen-inch softball games, and amenities, such as tennis courts.[34] The district valued the park's central place in the city, and the transportation links seemed strengthened by the opening of Meigs Field. In the decade after the war, it took some time to return to something resembling normalcy, and it was a different world that emerged.

Parking Lots, Protests, and Mayhem:
Grant Park in the Daley Era

Chicago emerged from the Great Depression and World War II poised for a bright future. The city had a large population that had survived the Great Depression and had contributed significantly to the war effort. If you asked the man on the street in the 1950s if his downtown was on the decline or at all threatened, he would have scoffed. Business leaders would have found it inconceivable that their operations in Chicago and its periphery could ever see a decline. Yet, as Robert M. Fogelson shows in *Downtown: Its Rise and Fall, 1880–1950*, despite expectations, city centers nationally would begin to decline.[1] During this monumental transition, Richard J. Daley served as mayor of Chicago. From 1955 to 1976, he led the city through what emerged as one of the most difficult periods in its history.

Chicagoans elected Daley mayor in May 1955. During his tenure as mayor, the city experienced its first decline in population. The 1950 census marked a peak in the city's population at 3,620,962. At the same time, the surrounding eight counties saw a rise in population, corresponding to their increased economic importance. In an era of complex change, Daley displayed a conservatism that was borne out of Chicago's ethnic neighborhoods.[2]

Yet, in this era, Grant Park's landscape represented a kind of changelessness. Its orderly walkways, lions in front of the Art Institute, and its classically inspired design bespoke of community stability. The use of the park reflected the significant changes in society. The park, however, provided the backdrop for events in the civil rights movement, youth and antiwar protests, and mayhem of the early 1970s.

The Prudential: Symbol for an Age

Grant Park provided Chicagoans a front-row seat from which to view the construction of the Prudential Building, the first major skyscraper built near the Loop since the onset of the Great Depression.[3] Developers set to work on its construction in 1952 on the northeast corner of Randolph Street and Michigan Avenue (see fig. 7.1). The architectural firm of Naess and Murphy completed what was, at forty-four stories, the city's tallest building in 1955, the same year Daley was elected mayor (see fig. 7.2). Featuring an observation deck that provided spectacular views of the park and lakefront, the building continued a long tradition of observation decks overlooking the park that went back to the Auditorium Building and the Aaron Montgomery Ward building at 6 North Michigan Avenue. Alfonso Iannelli, a sculptor who had worked with Frank Lloyd Wright and executed the bas-relief sculptures for the Adler Planetarium, designed the enormous Rock of Gibraltar, Prudential's corporate symbol, for the building.[4] The Prudential was representative of the new corporate organizations that had become synonymous with America in the post–World War II era. It also served as a potent symbol of the recovery from the Great Depression.

The construction of the Prudential Building became possible when the Illinois Central Railroad offered the air rights of its rail yards for the structure. Part of the building's foundation stood near the old depot and headquarters of the Illinois Central Railroad built in the 1850s and rebuilt after the Chicago Fire of 1871. The site was important for the Prudential's corporate image, with its corporate buildings located in prominent cities throughout the world.

The Chicago Park District, in anticipation of the increased parking demands that the Prudential Building would make on the area, constructed a large underground parking lot within Grant Park. Located between Randolph and Monroe streets along Michigan Avenue, the district provided parking for the new skyscraper and surrounding area and created an

Figure 7.1. Michigan Avenue and Randolph Street with peristyle, view north, ca. 1952 to 1954. Chicago Park District Special Collections.

additional revenue stream for the park district without resorting to surface parking. The idea for an underground parking lot had been floated earlier but was now an integral part of the park.

The Chicago Park District also improved the surface parking lot at Monroe Street. Built on an area of reclaimed land, it stood to the east of the expansive Illinois Central rail yards. Perhaps with this Monroe Street lot in mind, the Prudential Building did not build its own parking garage, although subsequent skyscrapers in Chicago, such as the Inland Steel Building, would.[5]

In the 1950s, traffic engineers, city officials, and local merchants struggled to meet the demand for public parking in the nation's cities. Many

Figure 7.2. Grant Park underground garage, Michigan Avenue and Randolph Street, view north, ca. 1954–55. Prudential Building is under construction in background. (14855–2) Chicago Park District Special Collections.

people believed that every attempt should be made to accommodate people who wanted to drive to a city's central business district. From Boston to San Francisco, cities attempted to find parking close to businesses. Some noteworthy examples of underground garages that featured green space above are Union Square in San Francisco and Pershing Square in Los Angeles.[6]

People wanted to park their cars downtown close to businesses or places of employment, which proved difficult in dense urban areas. One solution was to build costly underground garages. Others advocated the inexpensive, but addition-by-subtraction solution of tearing down buildings for a parking lot. In fact, the western end of the Loop became encircled by above-ground multilevel parking garages.

In Grant Park, the construction of an underground garage presented challenges, including the rerouting of traffic for a time on Michigan Avenue. With the completion of the parking garage in 1953, the district demonstrated that the park could be utilitarian by providing public parking. But the utilitarian approach also cost the city some of the architecturally noteworthy features of the park. In execution, the project eliminated one of the park's earliest design works—Edward Bennett's original peristyle of 1917. This semi-circular arrangement of Doric columns had become a landmark on the north end of Grant Park where Chicagoans and visitors alike gathered. The loss of the peristyle deprived the park of a noteworthy feature that had oriented visitors to the area. Additionally, the garage's engineers designed a ventilation system with vents that resembled oversized benches. Unfortunately, they were out of scale with the rest of the park and neither aesthetically pleasing nor useful for sitting. Additionally, workers tore out mature trees during construction that were replaced afterward with saplings.[7]

Attempting to meet the demands of ever-greater numbers of automobiles, almost every level of government, from the federal down to the smallest municipality, promoted the construction of new highways and roadways. Chicago had already constructed the Edens Expressway. With the opening of the Old Orchard Mall in suburban Skokie in 1956 and its abundant, free parking, people could easily drive to the shopping area and fill their car with goods. Taken together, expressways, the suburban malls, and the increase in suburban housing would transform the nation's residential patterns in subsequent decades, pulling people out of the city center. In 1956, the federal government passed the Interstate Highway Act, which promoted more highway building by providing significant funding for projects.

The expressways represented a significant investment in the city's and the region's infrastructure. They also had a dramatic impact as workers demolished homes and divided neighborhoods. According to historian Arnold Hirsch, these new highways separated poorer ethnic and African American neighborhoods from white and affluent areas. In the process, the city created a buffer around Chicago's Loop, including Grant Park, from surrounding black neighborhoods on the south and west sides.[8]

In 1955, the Department of Transportation began the construction of the Congress Street Expressway, which was rededicated as the Eisenhower Expressway in 1964. The Congress Street Expressway changed the most formal pedestrian entrance to Grant Park into a thoroughfare for cars (see fig. 7.3). This project, which included building much of the highway below grade, was expensive and created divisions among neighborhoods along its route. The scope of the project was so large that it was completed in sections and not finished until 1960. Workers removed stairs from the center of the design and constructed several lanes of traffic directly into the park.

Figure 7.3. Congress Street entrance to Grant Park, 1956. Chicago Park District Special Collections.

Automobiles now entered directly into the park rather than through the indirect route around the plaza. In essence, the former stately entrance became a well-decorated interchange for traffic between the expressway and Lake Shore Drive.

If the handling of design elements for the underground garage had been somewhat insensitive to Bennett's plan, then the alteration to the Congress Street entrance marked a serious disregard for the park's design and usage. Given the transportation needs of the city, it can be argued that the city and Chicago Park District acted responsibly, but in the process, they fundamentally changed the visitor's park experience.

The Congress Expressway was not the only highway construction with an impact on the park. Since its opening, the Outer Drive had become an important north-south artery. As a part of the work on expressways, engineers substantially modified South Lake Shore Drive by 1955.[9]

As journalist Lois Wille notes on the voracious pace of highway construction, "when the John F. Kennedy Expressway to the Northwest area opened in 1961, traffic on North Lake Shore Drive fell off 20 percent. Seven years later it had risen to its old volume and eventually exceeded it." She wrote about a similar situation "on South Lake Shore Drive when the Dan Ryan Expressway to the South Side was opened."[10] Within Grant Park, Lake Shore Drive transitioned from a scenic boulevard into a major traffic artery.

The automobile played a role in further transforming the city's landscape, as the expressway made it possible to live farther from the city center. The suburbs attracted residents by offering comparatively inexpensive land and new housing, and faced with limited housing, racial tensions, and comparatively higher prices in the central city, many families moved out of the city.[11] The federal census for Chicago shows a steady decline in population between 1950 and 2000.[12]

These changes were not yet visibly apparent in the 1950s, however, as Grant Park still served as the city's front yard. In fact, the city received Queen Elizabeth II in grand style as she made her debut through Grant Park on July 6, 1959. That summer, the queen traveled extensively on the Great Lakes. Her Royal Majesty's visit was occasioned by the International Trade Fair at Navy Pier that celebrated the opening of the Saint Lawrence Seaway. The queen and Prince Philip had been touring the Canadian provinces and arrived in Chicago on board the royal yacht *Britannia*. On a bright summer day, the queen made her way into the city, much the way Daniel H. Burnham might have imagined when reflecting on his 1909 Plan of Chicago. In the 1950s era of drive-in theaters and carhops, the queen's visit hearkened back to an earlier era of ocean liners and luxury train cars. Although Grant Park featured yacht clubs and fronted onto Lake Michigan, no one had ever alighted on the shore in such a royal state.

Mayor Daley met Her Royal Highness as she came ashore in Grant Park. The city literally rolled out a red carpet, and the area where she disembarked has become known as Queen's Landing (see fig. 7.4). After being greeted by the mayor, Queen Elizabeth II and Prince Philip made their way to ceremonies near Buckingham Fountain. The queen spent only thirteen hours on land in Chicago, but her day was packed with activities, including lunch with Governor William G. Stratton at the Ambassador West Hotel. At the center of the visit was her appearance at the International Trade Fair at Navy Pier. She also made stops at the Museum of Science and Industry and the Art Institute of Chicago.[13] The queen may have noted the newly expanded grounds that included the Ferguson Building built in 1958 by Holabird and Root and Burgee.[14] The queen's evening ended with transfer out to the royal yacht *Britannia* just before midnight. In a farewell tribute, the sky was illuminated with fireworks.[15]

Figure 7.4. Queen Elizabeth II in Chicago, July 6, 1959. Chicago Park District Special Collections.

The 1960s in and around Grant Park

The 1960s were defined by a number of tensions and conflicts. With rapid suburbanization, Grant Park became less important, as each suburban homeowner became his or her own park superintendent and grounds-keeper. It also began to lose attraction as a location that offered cool lake breezes in the summertime since city residents could now sit in front of their window air conditioners and experience a cool breeze. The museums in Grant Park served a great number of people, and the Chicago Park District continued to offer various programs. Some programs, however, such as the summer concerts of the Grant Park Music Festival, experienced their lowest attendance, with most concerts drawing fewer than five thousand people.[16] Why attendance dropped is open to speculation. The drop may reflect the rise of the popularity of rock and roll over classical and jazz music or the greater availability of entertainment choices, especially television, in the post–World War II era.

The Chicago Park District also emphasized activities that accommodated the automobile, thereby creating a revenue stream with its parking garages. In the 1960s, the park district built the South Garage between Van Buren and Jackson Streets. Completed in 1961, the underground garage just south of the Art Institute benefited the museum as well as surrounding businesses.[17] The Art Institute reworked the landscaping and the construction of the Morton Wing in 1962 with Shaw, Metz, and Associates designing the modern addition. This also necessitated the repositioning of Lorado Taft's Fountain of the Great Lakes.[18]

Just south of Grant Park, the construction of the McCormick Place Convention Center in Burnham Park signaled a striking shift in the commercial use of the lakefront. Completed in 1960 on landfill created in the 1930s, McCormick Place included extensive roadways and surface parking lots that significantly altered the lakefront. The location of the convention center on the city's lakeshore marked another departure from the vision of keeping the entire lakeshore free of permanent commercial structures. The museums in Grant Park had already broken with that vision, but McCormick Place was a different model. While the museums served a public use, conventions and trade shows were the draw at McCormick Place.

At the time of McCormick Place's construction, few Chicagoans would have argued against a state-of-the-art convention center, but some looked askance at its location. In their eyes, the new complex as erected took up too much of the lakefront. Community leaders were stirred into political action by this nonpark usage. Ironically, the building's designers had constructed a structure that was decidedly inward-looking, dedicated to meetings and the display of goods. The architects did not design it to take full advantage of the lake views. In fact, the building had few windows, since the emphasis needed to be on the trade goods inside. The project also necessitated a significant interchange at McCormick Place that transformed Lake Shore Drive just to the south of Grant Park.[19]

In what opponents to the convention center consider poetic justice, the building burned down in 1967. There were some accusations that corners had been cut during the original construction, but this controversy quickly subsided as the second McCormick Place was rapidly rebuilt on the same location.[20] The debate surrounding the first and second McCormick Place did awaken some Chicagoans to political action.[21]

Civil Rights Protests on Chicago's Lakefront

During the 1960s, social and national figures of the civil-rights movement used Chicago's lakefront to bring greater attention to their cause. Grant Park provided an area to stage civil-rights marches, and just to the south, Soldier Field was a site for large rallies. The proximity of the park to the Loop also provided access to City Hall, where the protestors often marched to make their demands.

Chicago had already played a significant role in key events of the civil-rights movement with the widely reported funeral of fourteen-year-old Chicagoan Emmett Till in 1955. Up to that point, the civil-rights movement had been a "Southern" problem; Chicagoans demonstrated that issues of race and class were problems for the entire nation. One of the key events of the movement, the Illinois Rally for Civil Rights, took place at Soldier Field on June 21, 1964, featuring the Reverend Martin Luther King Jr. and other civil-rights leaders.

King had gained national prominence during the bus boycott in Birmingham, Alabama, in 1955. He was also becoming a national symbol and voice of the great number of local efforts taken up by ordinary citizens. In many communities, students, teachers, and laborers were staking a claim for equal citizenship by refusing to relinquish their seat on a bus or by ordering coffee at a lunch counter. In 1963, King's career reached its height with his role in the March on Washington and his "I Have a Dream" speech. In 1964, the Illinois Rally for Civil Rights brought King to Chicago. Organized by the Church Federation of Greater Chicago, the Chicago Urban League, and other local groups, the rally pushed for the passage of the Civil Rights Act of 1964 by the federal government.[22] A crowd of one hundred thousand had been expected to fill Soldier Field, but a summer rain kept the attendance down to half of that number.[23] The list of presenters focused on the strides made on a national level, with U.S. Senator Paul Douglas of Illinois addressing the crowd with a message from President Lyndon Baines Johnson.

Touching on themes that had become familiar to the nation, King asserted the need for "Negro youths to become educated" and said that the pace of change should not be slackened. He said, "There are places in the United States where we are moving at a horse-and-buggy pace to get a hamburger and a cup of coffee in a lunch counter." King affirmed successes to date but also avowed that there was much work to be done. The rally closed with Mahalia Jackson, the internationally known gospel singer from Chicago, leading the crowd in singing "We Shall Overcome."[24]

Legislative progress in the civil-rights movement in the United States appeared to move forward in July when King attended the signing of the Civil Rights Act of 1964 at the White House. King then emphasized that America's racial divide existed not only in the south but in northern cities as well. His appearance in Chicago in 1964 reflected the shift to social action on ghettos, poverty, hunger, and poor-quality education found across the nation, including northern cities. The primary issue for Chicago and other cities would be the desegregation of schools. King's international profile had reached its summit. He received the Nobel Peace Prize at the end of 1964. At the same time, he was facing increased challenges at home. In early 1965, police arrested King in Selma, Alabama, for protests related to voting rights. Later in the year, President Johnson signed into law the Voting Rights Act of 1965.

In Chicago, civil-rights events began to heat up. After World War II, the percentage of African Americans within the city had increased. The economic situation had also changed as the demand for unskilled labor declined. Public-school education became the flash point for this conflict as the need for skilled laborers increased. Because of inequities in education in both southern and northern cities, African Americans were at a distinct disadvantage, especially in the new job market that was evolving in the postwar era.

Sociologist Philip Hauser of the University of Chicago led a panel that investigated segregation in Chicago's schools. The group issued a report in 1964 that found segregation of the schools was not a deliberate policy but a result of longtime housing and economic trends. The report also asserted that African American students were at a significant disadvantage in gaining a "quality education."[25]

In Chicago, Benjamin Willis, the superintendent of schools, became the symbol of school segregation and inequality. He bought mobile classrooms, popularly referred to as "Willis Wagons," for the overcrowded schools instead of constructing needed new buildings. In response to Willis's policies, the Woodlawn Organization became the most vocal of the grassroots organizations that protested the segregated school system for its resulting educational inequality. The local media underreported these protests.[26]

That changed, however, on June 10, 1965, when civil-rights advocates gathered at Soldier Field to protest Willis's retention by the Chicago Board of Education. Just a few days earlier, the board of education had filed an injunction against the African American groups that planned on boycotting the segregated and overcrowded schools. In spite of the court injunction, during June 10–11, 1965, the Reverend Lynward Stevenson, president of the Woodlawn Organization, said that more than one hundred thousand children remained out of school because they were participating in the demonstration.[27] The Woodlawn Organization brought its protest to all of Chicago by staging a march to City Hall to express its dissatisfaction with the status quo.

The *Chicago Tribune* describes the event of June 10, 1965: "About 200 started the march from the parking lot at the south end of Soldiers' field. As they marched along the lake front and through Grant Park, groups along the sidewalk joined them. Civil rights officials estimated that by the time they reached the City Hall there were 500 to 700 marchers. City Hall observers, however, estimated the number at closer to 300." This group included "Albert Raby, convener of the Coordinating Council of Community Organization, and Dick Gregory, black comedian, [who] went to the fifth floor of City hall in an attempt to see Mayor Richard J. Daley." The newspaper noted that "police made no efforts to arrest or harass the demonstrators as they marched north in Lake Shore drive, east in Balbo drive, north in State street, west in Madison street, and north in La Salle street to City hall." This group then met up with people who just two days earlier had started picketing City Hall.[28]

The following day, June 11, Raby and others were involved in another protest. The story on the front page of the *Chicago Tribune* reads: "A march by civil rights demonstrators on City hall and a demonstration by pickets outside the hall were broken up by police yesterday in what was said to be the largest mass arrest in any civil rights disorder in the city's recent history." Police arrested 228 men, women, and children. The police had attempted to limit the protesters to one lane of traffic on Balbo Drive, whereas the previous day they had taken up two lanes of traffic. According to the paper, "the order to prevent a repetition of Thursday's march, when demonstrators blocked traffic in all streets they used, apparently came from an angry Mayor Daley."[29] The confrontations between police and marchers occurred on Balbo Drive near Columbus Drive within Grant Park, with other arrests occurring at City Hall.

The direct action campaign did not abate, and the protestors met the following day on June 12. This time, however, the protestors congregated at Buckingham Fountain, rather than at Soldier Field's south parking lot. The orderly group walked two abreast on the sidewalks on this third day of marching to City Hall. As Dempsey J. Travis, noted Chicago historian, writes, "The character of the march changed abruptly as the demonstrators turned west off State Street onto Madison Street. At that moment, the demonstrators rushed wildly to the center of State and Madison Streets and staged a sit-down in the heart of what was reputed to be the world's busiest corner. [T]heir actions tied up traffic for almost an hour. Chicago Police Commander Robert Lynskey raised his baton to signal for the police vans to move forward and arrest the demonstrators, who then backed up into the middle of the intersection in a circular wagon type formation."[30] At this protest, police arrested ninety-six marchers, including members of the clergy. The protesters had established a clear and effective behavioral pattern and continued to stage their protests at Buckingham Fountain, a central location that was close to the Loop. As the summer progressed, it became clear that the protesters planned on continuing regular marches from the park to City Hall.

The protests against educational inequality received a significant boost when Reverend King agreed to come to Chicago and take part in a march on July 26, 1965. During the weekend prior to the march, King worked tirelessly to encourage sympathetic white people to join the protest. In these appearances, King linked the civil-rights struggles of the south to the north. "'[I]f we could walk from Selma, Alabama to Montgomery with the Klan all around us then you can march in Chicago," Dr. King told his audiences at all eight of his stops during the day. "Bull Connor in Alabama found out what the power of numbers means. When the white power structure sees us on Monday, they too will know we mean business." Although King was in Chicago to protest the segregated school system, he broadened his focus. According to journalist Thomas Fitzpatrick, "he placed as much emphasis on inadequate housing, [and] lack of job opportunities as he did on segregation in the schools."[31] King hearkened back to the earlier civil-rights struggle but adjusted his agenda to include larger social-justice issues.

In drumming up participation for the march, King spoke at the village green in Winnetka, an affluent northern suburb. He said, "[W]e must learn to live together as brothers, or we will all perish together as fools." As he had done throughout his public life, King pulled together a wide range of themes, addressing the "American dream" and referencing "Jewish, Catholic, and Protestant persuasions—Martin Buber, St. Thomas Aquinas, and Paul Tillich."[32]

Largely because of King's reaching out to communities throughout the Chicagoland area, the march on July 26 attracted tens of thousands of people. Due to the many engagements he had in the days leading up to the march, King had to be treated for exhaustion on the morning of the march, and as the newspaper reports, "Dr. King was more than an hour late, and many of the marchers, who had been waiting for hours, were shouting that they wanted to get on with it." In a further complication, many of the marchers seemed to have been attracted by King's star power. As journalist Thomas Fitzpatrick writes, "[V]irtually all those standing in front of Buckingham fountain had come there with the idea that they were going to march side by side with Dr. King, the Nobel peace prize winner." People jostled to get near him, but bodyguards from his Southern Christian Leadership Conference (SCLC) gathered around him. Finally, the police came to clear a path for King and the other marchers for the entire trip.[33]

King had been successful in gathering a larger number of demonstrators, but the size of the crowd was a matter of dispute. "Police officials estimated it was 10,000. 'I know we had 30,000 standing in front of Buckingham fountain,' said the Rev. Ralph Abernathy, 'and I know we picked up another 70,000 on the way.' Dr. King estimated the crowd at 30,000." The newspaper reports, "[T]he marchers took up the entire streets, from curb to curb, in their 2½-mile trek from Buckingham fountain to the La Salle street side of City Hall, but there were no incidents. At one time the marchers stretched back for eight city blocks, but the long trip required less than an hour." In the end, "Dr. King asserted that the parade which he had just led would go down as one of the great marches in the history of the country."[34]

Once the group arrived at City Hall, King gave his memorable assessment of Chicago from a loudspeaker: "Chicago is the North's most segregated city. Negroes have continued to flee from behind the cotton curtain, but now they find that after years of indifference and exploitation, Chicago has not turned out to be the new Jerusalem. . . . [W]e are now protecting the educational and cultural shackles that are as binding as those of a Georgia chain gang. The chains have now been replaced by emotional stratagem. We march here today because we believe that Chicago, her citizens, and her social structure are in dire need of redemption and reform."[35] He also used his authority as a preacher to set the goal of the marchers in messianic terms.

Reflecting on the march, King said, "[T]he response to the march yesterday was beyond our greatest expectations, and I really think it was magnificent. I will certainly return if the Chicago leadership asks me to. If something isn't done about the school situation, we will have to have another massive march and school boycott." Although King would return to Chicago, he would not take part in this same kind of protest.

Albert Raby, the central organizer behind the protests, would conduct a total of forty-three marches, the largest being the one that King participated in.[36] These political demonstrations continued to use Grant Park as a staging area. As before, the demonstrators were attracted by the central location and proximity to City Hall, in addition to the lakefront being a highly visible location where the news media were compelled to give the protests prominent coverage.

At the end of the summer of 1965, the civil-rights movement took a decidedly different turn with the Watts riots in California. On August 11, 1965, a traffic stop in south central Los Angeles started six days of riots that resulted in thirty-four dead, thousands injured, and almost four thousand arrested with rioters significantly damaging their neighborhood by burning homes and businesses. During the rioting, King made his way to Los Angeles and argued for calm, but he was unable to stop the violence, which gave the renowned civil-rights leader considerable pause.[37] King reflected on the death and destruction in Los Angeles and considered his best course of action. He had already been expanding his activities to address the issues of joblessness, lack of good education, and the sense of despair that came with discrimination in America. Rather than focus his energies on Los Angeles, however, he turned his attention to Chicago.

It is said that King and the SCLC selected Chicago because they believed that the political leadership in Chicago had real power. Earl Bush, Mayor Richard J. Daley's press secretary, said, "King considered Daley to be in complete control of Chicago, which in a way he was. King thought that if Daley would go before a microphone and say, 'Let there be no more discrimination,' there wouldn't be." Bush continued his assessment, "King overestimated Mayor Daley's power. Daley did not have the power to make all men brothers, nor was brotherhood necessarily a priority for Daley, who was also concerned about white flight to the suburbs. He saw whites running, and the real issue to him was how to keep them from running. Daley had no answers, but he wasn't anti-black. He felt that he had to preserve the foundation of the city."[38] The situation in Chicago was extremely complex.

King and the SCLC went to Chicago in 1965 to carry out their "northern direct-action campaign to spotlight the myriad slum conditions, substandard housing, unequal job opportunities, racist real estate practices, police brutality and de facto segregation."[39] The earlier civil-rights movement had definable and discrete goals, but King began to believe that the roots of inequality were largely economic. It was one thing to desegregate but another to provide equal access to jobs, improved housing opportunities, and education. These were much broader concerns.

King and the SCLC's choice of Chicago elicited a wide range of responses. While many welcomed the civil-rights leader, others reacted negatively. Some people saw the SCLC leadership and King as outside agitators who were only causing trouble, resulting in tense and defensive reactions from all involved. In one case, Lester Hankerson, an SCLC leader, said, "[A] lot of folks here in Chicago won't even talk to us. I would still rather be working in Mississippi. People here are not interested in first class citizenship." Reflecting on the period, historian Dempsey Travis writes, "[I]n April, 1964, the Daley machine was able to elect a dead white man Thomas J. O'Brien to congress over a qualified young black woman by the name of Mrs. Brenetta Howell. Chicago Negroes were so apathetic and intimidated by the Daley machine that they would vote for Frankenstein and make him a winner if Mayor Daley put him on the ballot."[40] In spite of these rifts within the communities, King set his sights on moving to Chicago

In January 1966, King and his family moved into a four-room apartment on Chicago's West Side that was an example of substandard housing.[41] King received significant media coverage in 1966 for this and other causes. From his apartment, King and his associates worked to improve conditions in the neighborhood by bringing attention to the living situation on Chicago's West Side. King also met with gang members and other individuals to advocate for nonviolence. He worked with national and community organizations to push for open housing, often marching into all-white neighborhoods, which met with significant resistance and some violence. King's groups demanded that all housing be opened up to black persons.[42]

To gain greater attention for his cause, King planned another rally in Grant Park. This marked the third summer in a row that King would appear on Chicago's lakefront. Organizers designated July 10, 1966, as Freedom Sunday in Chicago. Given its large capacity, organizers hoped to draw one hundred thousand individuals to Soldier Field. Yet, just as the weather had not cooperated during the Illinois Rally for Civil Rights two years earlier, on this occasion, the city's residents struggled in 100-degree weather. As a result, between forty thousand and fifty thousand gathered at Soldier Field. Those who arrived at 12:15 P.M., when the gates opened found what shade there was, but those arriving later had to sit in the dangerously hot sun.[43]

Freedom Sunday featured many of the top names associated with the civil-rights movement in the mid-1960s, including actor Sidney Poitier, singer Harry Belafonte, Peter Yarrow of folk group Peter, Paul, and Mary, popular musician Stevie Wonder, Raby, comedian Gregory, and singer Mahalia Jackson.[44]

King was the featured speaker. He closed his comments, "[A]s we march, some silent onlooker, some detached spectator will probably ask where are these people coming from. The answer will come in the words of John the Revelator, 'These are they that are coming up out of great trials and tribulations.' . . . [T]hese are they who with tear-drenched eyes having had to stand over the coffins of four little beautiful innocent, unoffending Negro girls in Birmingham, and Emmett C. Till, and Medgar Evers in Mississippi."[45] In this statement, King tied the cause in Chicago to the martyrs of the civil-rights movement, including Till. In the process, he transformed and elevated the event. There was a national cause for justice, and King pulled Chicago into its heart.

In a symbolic gesture to link the events at Soldier Field to Chicago's power structure, many in the audience joined King on a march from the stadium though Grant Park and on to City Hall (see fig. 7.5). This march echoed the events of a year earlier when protestors had marched to the center of city government. On Freedom Sunday, however, King led approximately thirty-eight thousand marchers up to City Hall. There, he posted the demands of the nonviolent Freedom Fighters on the door, which was reminiscent of the action of Martin Luther in 1517 that marked the beginning of the Protestant Reformation. In King's case, the demands asked for better jobs and improved conditions for the poor and black persons in Chicago.[46] The events of Freedom Sunday occurred largely without major disturbance.

Figure 7.5. Reverend Martin Luther King Jr., Al Raby (on King's left), and Bernard Lee, King's assistant (on Raby's left), Grant Park, Chicago, 1966. Photograph by Bernard J. Kleina.

Other responses to the civil-rights movement in the summer of 1966 were violent, however. On June 12, a riot occurred on the West Side in response to a patrolman shooting Arceilis Cruz in the leg. Although this was among the most significant events, the summer would include a number of conflicts between minorities and the police.[47]

Another flash point during the summer was caused by the tactic of predominantly black civil-rights protesters marching through primarily white neighborhoods. The white residents often met marchers with a wave of angry words and occasionally violence. In one widely reported incident on August 6, white youths threw stones at the marchers and struck King, leaving a mark above his right ear. Travis reports, "As Dr. King rose to his feet with assistance from fellow demonstrators, he ripped off his tie and opened his shirt collar and said: 'I've never seen anything like it in my life. I think the people from Mississippi ought to come to Chicago to learn how to hate.'"[48] The opposition in the north was intergenerational and crossed gender lines.

After a tumultuous summer, King met with Mayor Daley at the Palmer House Hotel on August 26, 1966. Their "summit meeting" represented the end of a long process of negotiations and the direct-action campaign of marching into neighborhoods. The city said it would take action to improve housing in Chicago. The immediate result was that most of the marches ended, and tensions were defused. Some of the more militant segments decried the agreement, but King thought that the city would honestly attempt to address the grievances set out before them.[49] King then turned his attention away from Chicago to continue the call for civil rights on the national stage.

Democratic National Convention of 1968

Although civil-rights leaders, including King, used Grant Park as a staging area for marches related to their causes, protests in the park never gained the national historical recognition that the marches in Washington did. However, the park would become forever linked with the Vietnam War protests and general youth protests of the Democratic National Convention of 1968 (see fig. 7.6). The television coverage of this convention with its skirmishes between the Chicago Police Department and protesters has become part of the national memory and gave rise to the popular perception that Grant Park was chronically beset with demonstrations and conflict.

Figure 7.6. National Guard in Grant Park, 1968. Photograph by Bernard J. Kleina.

Chicago had looked forward with great anticipation to hosting the Democratic National Convention of 1968. Mayor Daley had long been considered one of the most important Democratic mayors in the nation. Chicago also had a long tradition of hosting successful conventions of both parties, many held in Grant Park. The 1968 convention would provide Daley with an opportunity to show off his city to the nation.

The year had gotten off to a tragic start for the country as it faced the Tet offensive in Vietnam, in which the North Vietnamese launched a massive, coordinated attack on South Vietnam. The U.S. government sent more than half a million American soldiers to Vietnam. In response to the stepped-up war effort, the year included a great number of war protests. In an era of network television, the combination of local and national coverage of the war provided an almost unending stream of violent images. The scenes of mayhem and tragedy tended to further traumatize and polarize the nation on whether U.S. troops belonged in Vietnam.

Violence and tragedy were not limited to the war, though. Chicago took center stage as the city's West Side violently reacted to the news of King's assassination on April 4, 1968, in Memphis, Tennessee. Similar outbursts of violence consumed other major metropolitan areas, including Los Angeles and Detroit. In Chicago, despite police attempts to quell the violence, rioters destroyed a score of blocks on the city's near West Side, and eleven black persons were killed. Even more shocking was the news that Mayor Daley had issued a "shoot-to-kill order" against the rioters. This information further exacerbated an already volatile situation between the police and citizens of Chicago.[50]

Politically, Richard Milhous Nixon emerged as the front-runner for the Republican Party and eventually secured the presidential nomination. The Democratic Party entered the election year in disarray with President Johnson's decision not to run for reelection. As the primaries unfolded, the party and the nation faced the incredible shock of Robert Francis Kennedy's assassination on June 5, 1968, in California, after winning that state's nomination as the Democratic nominee for president. As Chicago began preparations for the convention, the mayor and the police were aware of youth protests in New York as well as in France.[51] While the Democratic Party organized for its meeting in Chicago, protesters across the nation were also preparing activities targeting the convention.

The Democratic National Convention was held between August 26 and 28, 1968, in the Chicago International Amphitheater, but party fractures and social tensions were visible within the amphitheater and on the city's streets and its parks. Protestors shared a fierce opposition to the war in Vietnam, but there was a wide mix of opposition. Some sought to work within the

existing political system to end the war by support for any of the Democratic presidential candidates, Hubert H. Humphrey, Eugene McCarthy,
or George McGovern. Some veteran civil-rights leaders attended and also
operated within the party structure. The Youth International Party members, known as Yippies, and even hippies sought to tear down the existing
structure.[52] The protesters served to underline the "generation gap" between
the pre– and post–World War II generations. The earlier generation had
lived through and coped with the deprivations of the Great Depression and
World War II. The younger generation was perceived as having grown up in
a climate of postwar-era prosperity. If the youth did "not trust anyone over
thirty," then they must have cast a wary eye at most of the leadership of both
the host city and the Democratic Party. The party leadership's perspective
would not allow the protestors to crash their party and take control of the
convention and the city's public spaces. The city tightly controlled park
usage permits and deployed heavily armed patrols during the convention.[53]

The events surrounding the 1968 Democratic National Convention have
become almost the stuff of myth (see fig. 7.7). Many who lived through the
event can call up the televised images of the conflict within the amphitheater, with the antiwar position of candidate McCarthy, or the status-quo
position of Humphrey, who would ultimately win the nomination. U.S.

Figure 7.7. Chicago police clearing protesters from Grant Park, 1968. Photograph by Bernard J. Kleina.

Senator Abraham A. Ribicoff from Connecticut angered Daley by saying that "with George McGovern as President of the United States, we wouldn't have Gestapo tactics in the streets of Chicago." Tom Hayden and Abbie Hoffman, leaders of the Youth International Party, became household names as a result of their protests during the convention.[54]

Outside the convention hall, there was just as much activity. As the intensity of the protests escalated, Mayor Daley called in "11,900 Chicago police, 7,500 Illinois National Guardsmen, and 1,000 FBI and Secret Service agents."[55] On August 26, a group of approximately a thousand activists gathered to protest, most of them young adults. They congregated in the park near the Logan monument at Ninth Street and Michigan Avenue. The Chicago Police Department dispersed the group. On the same evening, a number of people remained in Lincoln Park, and there was considerable violence when the police fired tear gas. There were additional skirmishes in Lincoln Park on the evenings of August 27 and 28.[56]

The protests escalated on August 29 in Grant Park. During the day, a rally was held in the south end of the park. In an impressive show of force, National Guardsmen were positioned on the roof of the Field Museum, and a large police force was stationed in front of the Hilton Hotel on Michigan Avenue, which was the delegates' headquarters, across from Grant Park. The altercation began when a protester climbed the flagpole at the band shell in an attempt to lower the flag. When the police intervened and arrested him, the crowd surged to the flagpole, lowered the flag, and raised a red shirt in its place. Faced with this defiant act, the Chicago Police Department pushed through the crowd at the flagpole, clubbing a number of protesters who were surrounding the pole.[57] If the protesters had wanted to provoke a response, they had achieved their goal.

The police then endeavored to clear the area around the band shell. As the protesters made their way toward Michigan Avenue, a melee ensued with protesters chanting, "The whole world is watching!" The news media in place at the Hilton Hotel were in prime position to broadcast the events taking place in the park across the street. The images captured by the television crews came to symbolize the convention. The police finally gained control of the situation, but they had lost the public-relations campaign with the event frequently referred to as a police riot.[58] In the end, the "police announced that 589 persons had been arrested and more than 119 police and 100 demonstrators injured."[59] Any goodwill that the mayor had hoped to gain from the convention had been lost. The mayor's and Chicago's reputations were tarnished by the events of August 1968.

In the popular mind, Grant Park would be forever linked with this clash because the news media had captured such powerful images as the scenes of the King riots and the 1968 Democratic National Convention that would be rebroadcast for decades after to reflect the unrest that became symbolic of the 1960s. Nationally, the city became associated with racial tensions and conflicts associated with the youth culture. The public belief was that Chicago was unsafe. The events implied that Grant Park and the central city had become out of control and unsafe. Grant Park still possessed its verdant lawns and was populated by superb institutions, but many approached it, like the city around it, with some trepidation. Memories of the event continued with the high-profile trial of some of the defendants arrested during the convention who were known as the Chicago 8, later known as the Chicago 7, making people relive these events in court.

Riots and Crime: The Grant Park Riots and the Park's Nadir

In the wake of the turbulent 1960s, Mayor Daley hoped to restore order and revitalize the city center. As it had in the preceding two decades, Chicago's population declined in the 1970s to 3,369,357, while the surrounding eight counties' population exploded to 7,612,314.[60] Nationally, the early 1970s remained politically divisive with the war in Vietnam, the Watergate scandal, and the Supreme Court's *Roe v. Wade* decision, all stirring up debate and polarizing opinions. In Chicago, the economy suffered significant reversals with the close of the Union Stock Yards and heavy industries. It was not all negative news for Chicagoans, however, who saw the opening of the much-heralded tallest building in the world, the Sears Tower, in 1974. The city had also worked with state and federal partners to expand the University of Illinois at Chicago, just west of the Loop. The city continued to improve the expressway systems, which are seen as hallmarks of the Daley era, as the mayor worked to revive the declining downtown.[61]

The negative perception of Grant Park as an area for protest and violence only increased, however. A riot erupted on July 27, 1970, at the Grant Park band shell, where a melee broke out during the performance of a rock group called Fat Water. Led by a group of approximately four hundred youths, rioters stormed fences and rushed the stage of the park's band shell, damaging the sound and lighting equipment and throwing rocks and bottles. Some people believe the outburst began when a rumor spread that the popular group Sly and the Family Stone would not perform as scheduled. Because of the damage done to the sound equipment on the stage, the organizers did cancel Sly and the Family Stone's performance. This then sparked further rioting with a crowd of nearly a thousand demonstrators clashing with police throughout the night, both in Grant Park and the surrounding downtown area.

During the evening, rioters continued to throw rocks and bottles, resulting in many injuries and culminating in the police shooting warning shots into the air.[62] After many arrests and much property damage around the Loop, the Chicago Police Department gained control of the situation. The rioters were only a minority of the more than thirty-five thousand to fifty thousand people gathered in the park for the concerts, but the damage to public perception was done. In response to the riot, the Chicago Park District Board, wishing to avoid future confrontations, cancelled all remaining rock concerts at the Grant Park band shell.[63] Audiences, however, could still attend the classical and popular favorites that continued through the decade at the site.

By the early 1970s, the popular perception of Grant Park was at its lowest point. Some people asserted that the park invited violence with its spotty and poor lighting, combined with park buildings that had limited security.[64] It was the front-page news stories of murders in Grant Park, however, that further fed the perception that the park was now life-threateningly dangerous.

The Grant Park murders ushered in the darkest chapter in the park's history. On July 10, 1970, the battered body of Agnes Lehmann was discovered near the park's band shell.[65] The state charged Wilber McDonald with her death, linking McDonald to the crime by blood evidence and a shoe left at the scene of the crime. McDonald admitted having talked with Lehmann during the evening, but he contended that they had been attacked by a black youth. Although he maintained his innocence throughout his trial, he was convicted, and the court sentenced him to 100 to 150 years in prison.[66] It seemed as though the police had caught their man.

Two years later, the murders resumed with the discovery of a naked and badly beaten body in the park near bushes at Eleventh Street. The victim was Judith Bettelley of Stoke-on-Trent, England, who was found dead on September 5, 1972. The coroner ruled that the twenty-four-year-old had been murdered. Bettelley had been vacationing in Chicago and planned to return to England to take a job as an architect.[67]

Almost a year later, police investigated the murder of Irene Koutros. Her partially clad body was discovered in the north Grant Park garage. Koutros, a forty-one-year-old Chicago schoolteacher, had been stabbed to death in the front seat of her car on July 15, 1973.[68]

Later in the summer, on August 3, 1973, the *Chicago Tribune* reported that the body of Lee Alexis Wilson, a junior college student, was found in the bushes of the Stanley McCormick Court of the Art Institute of Chicago near Jackson Boulevard and Michigan Avenue. A twelve-year-old boy had discovered the body while he was playing in the bushes and notified the guards at the Art Institute. The newspaper account related that "blood spots were found at a point 20 yards north of where the body was found, indicating she may have been struck first at this point and then dragged into the bushes." Police noted the similarities between this murder and that of Bettelley's a year earlier. Upon further investigation, Wilson had been stabbed, and a gruesome discovery was that her assailant had gnawed on her body.[69]

Editorials and newspaper articles from this period tended to focus on the dangers of Chicago's urban areas, especially within its park system. A *Chicago Tribune* editorial published a week after Wilson's murder expressed outrage at the murders: "That women should be killed in public places in the front yard of downtown Chicago is shocking and shameful." The author suggested that the public, especially women, should take great care in their use of the city's parks: "[I]ndeed, such parks are more likely to be frequented by muggers, rapists, and killers, among others, than are out-of-the-way places. Broad daylight is not sufficient protection."[70] A climate of fear and outrage was apparent.

In a tragic chance encounter, David and Judith Elaine Ott and their twenty-month-old son were on a four-hour train stopover in Chicago when they decided to walk over to Grant Park. Judith Ott had gone to use the restroom when she was attacked and stabbed to death. Her husband, David Ott, responded when Chicago Park District employees yelled that a man running from the scene had just murdered a woman. Ott chased the perpetrator down, unaware that it was his wife who had just been killed.[71] Judith Ott was the third woman killed in Grant Park in that month and the fourth in the past year.

David Ott had captured forty-nine-year-old Lester Harrison. Harrison later admitted to killing four of the women in Grant Park, relating how hurting and murdering women sexually aroused him. The murderer had a long history as a violent criminal, including battery, armed robbery, and rape and had been remanded on several occasions to Menard State Prison for the criminally insane.[72] Harrison stated that he played no role in Koutros's death. With Harrison's capture and confession, the state released McDonald, who had been tried and convicted in 1970 of the murder of Lehmann. In January 1974, police charged nineteen-year-old Ray Anthony Cooper with the 1973 murder of Koutros in the Grant Park underground garage. Cooper had been on probation at the time for a theft charge. He later was charged with a rape in the First National Bank building.[73]

The events in the Grant Park murders reflect the greatest fears of the 1970s. Women were brutally murdered by a sexual deviant. An innocent man was charged, tried, and convicted of murder. Meanwhile, the murders continued. Then to make matters worse, another murderer was on the loose, having recently been released from prison. These scenarios were repeatedly played out in television and movie dramas. The theme of violence unchecked was reflected in the Dirty Harry movies, where vigilante justice is seen as a viable solution to an inept justice and police system in cities where killers roamed.

The day after the last of these murders, an article appeared in the *Chicago Tribune* outlining a program entitled "Parks and Playgrounds Safety." Approved by the Chicago–Cook County Commission on Criminal Justice, the program urged that federal anticrime funds available to the state be used to recruit, train, and organize ordinary citizens to assist police in preventing park crimes.[74] Clearly, the city had to take even more serious measures to change both the perceptions and the realities of public safety in its parks.

While it was statistically unlikely that a visitor to Grant Park would be murdered, the public perception was that the park was not safe. By 1975, a newspaper survey stated that only 25 percent of Chicagoans would even suggest a visit to Grant Park.[75] This was not a ringing endorsement for the city's front yard.

Yet, it wasn't just Chicago. The nation as a whole had concerns about violence in its major cities. Considerable statistical evidence from the 1960s supports the belief that these cities, especially Chicago, experienced rising homicide rates. Frank Zimring, lawyer and educator, asserts that this increase was related in part to the "increased availability of handguns. . . . Between 1965 and 1974, the homicide rate in U.S. cities doubled, and it hovered at that level until the late 1990s."[76] However, the Grant Park murders were all done without handguns. Chicago's significant increase in violent crime, coupled with the public's perception, made Chicago's downtown, including Grant Park, a place to avoid. This marked a low point for the park; it still possessed stately lawns and cultural institutions, but somehow the manicured gardens did not reflect a controlled space.

A Proposed New Band Shell

The Chicago Park District discussed the idea of building a new band shell in a move to improve the security of the park and to increase the utility of the north end of the park. The 1930s-era band shell on the south end of the park had lasted longer than had been planned for or expected. Several groups had proposed replacement band shells, but none of the plans ever moved past the conceptual phase. In 1963, the Chicago Park District proposed a band shell for Butler Field with part of the money coming from the Montgomery Ward Foundation. Ironically, this was defeated by Ward's court decision that required the unanimous consent of all Michigan Avenue property owners. In 1966, the Chicago Community Trust put forth a proposal that was slated for Butler Field but never moved beyond the drawing board.[77] In 1972, a new plan was proposed for the north end of the park, but a number of Michigan

Avenue property owners expressed their opposition to this notion. In a capitulation to the inability to get a new band shell constructed, in 1975, the Chicago Park District dedicated the old band shell to James C. Petrillo, who was then eighty-one years old and was recognized for starting the free concert series during the Great Depression.[78]

Although plans for the new band shell were repeatedly defeated, the concept of an underground garage survived. The Chicago Park District pushed forward with the construction of the parking garage on the north end of the park at Monroe Street, even though it would not include a band shell. The district planned to cover the top with landscaping and some amenities, but the project evolved to eventually include tennis courts, an ice rink, and chess and checker facilities.[79] The plan reflected the trend during the Daley era of excavating parking garages. The underground garage did replace a surface lot, so, arguably, it led to some increase in park land and additional amenities. The Monroe Street underground garage opened in 1976, during the nation's bicentennial, and the area above it was renamed Daley Bicentennial Plaza after Mayor Richard J. Daley's death in 1976. During his tenure as mayor, Daley remained popular and continued to win reelection. Today, he is remembered as the last of the big-city bosses.[80]

During this time of social and political change, a new movement was mobilizing in Chicago. Unlike the massive political unrest that characterized the 1960s, the 1970s brought an increased appreciation for the value of open space, not only in rural and suburban areas but also in the city's core. Pulitzer Prize–winning journalist Lois Wille in her book *Forever Open, Clear, and Free*, published in 1972, recounts the history of the lakefront and Grant Park, emphasizing the importance of open space. Some groups, such as the Openlands Project, had been advocating for a wide range of planning issues since the 1960s. Reflecting the environmental movement, these groups asserted the core concept that "nature" can be found in cities and also made a case for creating more open areas in northeastern Illinois.[81] Wille's book serves as a touchstone for the Chicagoland community that mobilized a great number of people to take action. This general sense of environmental advocacy resulted in the founding of Friends of the Parks in 1975, which provided grassroots support for Chicago's parks.[82] These organizations and Wille's call to action mobilized the revitalization of Chicago's parks. A new era was dawning for Grant Park.

8

The Park Reenvisioned and Renewed

During the late 1970s and early 1980s, Chicagoans sowed the seeds for significant change for Grant Park. Chicagoans looked to transform their city while the changing economy created urban challenges that were marked by depopulation and deindustrialization. At the same time, Americans were becoming energized by the environmental movement and gaining a greater appreciation of green space. Many people became more active, which brought them out to parks to jog, bike, or participate in team sports. Outdoor festivals began to fill Grant Park. As a result, Grant Park reclaimed a central place for the community. With activities ranging from music festivals to Fourth of July celebrations, Grant Park emerged as a park triumphant.

Bringing People Back to the Park

The late 1970s saw an increased demand for open space for sports. Within the ethos of environmentalism and physical fitness, people looked to the parks as not only green space within the city limits but also as a resource for maintaining a healthy lifestyle. Park districts across the country met this demand. The Chicago Park District built tennis courts at the Daley Bicentennial Plaza, and enthusiasts jogged in Grant Park and played tennis. Inaugurated by Friends of the Park, the first Chicago Marathon was run in 1977, beginning and ending its 26.2-mile loop in Grant Park.

Reversing a decades-long trend, the Chicago Park District garnered enough support to move forward with a new band shell in the park's northern section in Butler Field (see fig. 8.1).[1] In 1978, the park district constructed the new "demountable" Petrillo Music Shell directly east of the Art Institute of Chicago. This new performance venue was designed to be disassembled, but this proved expensive and time consuming, so it became a permanent structure. Although not as attractive as the art-deco band shell on the south end of the park, the new shell provided a significant step up from its worn-out predecessor.[2]

Critics decried the squat appearance of the band shell, with one reviewer commenting, "The park district's shell design looks like a gigantic doorstop and is in sympathy with nothing near the site."[3] Critics notwithstanding, the new band shell reflected contemporary design, and its modernity reflected the recent additions to the School of the Art Institute and its Columbus Street entrance across the street from the band shell. Over time, the park district landscaped the area around the band shell with trees and shrubs, which served to shield the audience's view of the street. The new venue offered additional amenities, including dressing rooms, locker rooms,

Figure 8.1. Petrillo band shell, Grant Park, July 25, 1997. Chicago Park District Special Collections.

restrooms, lounges, mechanical and electrical areas, and a sound room. The band shell featured a screen that could be closed for rehearsals during inclement weather.[4] The Grant Park Music Festival Orchestra, the resident orchestra, performed regularly in its new home.

The design provided seating for 5,022 guests on removable benches, and the grassy area of Butler Field could accommodate 35,000 more.[5] The new band shell's location on the north end of the park reflected, at least in part, the increase in residential construction nearby. Developers built a number of high rises along Randolph Street, and downtown urban living had some significant successes, notably Bertrand Goldberg's iconic Marina City at 300 North State Street. The southern end of the park remained in proximity to rail yards and light industry, but business leaders worked with the city and other interested parties to construct a new neighborhood there. Journalist Lois Wille notes, "[B]y 1997, the desolate south Loop of 1972 had blossomed into a thriving new town of 14,500." Over the coming decades, developers rebuilt the South Loop into a desirable residential area, featuring the uniquely elegant renovations of Dearborn Park I and Central Station.[6]

A new era in Grant Park's history was unfolding when the city selected Butler Field as the staging area for an outdoor Mass celebrated by the newly elected head of the Roman Catholic Church, Pope John Paul II, when he traveled to Chicago in October 1979. More than one million people attended the Mass, which was preceded by an ethnic festival featuring Hungarian, Irish, Cuban, Mexican, Korean, and German choirs and the Polish Millennium Chorus. Rather than utilize the new band shell, workers erected a special dais for the Mass (see fig. 8.2).[7] People walked in the streets and gathered peacefully with the support of local police and other civil services. This was in stark contrast to the violent protests that had marred the park's reputation since 1968.

In spite of the enormous number of worshipers and curious onlookers, Grant Park demonstrated its ability to assemble large crowds with the efficient coordination of traffic control, medical services, and toilets. In another action that portended much for the future of large gatherings in the park, the city closed Madison and Jackson Streets to accommodate pedestrians. The street closures would become routine to accommodate crowds in the park, leaving the streets open only to pedestrian traffic. While many forces affected the physical evolution of Grant Park, the pope's visit in 1979 significantly influenced the future cultural direction of park use (see fig. 8.3). Grant Park returned to being Chicago's location for civic celebration and inspired others to use the park for major events. After more than a decade of negative press, the pope's visit to Grant Park transformed the public perception of Grant Park.

Figure 8.2. Construction of platform for papal Mass, Grant Park, 1979. Photograph by Jack Lenahan.

Figure 8.3. Pope John Paul II Mass, Grant Park, October 5, 1979. Chicago Park District Special Collections.

The first of the perennial music festivals that would become a summer staple of Grant Park, the Chicago Jazz Festival, was organized in 1980. The selection of jazz as the showcase music reflected an expansion of the diverse offerings within Grant Park. The Jazz Institute of Chicago, the Mayor's Office of Special Events, and numerous private partners were involved with the festival, and it was able to draw marquee-name performers from year 1. Chicago jazz favorites Benny Goodman and the Art Ensemble of Chicago have appeared as well as jazz icons Miles Davis, Ella Fitzgerald, and Wynton Marsalis. The Jazz Festival draws visitors from around the globe and has become a cornerstone of the city's summer festival schedule.

Other annual events were piloted within a few years of the success of the Jazz Festival. The first Taste of Chicago was held on North Michigan Avenue in 1980 but eventually made its way into Grant Park. The festival routinely attracted over one million visitors each year with programming that lasted more than a week and culminating in the city's largest Fourth of July celebration.[8] It is the largest of Chicago's street fairs, with food vendors from city neighborhoods and restaurants representing a wide range of ethnic tastes. The format, however, continues to evolve with new city administrations.

The Chicago Blues Festival started in 1984, with Gospelfest added in 1985. The city created the innovative Department of Cultural Affairs to act as the liaison with the increasing number of groups interested in sponsoring events that would attract people of all ages, races, and ethnicities. Drawing on the model of the Grant Park Music Festival, these events were free and open to the public. Because of a partnership between corporate sponsors and the city, businesses, such as hotels and restaurants, were able to generate significant revenue from these events to the benefit of the parties involved.

In the 1980s, the city and the Chicago Park District undertook a comprehensive self-assessment to help guide the development of the next plan for Grant Park and all the parks in the system. Reflecting national trends, the Chicago Park District and the city took stock of their parklands in 1982 and chose to reinvest in these "treasures." The park district made informed choices based on historical research, a preservation ethic, and comprehensive design concerns. In addition, perhaps reflecting the popular advocacy of the 1960s and 1970s, the district allowed its thinking to be influenced by outdoor enthusiasts, preservationists, and advocacy groups.

By 1987, the district had uncovered a great number of park records in its back rooms and administrative offices. These records included "letters, drawings, news clippings, hand-colored glass negatives, and European books and maps from the turn of the century," which provided the opportunity to recover the park's history. The district continued to move forward with the study of the park and its preservation program.[9]

In the early 1980s, the city council had become entangled in a conflict known as "council wars." Mayor Harold Washington, the first African American mayor of the city, battled with the city council, with one area of contention being the patronage system. Washington initiated a process that led to a more inclusive city government and marked an important transition within the city, eventually resulting in greater professionalism within the Chicago Park District's ranks.[10] The city increased its cultural offerings in the late 1980s with the addition of the Mexican Fine Arts Museum and the much-needed renovation of Navy Pier, which began in 1989.

In the 1990s, the Petrillo Music Shell became associated with another milestone in the city's history. Although Chicago has been touted nationally as a sports town, the city had celebrated few championship teams in the twentieth century. The first notable exception was the 1985 Chicago Bears. Then in the 1990s, the Chicago Bears, White Sox, Cubs, and Bulls all vied for public attention. Chicagoans heaped a great deal of adulation on Michael Jordan and the Bulls, which dominated the National Basketball Association and won championships in 1991, 1992, 1993, and again in 1996, 1997, and 1998. In an era of expensive and scarce tickets to games, victory celebrations at the Petrillo Music Shell provided many Chicagoans their only opportunity to cheer for their team in person after a championship. As the celebratory raising of championship trophies became a fairly regular occurrence, players often used the phrase "one more game until Grant Park." In these moments of community celebration, the city used Grant Park as the central location for featuring its sports heroes.

Popular festivals brought throngs of people into the park. Over time, these events grew so large that some roads through the park were closed for weeks at a time during festivals. For example, Columbus Drive between Congress and Monroe was regularly closed for the Taste of Chicago, which had a significant positive impact on the enjoyment of the park for visitors. At certain times, pedestrians take precedence over traffic concerns within the park, a reversal from the Richard J. Daley era. With no traffic to contend with, park visitors are free to stroll around large roadways and the park.

Chicago Park District: Planning for Change

Throughout the early 1990s, improvements in operations continued for the Chicago Park District. Unwanted and underutilized programs were eliminated, and the management of Lincoln Park Zoo, Soldier Field, parking garages and lots, information systems, medical and risk-management services, and internal janitorial operations were privatized. As an example of the savings realized by these changes in management, the park district saw a positive turnaround within two years of nearly $1 million at its golf courses, operated by Kemper Golf Management. Soldier Field also realized the first net-revenue gain in its fifty-plus-year history.[11]

During a restructuring in 1992, the park district determined that Grant Park did not have a single, definitive plan. The city drafted the Grant Park Design Guidelines, a thoughtful and site-sensitive document that set out a comprehensive guide for the district to prepare for new and significant changes in the park.[12] It notes, "With the publication of Daniel Burnham's Chicago Plan of 1909, Grant Park was designated to become 'the formal focal point, the intellectual center of Chicago.' This goal was partially achieved in the 1920s when most of present day Grant Park was constructed. However the potential of Grant Park to provide a full spectrum of leisure time experiences has never been fully developed. . . . Our priceless legacy is at a critical crossroads. Years of use have taken a fearful toll, and have created new and substantial needs. These must be met if Grant Park is going to flourish in the 21st century. The Chicago Park District is faced with the call of accommodating future uses while renewing the glory of Grant Park's historic past."[13]

The Chicago Park District's Office of Research and Planning studied the strengths and weaknesses of the park, publishing an assessment of Grant Park on July 1, 1992. For the most part, the Grant Park Design Guidelines were used to carry out work in the park and to accomplish goals, such as historic rehabilitation intended to recover the park's historic character, and, where practical, to extend the traditions of its design. Another goal of parkland consolidation attempted "to incorporate all the land within the traditional park boundaries—Randolph Street, Michigan Avenue, Roosevelt Road and Lake Michigan—into a unified scheme for the development and use of the park."[14]

Other qualitative goals included "use and activation" because the district realized that "the variety and duration of uses should be expanded if the potential of the expanded and more unified park is to be realized. Currently, only a handful of the major spaces in Grant Park are programmed for more than one particular function. Activity, even in or near those areas designated for passive uses, increases safety and security." It also recognized the need to make the sprawling lands of the park more manageable and accessible: "Large areas are hard to get to or through and once you get there it is hard to know where else to go. The multi-level Randolph Street structure and the IC trench from Randolph to Roosevelt Road are especially disruptive in this regard. Grant Park needs a comprehensive program of signage to explain the physical layout of the park and to identify the range of activities."[15]

The guidelines also laid out the need for structures and infrastructure: "Convenient, safe and clean toilet facilities are almost nonexistent. Food services are available but limited, and significant opportunities to make

Grant Park a good place to have a meal or snack have been missed." In closing, the Chicago Park District recognized the "primary task of providing recreational, cultural and leisure time opportunities."[16]

The report also addressed the issue of reforestation: "Perhaps the most basic need for Grant Park is the most obvious: the park needs more trees, shrubbery, and flowers. Grant Park had one of the largest stands of American Elm trees anywhere. Spectacular displays of flowering crabapples, lilacs and other ornamentals have declined and vanished over time." In conclusion, the Chicago Park District asserted, "As the gateway to our business, civic and cultural institutions, the condition of Grant Park is symbolic of the economic health and civic well-being of our city."[17] The push was for the reinvestment in downtown to be met by reinvestment in Grant Park. Fortunately for Grant Park, the economic boom of the late 1990s provided the resources and vision for the city to move forward with improvements.

One key driver to these improvements was the importance of the convention and tourist business in Chicago. Since the 1870s, Chicago had been a national leader for conventions and trade shows. Grant Park had for a time played a central role in this field as the site of the Inter-State Exposition Building, which was used until the 1890s. In the twentieth century, much of this display was slated for the lakefront center south of the park, at McCormick Place, which had become a sprawling complex. Grant Park, with its central location and iconic status, has become increasingly important as one of the value-added incentives for groups selecting Chicago as their meeting place. With the increased competition from "sun belt" cities for trade shows, part of Chicago's package has been its world-class parks and cultural offerings just steps from its hotels. As part of a concerted effort, the city renewed its efforts to improve and maintain the park's landscape and provide tourist amenities. As a result, on any given weekend, tourists and visitors from Chicago's suburbs enjoy Grant Park's museums, paths, and lawns.

Chicagoans and visitors alike continued to benefit from innovations offered by Grant Park's institutions. Reflecting national trends, institutions expanded their complexes and featured blockbuster expositions, beginning with the 1977 King Tut exhibit at the Field Museum. The Art Institute, Adler Planetarium, Shedd Aquarium, and Field Museum all featured large exhibits, dining, and shopping opportunities, the quality of which they worked to improve over the years as they realized how much these offerings influenced attendance. The museums also provided safe and well-lighted parking as part of their larger plans to meet the needs of their visitors. Internally, the institutions professionalized their staffs and increased financial stability through capital campaigns. The Loop also increased in population, especially with the energy and around-the-clock presence of students in expanded programs of School of the Art Institute of Chicago, DePaul University's Loop campus, Columbia College, Roosevelt University, and other educational institutions. The largely young and diverse student body has brought additional foot traffic to the Loop and Grant Park.

Changes in the Grant Park Landscape

While the core design for Grant Park remained in place, the Chicago Park District incorporated a great number of improvements between 1976 and the late 1990s, creating a dynamic landscape. Starting in the late 1970s, the park district and the Art Institute of Chicago made a number of changes to the northern end of Grant Park. In early 1978, the park dedicated the Daley Bicentennial Plaza, built on top of the Monroe Street underground garage (see fig. 8.4). Although this modernist architectural style broke with the park's neoclassical past, it represents a significant investment. The design features tennis courts, chess tables, an outdoor skating area, and a bunker-like field house, serving the new populace that has moved into the high-rise developments built nearby.

Figure 8.4. Daley Bicentennial Plaza under construction, October 13, 1976. Chicago Park District Special Collections.

In 1977, the Art Institute created a new, modern face on its east side, facing Grant Park and the Petrillo Band Shell. The architectural firm of Skidmore, Owings, and Merrill designed the Columbus Drive addition and expanded the School of the Art Institute. The firm also designed a new eastern entrance into the museum to accommodate tour buses. The addition houses the Adler and Sullivan's Trading Room, rescued from the Chicago Stock Exchange Building, which had been salvaged when the building was demolished in 1972.[18] The exterior features several fountains, with the northeast section at Monroe and Columbus Drive incorporating the entrance arch of the stock-exchange building with Sullivan's signature organic ornamentation.[19] The Art Institute presented these remnants of Chicago's architectural past as stand-alone works of art.

Hammond, Beeby, and Babka designed the Daniel F. and Ada L. Rice addition to the Art Institute of Chicago in 1988 to house the modern-art collection. In 1991, the firm also completed Chicago's new Harold Washington Public Library, located downtown on Congress Street, just blocks away. The design reflects the city's nineteenth-century past with a modernist twist. During this same period, the Art Institute added a sculpture garden north of its main entrance.

The School of the Art Institute now had room for a wide range of educational activities. Often lost in the stunning treasures of the Art Institute were the school and its dynamic influence on the entire organization. While conserving and displaying art remained the heart of the museum's operations, training future artists and grounding them in the world's artistic tradition have remained central. The Art Institute's board also moved forward with an improvement along Michigan Avenue that included a new design for its south garden in 1977.[20]

While the northernmost section of Grant Park underwent significant transformation, the middle third of the park was where some of the most successful design elements and preservation sensibilities were in evidence. The incorporation of historical street lamps and additional gardens demonstrates the impact of solid design choices, which recaptured and improved many of the original design elements in the park.

Continuing a tradition of placing memorials and sculpture within the park, the Chicago Park District reinstalled the Spirit of Music/Theodore Thomas Memorial at Michigan Avenue in 1991. The South Park Commission had originally installed the figure south of the Art Institute but then removed it and placed the central figure as part of Edward H. Bennett's 1917 peristyle. The Spirit of Music was removed along with the peristyle when the city built the underground garage in 1953. In 1991, the district selected a new location for the sculpture closer to Symphony Center, with an eye toward design restoration and preservation. In its new location, the memorial better related to the living monument of Thomas's work and served as a reminder of his influence as conductor and guiding light of the Chicago Symphony Orchestra. The statue of the Spirit of Music stands atop a pedestal, and the bas-relief furniture features Thomas and orchestra members to create a successful sculptural ensemble. Later, the park district added an elevated stand for performers and an area for dancing. It became a popular destination featuring world music, dance lessons, refreshments, and restrooms.[21]

In 1986, the city realigned Lake Shore Drive north of Monroe Street. For years, drivers traveling on this route had encountered a dangerous curving zigzag. Traffic engineers greatly improved the safety of the roadway by making it a longer and more gradual curve. The park district created some parkland where the road had previously been. The restructure of the drive intentionally left standing the massive supports of the previous roadway at Randolph Street. In the 1990s, part of the former roadway became the Richard and Annette Block Cancer Survivor Park, featuring a Positive Mental Attitude walk. Its construction was part of an effort to create similar parks nationwide.

In a notable improvement, the city's transportation department undertook the renovation of Congress Plaza in the mid-1990s. Bennett had designed and witnessed the construction of the main entrance to Grant Park in 1929, which provided one of his crowning glories for the park. By 1956, the Congress Expressway surged through with six lanes of traffic and obliterated the grand staircase because traffic engineers had transformed this part of the park into an interchange. Bennett designed it with pedestrians in mind, but those on foot could no longer easily navigate the lanes of traffic, and it became an entry that did not easily lead pedestrians into the park.

The city and the *Chicago Tribune* pronounced in 1994 that the "new front door for Grant Park, lifeless city plaza, once a grand entry, will be reborn in [a] $9-million project." The city had decided to renovate the long-neglected plaza, including adding design-appropriate streetlights. Stan Kaderbek, the chief bridge engineer for the city's transportation department, said, "[W]hen this thing [the Expressway] was put through, the appendages, all that was left of the grand plaza, lost all meaning. . . . Restoring the plaza sections to usefulness was strongly supported by Mayor Richard M. Daley, and it reflects a trend in recent years by city officials, from the mayor on down, to recognize the importance of architectural attractiveness in restorations and new construction."[22] The architectural plans reflect a great deal of sensitivity to the original design, with the city providing a majority of the economic resources for the project.

In line with the redesigned Congress Street entrance and focused within the heart of the park, the park district conducted a $2.8 million restoration of Buckingham Fountain in 1994. Contractors dismantled the fountain during a nine-month period and replaced much of its concrete core. Kate S. Buckingham, whose family made its fortune in the grain trade, created an endowment for the upkeep of the fountain in perpetuity at no taxpayer expense, even providing the funding for the multi-million-dollar restoration. The fund is administered by the Art Institute, another Chicago institution Buckingham supported generously. Like many seamless restorations, visitors might not be able to discern the changes, although the district hired a firm to install a stronger and more varied light show.[23] Chicagoans glory in their great fountain, and its annual switching-on is one of the official marks of the arrival of spring.

In 1997, the park district further improved the area surrounding Buckingham Fountain because visitors would make the long walk to the fountain only to realize that it did not provide places to sit, have any restrooms, or sell refreshments. The district built two refreshment stands and four low-profile and site-sensitive buildings housing two restrooms. The district also paid great attention to detail, ensuring that modest signage and building placement would not interfere with the view of the lake or fountain.[24]

In line with the greening of the city, the Chicago Park District restored and improved its plantings. With these changes, the district made the park more accommodating to its users and created a location to relax and enjoy the views of the park, particularly the stunning fountain. The city also improved Michigan Avenue and installed new streetlights. With the heart of the park now significantly renovated, the Chicago Park District had demonstrated a continuing sensitivity to the park's overall design.

The Museum Campus: Rebuild and Reinvest

While the northern parts of the park saw significant improvements, needs in the southern third of the park warranted complete reinvention. These changes included the considerable modification of traffic routes and landscaping to create the Museum Campus. Lake Shore Drive had wrapped both sides of the Field Museum, leaving it an island in a sea of traffic. Rerouting the drive consolidated traffic lanes on the west side of the museum complex, locating the Field Museum, Shedd Aquarium, and Adler Planetarium on the same side of the drive and providing a pedestrian passageway under the new Lake Shore Drive. Within this newly unified park area, each of Chicago's major cultural institutions—the Field Museum, Shedd Aquarium, and Adler Planetarium—also underwent significant modifications beginning in 1977. South of the museum campus, the park district incorporated areas of Burnham Park into a more cohesive, integrated landscape plan and executed a complete renovation of Soldier Field.

The trustees of the Field Museum hired Harry Weese and Associates to renovate its massive building.[25] The museum's wondrous neoclassical elements have their best display in the central hall with its enormous columns. The hall's impressive interior features early-twentieth-century light fixtures with large filament bulbs. In 2004, the museum undertook the construction of a new underground collection center on the east side of the building. Parking for the Field Museum was also significantly enhanced with the addition of parking garages as part of the reconstructed Soldier Field.

Since 1929, the Shedd Aquarium had been tucked away along the lakeshore. In 1990, the aquarium's board moved forward with a spectacular addition to the national landmark building, originally designed by the architectural firm of Graham, Probst, and White. The board selected the firm of Lohan and Associates to build the Shedd Oceanarium.[26] The architectural firm drafted a plan that required additional landfill and a reworking of the shoreline for the addition, which faces the lake. The design provides one of the most spectacular sight lines in the city. Visitors barely discern the distinction between the massive interior tank and the adjoining lake from the view line of the public space. The Shedd staff focused its attention on America's Pacific Northwest, capturing beluga whales, Pacific white-sided dolphins, harbor seals, and sea otters for the newly installed tanks. The new addition also features a food court and a more upscale dining experience. The museum emerged revitalized, with heralded new permanent installations including exhibits, such as Amazon Rising and the Wild Reef.[27]

Further east on the museum peninsula, the Adler Planetarium and Astronomical Museum enlisted Lohan and Associates for a renovated entrance in 1981 and an addition in the 1990s featuring a new café and a history-of-astronomy research center. After a decade of significant expansion, the Adler capped this period with its celebrated Sky Pavilion, which features exhibit galleries, a telescope terrace, and a lakefront restaurant.[28] Lohan and Associates created a visionary design that ties the planetarium to the surrounding landscape.

Beyond the institutions themselves, the Chicago Park District worked closely with the Chicago Department of Transportation to transform the north and south ends of Grant Park. In the mid-1990s, the district worked with a number of parties, including engineering firm Teng and Associates, to completely renovate the landscaping at the south end of Grant Park, including the traffic lanes. The complex work of reconfiguring Lake Shore Drive was completed in 1996. The mayor's office reported that as a result of this construction, there had been an enlargement of "Grant and Burnham Parks by 17.5 acres."[29]

With consultation from landscape architect Lawrence Halprin, a rolling landscape was created that differed significantly from the flat uniformity of much of the rest of the park. The changes included a new signage system and pedestrian viaducts, advocated by city project manager Richard Kinczyk, so that visitors could move through the park without crossing traffic.[30] The district also included concessions, such as food service, additional seating, and, for several years, occasional seasonal attractions, such as a merry-go-round. Visitors now had a new park destination that helped them when they planned their visits to the Field Museum, Adler Planetarium, and Shedd Aquarium. As one journalist notes, the museum campus creates "a cultural and recreational mecca that is, in a sense, a permanent world's fair, with the earth, the sea and the sky (the respective subjects of the Field, the Shedd and the Adler) as its main exhibits."[31] The comprehensive plan for the whole area has unified the landscape in appearance and provided a fitting setting for these three cultural institutions. In 1998, Mayor Richard M. Daley, son of the first Mayor Daley, dedicated the museum campus to the citizens of Chicago: "[T]he museum campus ranks as one of the most significant additions to the Chicago lakefront in generations."[32]

The Chicago Park District manages the Museum Campus, fifty-seven acres housing three institutions that collectively attract more than four million visitors each year. While elements of the plans date back to the 1980s, Mayor Richard M. Daley took the lead in 1995 for this complex, large-scale project, which "is accessible by foot, bike, roller blades, taxi, water taxi, car and public transportation."[33] In conception, it harmonizes both active and passive recreation.

In improving the whole, Mayor Daley in the 1990s supported the "classically inspired renovation of the Roosevelt Road bridge that crosses the Chicago River. The bridge allowed Roosevelt Road to leap the railroad tracks that have always separated it and West Siders from the lakefront."[34] Within Grant Park, the mayor demonstrated his penchant for greenery and preservation. Some of the improvements were completed by the time of the Democratic National Convention of 1996, and the convention provided an opportunity to push other projects to completion. For Grant Park, the convention was a chance to showcase the massive renovations and host a national event without major incident.

In the 1990s, smaller sections of work started to amount to something. As one journalist commented, the mayor "has turned South Michigan Avenue into a preservation showplace, with historical street lamps, plazas, viaducts, fountains and gardens—which admittedly seemed timed to be ready for the Democratic National Convention, but nonetheless represent the best of the city's big spruce-up."[35] The Chicago Park District had renovated the city's "front yard" in a way that previously would have seemed inconceivable.

Controversial Change South of Grant Park

During the 1990s, the city was conducting work on an enormous scale. This was especially true of the area around Grant Park, where the spectacular building boom of the 1990s fueled some of the city's most high-profile projects. Residential construction took place all around Grant Park with diverse projects, including condominium conversions, dormitories for college students, single-family townhomes, and high-rises. Realtors listed among their top selling points access to Grant Park and its cultural offerings, the restaurants, bike and walking paths, and easy access to transportation. The attraction proved so great that Mayor Richard M. Daley, a lifelong resident of Bridgeport on the South Side, moved with his family in 1993 to the Central Station development.[36] The city's tourism industry began to capitalize on the image of the skyline from Grant Park as the unofficial emblem of the city.

Other locations just outside of Grant Park received significant attention. One of the most controversial and publicized was the city's closing of Meigs Field on Northerly Island, at the east end of the museum peninsula. The airport's fifty-year lease on the land terminated in 1997 but was extended for a time. Many advocates desired a permanent air presence at this site and noted the positive impact this airport had in providing access to downtown businesses.[37] The city, however, in a bold stroke, destroyed the tarmac on March 31, 2003. The hue and cry from the airport supporters has been significant ever since the clandestine midnight closing with many protesters unhappy with what they perceived as lack of adequate public comment.

Initially, the Chicago Park District used the former Meigs terminal building as a field house. With the airport's closure, the mayor and the Chicago Park District advanced a plan for Northerly Island that featured ecological areas and nature programs. Advisers from the mayor's office arrived at an innovative solution to pay for this work, with the park district entering into a short-term contract for a music pavilion with revenue from the concerts providing funds for the proposed plans. In June 2005, the Charter One Pavilion opened with seating for 7,500. During its first season, it hosted a number of popular concerts and a Hurricane Katrina relief benefit.[38]

Chicagoans also focused their attention on the controversial changes to Soldier Field, which was largely underutilized and a bit of a white elephant. Unlike their split allegiance to two baseball teams, Chicagoans share a passion in football for the Chicago Bears. The South Park Commissioners built Grant Park Stadium (Soldier Field) from 1922 to 1926.[39] Although the stadium hosted some spectacular events, such as the Dempsey-Tunney fight in 1927, it drew its largest crowd when 260,000 faithful attended the large Catholic celebration, the Marian Year Tribute, on September 8, 1954.[40]

Given the stadium's prominent location, the Chicago Bears moved their home from Wrigley Field to Soldier Field in 1971. The stadium was renovated numerous times, in 1979, in 1982, and in 1988 with the addition of fifty-six skyboxes. For the World Cup soccer games in 1994, the city undertook a major renovation of the stadium, following a national stadium-building boom in the 1990s that rivaled the building boom of the 1920s. As part of this trend, in 2001, the Chicago Plan Commission passed the $587 million Soldier Field rehabilitation project. Essentially, the plan was to build a new stadium within the structure's neoclassical colonnades.[41] Criticism came from a number of camps and included those who questioned the plan, the location, the process, and the public funding of changes that essentially benefited a private organization—the Bears.

Reflecting the choice of architect for the recent museum renovations, the city, the Chicago Park District, and the Bears selected Lohan and Associates for this project as well. The architectural firm with principal Dirk Lohan had displayed great sensitivity in the additions to the Shedd Aquarium and the Adler Planetarium. In each case, the firm had created imaginative and cohesive additions that artfully blended with the historically significant structures. The firm's success, in part, resulted from maintaining intact the front façades of the iconic structures while blending their additions to the lake sides of the buildings. The architects also made structures that were outward looking and took advantage of their spectacular settings.

The architectural design for Soldier Field, however, obscured the visual impact of the colonnades by having the new stadium loom over them. Unfortunately, the renovation did not share the same success as those of the museums, and in 2006, Soldier Field lost its national-historic-landmark designation. The National Park System Advisory Board said the glass bowl–shaped stadium set inside the colonnades of the old Soldier Field had destroyed the stadium's historic character. In a positive light, the new landscaping yielded a great deal more useful parkland and features underground parking as a replacement for the previous unsightly surface lots, which better served the parking needs of the nearby Museum Campus.

The landscaping plan for Soldier Field also included the demolition of the Chicago Park District's former administrative building at 425 East McFetridge Drive, which was designed by Holabird and Root and built in 1939. The Chicago Park District removed this structure and landscaped the area to feature a water wall dedicated to the nation's armed forces. The new landscape also features an interactive children's garden just north of the old administrative building site.[42]

Soldier Field represented not only the home of professional sports but also a war memorial and a federally recognized structure. Veterans and others were concerned about the possible loss of a significant war memorial dedicated to those who had served in the military. Assurances were made that the structure's name would not change, a concern in an era of corporate naming rights. The Chicago Park District made efforts to expand the official role of Soldier Field's memorial with little modifications to the colonnades and other architectural features. In contrast, Navy Pier, dedicated to those who had served in the U.S. Navy, also had undergone considerable redesign, but its major modification did not receive much public criticism.

The Bears opened their renovated stadium in 2003 to enthusiastic reviews from fans. Among the first teams to play at the stadium was the Chicago Fire, a Major League Soccer team, which started its 2003 season in Naperville, a suburb thirty miles west, but played some of its remaining games at Soldier Field. Unlike the critics, most fans were thrilled with their new stadium.

Although outside of the boundaries of Grant Park, these high-profile and controversial changes to Meigs Field and Soldier Field have maintained popular attention on the city's lakefront. The projects have had a significant impact on the south end of Grant Park. Ultimately, they demonstrate that Chicagoans and special-interest groups take seriously their charge to be watchdogs for the lakefront. These cases also reflect the degree to which the lakefront remains a dynamic landscape.

Grant Park and a Comprehensive Approach to the Lakefront

With the theme of change in mind, Blair Kamin, architecture critic for the *Chicago Tribune*, examined Chicago's lakefront in 1998 in his Pulitzer Prize–winning six-part series, "Reinventing the Lakefront." In the series, Kamin contrasts the overcrowded nature of Lincoln Park with Grant Park, which teemed with visitors during the summer festivals but was otherwise underutilized. With the city's coffers then brimming and many lakefront projects in the offing, he wondered if the city could provide a comprehensive and unified approach to all of these projects. Kamin's critical eye rested on high profile projects at Navy Pier, Soldier Field, Meigs Field, Burnham Park, and the South Works plant, the vacant and expansive former U.S. Steel plant on the far south side of the city.[43]

The *Chicago Tribune* series provided a prescient snapshot of the park. The series was reprinted and included an editorial that notes, "It is time to look past the civic myth that is the perfect lakefront and confront the not-so-glamorous reality. . . . Kamin's series is timely because more than $500 million worth of physical improvements are planned over the next few years. And yet, there is no single agency—much less, vision—deciding how these improvements may intertwine." The editor provided specific examples: "[S]o the state will rebuild South Lake Shore Drive taking little heed of the Army Corps of Engineers' redo of the sea wall that protects adjacent Burnham Park. And the city will install a busway along the sunken Metra tracks through Grant Park, connecting McCormick Place to the new Millennium music park at Randolph Street but strangely leaving Navy Pier stranded beyond walking distance."[44] In the late 1990s and the first years of the new millennium, Kamin called for a comprehensive assessment of the lakefront. Yet, there was a spectacular project waiting in the wings.

Millennium Park

The city and the Chicago Park District brought together vast resources and partners to reclaim acres of land for park use. On the south end of Grant Park, visitors now strolled through a landscape where once busy highways were. Visitors found the Museum Campus landscape almost as enjoyable as the cultural institutions that drew them there in the first place. With the improvements to the south end of Grant Park complete, it was time to focus attention on the north end and bring it up to the new standards for Grant Park. Those improvements were laid out in the Millennium Park plan (see fig. 8.5).

Figure 8.5. Millennium Park, aerial view, opening weekend 2004. City of Chicago/Peter J. Schulz/Walter S. Mitchell.

Mayor Richard M. Daley said, "This civic project is unprecedented in its size and scale and has taken the commitment of many individuals and organizations to make Millennium Park a reality. It recognizes and enhances the foresight of those who came before us who worked to keep the lakefront the crowning jewel of our city."[45] Although the final results received positive reviews and the individual components were deemed spectacular, the project had its share of controversy during its development.

The kernel of the idea for Millennium Park was inspired by a number of postwar plans that the Chicago Park District had proposed to replace Grant Park's band shell. These plans featured a central music pavilion that could include a theater on the north end of Grant Park. The Illinois Central's rail yards, which had been a constant problem in previous proposals, presented an opportunity for redevelopment and the focus of the new plan in the late 1990s. Chicago journalist Jonathan Black writes, "The railroad property was considered inviolate, and it was—until Chicago's great green crusader, Mayor Daley, negotiated the air rights from the railroad in 1998. An underground garage would pay for much of the new park. McDonough Associates was hired to engineer the garage; Skidmore, Owings & Merrill was hired to design the park."[46] Michigan Avenue property owners could not easily object to a project that would transform an unsightly postindustrial landscape into park usage. In this case, the Illinois Central Railroad, which had saved the park from lake erosion in the 1850s, would now provide the site for a park that would gain international attention.

When the city had built its new downtown library, it rededicated the old library at 78 East Washington Street as the Chicago Cultural Center.[47] In a successful adaptive reuse, Holabird and Root renovated and modernized the building in 1977, and the Chicago Cultural Center has been the cornerstone for activities on the north end of the park since the 1990s. The Office of Cultural Affairs, under Lois Weisberg, operated a wide range of activities at the north end of Grant Park along Michigan Avenue. With Chicago being one of the host cities for the World Cup in 1994, the Cultural Center expanded its role and hosted musical, artistic, and other programs. The success of the Cultural Center programs demonstrates the potential draw of visitors to renovated park grounds and facilities at the north end of Grant Park.

Mayor Richard M. Daley appointed Ed Uhlir as design director of the Millennium Park Project. Uhlir had served as the director of architecture, engineering, and planning and later director of research and planning at the Chicago Park District. Although located within the historical boundaries of Grant Park, the proposal for Millennium Park set it apart so much that it can almost be viewed as its own park. The renovated area is bounded by Michigan Avenue, Columbus Drive, Randolph Street, and Monroe Street.[48]

In the late 1990s, the world-renowned architectural firm of Skidmore, Owings, and Merrill (SOM) developed a comparatively straightforward design for the Millennium Park project that featured a modest new band shell. In time, the idea for the park expanded and included additional parking because the city desired underground garages as revenue to help pay for the park project. The city hired two engineering firms, McDonough and Teng and Associates, to complete the garages. McDonough undertook the design for Millennium Park garage, with twenty-two-hundred spaces and the foundational support for the band shell. Teng would renovate the eighteen-hundred-space Grant Park North Garage. The firms immediately ran into problems, as the support columns for the new garage cracked, and the old garage was crumbling. At that point, the city incurred cost overruns, and there were reports that the budget issues strained communications among all the parties involved.[49]

By big-city standards, the budget had started at a relatively modest $150 million to $270 million and then rose to $300 million. In addition to cost overruns, the project fell significantly behind schedule. Originally slated to be completed before 2000, the project was nowhere near completion as the millennium passed. The *Chicago Tribune* ran a series of tough investigative pieces charging sloppy management, misuse of TIF (tax increment financing) funds, murky accounting, and cronyism. As the construction continued, the working relationship between the architectural and engineering firms purportedly deteriorated, and mistakes led to public finger-pointing among the "collaborators."[50]

Despite the cost issues and riding the continuing economic prosperity of the 1990s, the project grew by leaps and bounds. While reclaiming park land from rail yards would have made the project a success, the price tag would have been shocking for just parking spaces and green lawn. Rather, a public and private partnership emerged that featured a number of "enhancements" to the park to make the entire renovation have a significant impact and be newsworthy. It also provided an opportunity to talk civic-minded Chicagoans into supporting the project by paying for certain added architectural and sculptural features by world-renowned designers. As a tribute to the millennium, the city provided a compelling vision for this section of the park, enlisting some of the metropolis's most powerful and influential business leaders to garner support for the project. The city could allocate money for a park, but extra value would be provided through these "enhancements." John Bryan of Sara Lee Corporation supported the project. Long associated with the National Trust for Historic Preservation, Bryan brought on a whole range of people who might be interested in improving the park. He encouraged people to participate as a way to give back to the city in a tangible way. The city enticed the public with news of each stunning addition, creating a year-round destination with significant public programs and works of art. As one writer described it, "Gone were those nothing walkways and prosaic planting. In their place—Art! Music! Design!"[51]

Providing an international profile for the project, Frank Gehry signed on to design a band shell for the park. The architect had long-term ties with Chicago's Pritzker family, having won the Pritzker Prize for architecture in 1989. His designs for the Guggenheim Museum in Bilbao, Spain (1997), and the Disney Concert Hall in Los Angeles (2003) were among the most-discussed architectural designs in the world. Building on this excitement, the Museum of Contemporary Art in Chicago featured Gehry in an exhibit. One of the most celebrated architects in the world, Gehry delivered a swirling silver design for the band shell that did not disappoint those looking for a bold statement. While it may not be everyone's cup of tea, the city now has a centerpiece that is an unmistakable landmark. Gehry also designed the BP Pedestrian Bridge, which serves to break Millennium Park out of its architectural room and allows pedestrians to cross over busy Columbus Drive via its serpentine span.

The Public Building Commission of Chicago announced that "Millennium Park will be Chicago's newest world-class destination for families, tourists and convention-goers, and it will guarantee new jobs and revenues in Chicago for decades to come. Conservative estimates say it could generate $100 million to $150 million of new tourist revenues each year."[52] Within these calculations, the project would repay the city in just a few years.

The enormous and heavy band shell required additional foundational supports. The city also commissioned a sculpture by Anish Kapoor, which weighed 110 tons and required additional architectural support. Each one represented engineering challenges for SOM's engineering of the underground garages, which were to provide funding for the park project. Each new modification in the park, from additional fountains to a new dance theater, required changes to the plan, and that meant change orders, which created cost overruns and affected the project's bottom line by reducing the number of parking spaces.[53]

The city opened its first feature in Millennium Park at the end of 2001, the McCormick Tribune Plaza and Ice Rink. The outdoor rink, designed to be open from November to February, evokes other festive, urban ice-skating venues, such as the Rockefeller Center in New York City. Two years later, the Park Grille opened, using the rink area for outdoor dining and events in the summer. The mayor returned to Millennium Park in October 2002 to dedicate Wrigley Square. The square features a peristyle, which is a tip of the hat to Bennett's earlier design. At this corner decades earlier, Bennett had first realized his neoclassical designs for Grant Park with his balustrades. In 1917, he had crowned his work with a classically inspired peristyle, a series of columns enclosing a court and fountain. This popular landmark became a much-loved feature of the park, but it had been removed in 1953. The new peristyle features a fountain and serves as a cornerstone for the park. The names of private-sector donors of more than $1 million are featured here, in recognition of donations that provided well over $100 million for the park.

The next feature to open was the Joan W. and Irving V. Harris Theater for Music and Dance. The architectural firm of Hammond Beeby Rupert Ainge designed the fifteen-hundred-seat theater that opened in 2003. The Music and Dance Theater Chicago serves mid-sized performing arts organizations and represents an attempt to address the need for a medium-size theater. The Harris Theater brought together a number of partners under one roof, providing ballet, folk dance, and other musical offerings.[54] It features a terrace and connects to the underground Millennium Park garage. The theater's trustees, representing a privately funded arts organization, lease the land from the City of Chicago. While the theater challenges the historical "forever open, clear and free" designation, most people agree it is a valuable addition to the Randolph Street Theater District.

In July 2004, the much-awaited Gehry-designed music pavilion was dedicated in honor of the Pritzker family. Although some in the Petrillo family expressed disappointment, the band shell was designated the Pritzker Pavilion.[55] Gehry applied space-age technology to create the frame that enthralls visitors. The classical Grant Park Music Festival Orchestra and Chorus are permanently based at the site. The pavilion is equipped with fixed seating for four thousand and is surrounded by ninety-five thousand square feet of lawn that accommodates eleven thousand more people. Designed to be enclosed, the stage can be used year-round. Central to this concept, the seating area is covered by metal latticework, which holds the sound system, arching over the audience area. SOM designed this practical work that contributes to one of the most refined outdoor spaces in the city.

The AT&T, formerly SBC, Plaza features Kapoor's sculpture Cloud Gate. Kapoor designed the 168-piece elliptical stainless-steel sculpture to literally reflect the park and city around it. Kapoor was an unexpected choice for the commission since he had never been commissioned for an installation in the United States.[56] Ned Cramer, the former curator for the Chicago Architecture Foundation, said, "The Kapoor is an incredibly daring choice for the city. . . . It should be as significant as the Picasso on Daley Center Plaza."[57] The heavy stainless-steel sculpture spent much of 2005 under a tent as the seams from its steel plates were buffed out to give a seamless appearance. In some ways, this work of art serves as a carnival mirror, and in other ways, it is an entryway that creates an area for the interaction of park visitors. Already, the silver sculpture has become the unofficial symbol of the city, with most Chicagoans referring to it as "the bean" because of its shape.

If Cloud Gate has become one of the most-beloved features of the new park, perhaps the most-surprising is the Crown Fountain, originally referred to as the Millennium Fountain (see fig. 8.6). The two, fifty-foot-tall glass towers designed by Jaume Plensa from Barcelona, feature LED images of faces of Chicago's diverse citizens and photos that slowly but continuously change.[58] The highlight occurs when spouts of water seemingly shoot from the mouths of those portrayed, closely followed by a cascade of water over the towers. The donors of the fountain are the Crown and Goodman families of Chicago, who gave the multi-million-dollar gift that paid for the delightful work of art.

Figure 8.6. Crown Fountain, by Jaume Plensa. City of Chicago/Peter J. Schulz/Walter S. Mitchell.

Located at the southwest corner of Millennium Park, at Michigan Avenue and Monroe Street, the fountain's towers stand on a black-granite reflecting pool that is over two hundred feet long and almost fifty feet wide. In warm weather, spectators watch as bathing-suit-clad children and even some adults treat the fountain like a municipal plunge and splash around with great joy. Plensa's fountain provides a unique park experience, enjoyable both when the park is relatively empty as well as when the area around the fountain is packed with drenched revelers and those surrounding the reflective pool. With this unique concept, the artist has created a revolutionary interpretation of a fountain and wonderfully interactive work of art.[59]

One of the most rewarding additions in Millennium Park is the Lurie Gardens, named in honor of Ann Lurie, a Chicago philanthropist who became the major donor for the garden and its upkeep.[60] Kathryn Gustafson, Piet Oudolf, and Robert Israel conceived the garden's design, which utilizes plants, architecture, and lighting to create a distinctive environment. It features walkways, a water feature, fifteen-foot-high hedges, and discrete seating areas. The garden is linked to the western end of the park via the Bank One Promenade, an area that is often used for special events. The designers selected a wide variety of plants to enhance the visitor's experience, depending on the season and the year. The plantings are designed to mature in place so the garden will not be fully realized until almost a generation after its creation.[61] The landscape hearkens back to the city's earliest history and celebrates its glorious present. The scope of Millennium Park was designed to accommodate both strollers and bikers and includes features such as the Millennium Park Bike Station with cycle storage and other services, including bike repair.[62]

The city sought naming rights to help defray the cost of redesigning and enhancing the park. For example, the park has the Chase Promenade, a tree-lined walkway of several blocks, which the Bank One Foundation funded.[63] The Boeing Company sponsored the Boeing Galleries, a terrace near the Crown Fountain for public exhibitions.[64] Exelon Company funded the Exelon Pavilions. Renowned Italian architect Renzo Piano designed the two pavilions closest to the Art Institute of Chicago in anticipation of the new Modern Wing at the museum.[65]

In a populist mode, the Millennium Mosaic features the work of five thousand "children and adults who, in 1999, created individual tiles for the mosaic. These were composed and installed as a free-form mural at the Randolph Street entrance to the garage built underneath the park."[66] Architecturally, Metra's Millennium Station at Randolph Street is worth a look because it reminds visitors of the history of the park and its rail yards.[67]

Chicagoans still struggle to put this project in perspective. Jonathan Black, Chicago journalist and author, observes, "[I]n terms of a rehabbed cityscape, the sheer scope of the project knows few rivals. The Washington Mall, maybe, or plans for Ground Zero. Certainly it's hard to name a single other recent undertaking that is so complete and with so many separate engineering challenges. . . . Millennium Park will be a worthy creation for all time. It will define Chicago to the entire world as America's greatest city." In February 2004, the city reported the cost of the project at $470 million, with $270 million provided by the city and a majority of the remaining costs donated by the private sector.[68]

With a bold stroke, the Millennium Park project reclaimed unsightly and underutilized rail yards located on the north end of the park for 150 years and with a great deal of time, talent, and resources created a unique landscape of international renown.[69] Constructed largely within one of Grant Park's "rooms," Millennium Park offers free concerts, fine dining, and world-class architecture. Extending over 24.5 acres, the park officially opened in July 2004, but some features within the park opened earlier with individual ribbon cuttings made possible through a combination of public and private partnerships. The renovated north section of Grant Park has become a large draw for both tourists and residents. It has also become a source of pride for the city and the center point for some of the largest cultural and civic events of the first two decades of the new millennium.

The park has been able to provide effective crowd management, allowing visitors to navigate the park without the interference of traffic. One control method is to temporarily gate sections of the park and charge admission to events. A notable example is the relocation of Lollapalooza to Grant Park. The popular music show began in 1991 as a traveling concert series. The alternative-rock format fueled the festival for several years, but the festival lost steam in 1998, a year in which the concerts were cancelled. After some attempts to resurrect itself, Lollapalooza became a destination concert in Grant Park. Large numbers of mostly young concert-goers attended performances by musicians on multiple stages. Lady Gaga, Radiohead, and Kanye West have all made their way to Grant Park for the August concerts that feature headliners as well as up-and-comers. Lollapalooza represents a significant new trend of requiring admission to enter the public park and providing a revenue stream for the city.

Beyond programming, a new modern-art installation was placed on the southern end of part of Grant Park. On November 16, 2006, the public first viewed the permanent installation, Agora. Conceived by Polish artist Magdalena Abakanowicz, 106 cast-iron figures create a striking landscape.

The larger-than-life torsos occupy an area northeast of Michigan Avenue and Roosevelt Road and provide a way to mark the southern entrance to the park.[70] The installation is located near the Rosenberg Statue, the first statue in the park.

Demonstrating that the park will continue to surprise, in May 2009, the Art Institute of Chicago dedicated the latest addition to its sizable complex. The oldest cultural institution in the park secured world-renowned architect Renzo Piano to design the Modern Wing that is situated adjacent to Millennium Park (see fig. 8.7). The elegant, glass structure features a 620-foot-long pedestrian bridge that connects the Art Institute to Millennium Park. Visitors can walk on the bridge and visit a sculpture garden without entering the museum. Park visitors are removed from the Monroe Street traffic and, from the bridge, enjoy expansive views of the park and the skyline. The galleries provide additional space for collections and a third-floor restaurant cleverly named Terzo Piano.

President Obama in Grant Park

Reflecting the local, national, and global nature of Grant Park, President-elect Barack Obama gave his first election victory speech in the park. Obama, a long-time resident of Chicago, became the first African American elected to the office of President of the United States. Late on November 4, 2008, and into the early morning of the next day, approximately one hundred thousand people gathered on a cold autumn night to celebrate the victory. Oprah Winfrey and Spike Lee made their way into the ticketed area, and many thousands more gathered in the park to hear Obama's speech, which was broadcast around the globe.

Having lived in Chicago and been elected a representative of the State of Illinois, Obama gave his victory speech on a stage in Chicago's park. Obama had campaigned for twenty-one months, and in this speech, as he had done from the beginning of his campaign, he quoted Abraham Lincoln: "[A]s Lincoln said to a nation far more divided than ours: 'We are not enemies, but friends . . . though passion may have strained it must not break our bonds of affection.' And to those Americans whose support I have yet to earn—I may not have won your vote tonight, but I hear your voices, I need your help, and I will be your president too."[71] As the front yard and community gathering place, Grant Park provided the appropriate location for the celebration.

Grant Park Triumphant

As Chicago continues to acknowledge the development of tourism as a major focus of its economy, it has used its front yard as a calling card to the world. Tourists have helped pay for park improvements and programs through hotel and restaurant taxes. After losing population for half a century, Chicago recorded a population increase in the 2000 census. Some residents have moved near the park to enjoy its cultural amenities and landscape. The real estate around the park, and Millennium Park in particular, has become some of the most sought-after property in the city.

Every year, Grant Park rises veiled from the summer's lake mist, with the buzzing of automobiles making their way along Lake Shore Drive. It is the trees and the lake that the driver notices and occasional glimpses of the park's features. There are fleeting views of the silver Pritzker Pavilion glinting in the sun. Pedestrians make their way through the park. Visitors and residents check the schedule for special programs, the various music festivals, and the enormous Taste of Chicago. Many local residents plan their time around softball, soccer, and other sports activities. Others use the lakefront as a bicycle route or jog on the long, straight paths of the park. Every October is highlighted with the Chicago Marathon, while each winter bears witness to the return of the park's ice skaters. Any time of the year, Grant Park provides spectacular views that include the park, the city, and

Figure 8.7. Renzo Piano's addition to the Art Institute of Chicago, June 2009.

Figure 8.8. View of Chicago from the Adler Planetarium. Photograph by Bernard J. Kleina.

the lake (see fig. 8.8). The cultural organizations in the park represent some of the most dynamic offerings in the city.

In a real sense, Grant Park is unique in the city, nation, and world. Visitors enjoy the park's central location, as they have since its earliest days. From the fairgoers of the late 1800s through the conventions, riots, and celebrations, Grant Park has seen its moments of triumph, tragedy, terror, and turmoil. But it has both reflected the times and directed them as well. Grant Park is Chicago's urban mirror that provides a reflection of the city's development and acts as a fascinating lens through which to view the city's history.

Notes • Bibliography • Index

Notes

1. Early Park History: Lake, Land, and Place

1. Quoted in Quaife, *Development of Chicago*, 177.

2. Cronon, *Nature's Metropolis*, 13–19, 31–41, 55. For more information, see Abbott, *Boosters and Businessmen*.

3. Andreas, *History of Chicago*, 165–73. For more information, see Ranney, *Prairie Passage*; Lamb, "I&M Canal."

4. Conzen, "Historical and Geographical Development," 7.

5. "Fort Dearborn," clipping file, Chicago Historical Society; Nash, *Wilderness and the American Mind*, 23.

6. Conzen, "Historical and Geographical Development," 6; Fink, *Grant Park Tomorrow*, 223.

7. Bluestone, *Constructing Chicago*, 13.

8. Larson, *Those Army Engineers*, 15–30.

9. Miller, *City of the Century*, 68–70.

10. Bluestone, *Constructing Chicago*, 29.

11. Quoted in Quaife, *Development of Chicago 1674–1914*, 177.

12. Fink, *Grant Park Tomorrow*, 222; Pierce, *History of Chicago*, 1:362–63; Ayer, *Lake-Front Questions*, 16.

13. Lois Wille, *Forever Open* (1972), 22; *Chicago Democrat*, November 4, 1835.

14. Conzen and Carr, *Illinois and Michigan Canal*, 7; Grossman, Keating, and Reiff, *Encyclopedia of Chicago*, 1011. For more information, see Conzen, "1848."

15. Wille, *Forever Open*, 23.

16. Ibid.

17. Fink, *Grant Park Tomorrow*, 14–17; Chicago Common Council, *Chicago Common Council Proceedings*, 1839/39, doc. 55.

18. Bluestone, *Constructing Chicago*, 17.

19. Fink, *Grant Park Tomorrow*, 17.

20. Chicago Common Council, *Chicago Common Council Proceedings*, April 14, 1837.

21. "Crawford, James and William."

22. Chicago Common Council, *Chicago Common Council Proceedings*, August 28, 1837.

23. *City of Chicago v. A. Montgomery Ward*, 169 IL 392.

24. Fink, *Grant Park Tomorrow*, 222; Clayton, *Illinois Fact Book*, 38.

25. Chicago Common Council, *Chicago Common Council Proceedings*, August 10, 1847. The common council designated this area as Lake Park, as well as the area that became Dearborn Park. Fink, *Grant Park Tomorrow*, 17.

26. Quoted in Pierce, *History of Chicago*, 1:362.

27. Fink, *Grant Park Tomorrow*, 18.

28. Pierce, *History of Chicago*, 2:340, 1:363.

29. Bluestone, *Constructing Chicago*, 18.

30. Cronon, *Nature's Metropolis*, 56; Wille, *Forever Open*, 26; Stover, *History of the Illinois Central Railroad*, 43.

31. *Chicago Democrat*, August 9, 1849.

32. *Chicago Daily Journal*, March 17, 1849.

33. Wille, *Forever Open*, 26–37; Chicago City Council, *Chicago City Council Proceedings*, files and Chicago Common Council, *Chicago Common Council Proceedings*, Special Committee on Lake Shore Protection, September 6, 1850.

34. Stover, *History of the Illinois Central Railroad*, 15, 43.

35. Chicago Common Council, *Chicago Common Council of Chicago Proceedings*, files 1851/52: 1315, 1256A, 1255A; Chicago Common Council, *Common Council of Chicago Proceedings*, files, 1851/52: 1313; Stover, *History of the Illinois Central Railroad*, 43.

36. Pierce, *History of Chicago*, 2:48–49.

37. Stover, *History of the Illinois Central Railroad*, 44; Chicago Common Council, *Chicago Common Council Proceedings*, files, 1851/52, 1376.

38. Stover, *History of the Illinois Central Railroad*, 44.

39. Ibid., 74–77.

40. *Illinois Central Railroad Company*, 2.

41. Pierce, *History of Chicago*, 2:340.

42. *Daily Democratic Press*, August 19, 1853.

43. Ibid.

44. Ibid.

45. Schuyler, *New Urban Landscape*, 59.

46. "Thoroughfares," 610.

47. Peckham, "Chicago—A Mean Spot," 167.

48. Cook, *Bygone Days in Chicago*, 339–41.

49. Sheahan, *Chicago Illustrated*, part 1, n.p., and part 2, cover page.

50. Ibid., part 1, n.p., and part 10, n.p.

51. Cook, *Bygone Days in Chicago*, 341–43.

52. Ibid., 343.

53. Mayer and Wade, *Chicago*, 186, 234–38.

54. Pierce, *History of Chicago*, 2:341.

55. Board of Public Works, *Third Annual Report*, 24.

56. Pierce, *History of Chicago*, 2:340.

57. Sautter and Burke, *Inside the Wigwam*, 2, 18, 20.

58. Karamanski, *Rally 'Round the Flag*, 201–7.

59. Sautter and Burke, *Inside the Wigwam*, 20.

60. Ibid., 18–20.

61. *Chicago Tribune*, August 31, 1864.

62. *Chicago Times*, August 30, 1864; Sautter and Burke, *Inside the Wigwam*, 24.

63. For more information, see Angle, "Chicago's Second National Convention"; *New York Times*, September 2, 1864.
64. Kunhardt and Kunhardt, *Twenty Days*, 235.
65. *Chicago Tribune*, May 2, 1865.
66. Kunhardt and Kunhardt, *Twenty Days*, 235.
67. *Chicago Tribune*, May 2, 1865.
68. Kunhardt and Kunhardt, *Twenty Days*, 237.
69. Pierce, *History of Chicago*, 2:340–41; Einhorn, *Property Rules*, 104–43. For more information, see Rauch, *Public Parks*; Cranz, *Politics of Park Design*.
70. Andreas, *History of Chicago*, 3:167.
71. Pierce, *History of Chicago*, 2: 342–45; Andreas, *History of Chicago*, 3:167–89.
72. Mayer and Wade, *Chicago*, 100–101; Bluestone, *Constructing Chicago*, 21.
73. Board of Public Works, *Seventh Annual Report*, 36; Board of Public Works, *Eighth Annual Report*, 51; Colten, "Chicago's Waste Lands," 124–42.
74. Board of Public Works, *Ninth Annual Report*, 75. The map "Plan of Lake Park" is between pages 76 and 77.
75. Bluestone, *Constructing Chicago*, 37–61.
76. Roy Lubove, *H. W. S. Cleveland*, ix; Bluestone, *Constructing Chicago*, 22.
77. Cleveland, *Public Grounds of Chicago*, 15.
78. Einhorn, *Property Rules*, 129.
79. Cleveland, *Public Grounds of Chicago*, 15.
80. Board of Public Works, *Tenth Annual Report*, 52.
81. For more information, see Board of Public Works, *Ninth Annual Report*, 75. The map "Plan of Lake Park" is between pages 76 and 77.
82. Ibid., *Tenth Annual Report*, 53–54.
83. Colten, "Chicago's Waste Lands," 128.
84. Bluestone, *Constructing Chicago*, 33.
85. Chicago Common Council, *Chicago Common Council Proceeding Files* 1868/69: 2138, 3163, and 1869/70: 144-I, 744, Andreas, *History of Chicago*, 3:191; Wille, *Forever Open*, 36–37.
86. Andreas, *History of Chicago*, 3:191; Pierce, *History of Chicago*, 2:342.
87. *Chicago Tribune*, February 18, 1869.
88. Pierce, *History of Chicago*, 2:296.
89. *Chicago Tribune*, February 18, 1869.
90. Ibid.
91. Pierce, *History of Chicago*, 2:296.
92. Andreas, *History of Chicago*, 3:191.
93. Pierce, *History of Chicago*, 2:296; Bluestone, *Constructing Chicago*, 33; *Illinois Central Railroad v. Illinois*, 146 U.S. 387 (1892).

2. Lake Park: A Cultural and Civic Center

1. *Chicago Tribune*, October 11, 1871; "Chicago Fire."
2. *Chicago Tribune*, October 11, 1871; Cromie, *Great Chicago Fire*, 89–91.
3. *Chicago Tribune*, October 20, 1871.
4. *Chicago Tribune*, November 16, 1871; Andreas, *History of Chicago*, 3:62; *Chicago Tribune*, October 14, 1871.
5. *Chicago Tribune*, October 14, 1871.
6. *Chicago Tribune*, October 18, 1871.

7. *Chicago Tribune*, October 14, 1871.

8. Andreas, *History of Chicago*, 3:192.

9. Colbert and Chamberlain, *Chicago and the Great Conflagration*, 140; *Chicago Tribune*, October 28, 1871.

10. Board of Public Works, *Thirteenth Annual Report*, 19; Board of Public Works, *Twelfth Annual Report*, 43.

11. Board of Public Works, *Thirteenth Annual Report*, 19–20.

12. Board of Public Works, *Fourteenth Annual Report*, 19–20.

13. Berger, *They Built Chicago*, 95; *Inter-State Exposition Souvenir*, n.p., 24; "Its Career Is Ended," *Chicago Tribune*, January 19, 1892.

14. Allwood, *Great Exhibitions*, 7–41.

15. Spiess, "Exhibitions and Expositions in 19th Century Cincinnati," 170–92. For more information, see *Books of the Fairs*.

16. *Inter-State Exposition Souvenir*, 25. For more information, see Moffat, *L*; Cudahy, *Destination: Loop*.

17. *Inter-State Exposition Souvenir*, 25; Lowe, *Lost Chicago*, 107.

18. *Inter-State Exposition Souvenir*, 39, 43.

19. Duis and Holt, "Chicago as It Was," 72, 74; *Inter-State Exposition Souvenir*, 40.

20. *Inter-State Exposition Souvenir*, 25, 42, 45.

21. Ibid., 46.

22. Ibid., 47.

23. *Inter-State Exposition Souvenir*, 33–34; Duis and Holt, "Chicago as It Was," 73.

24. *Inter-State Exposition Souvenir*.

25. Spiess, "Exhibitions and Expositions in 19th Century Cincinnati," 170–92.

26. Andreas, *History of Chicago*, 3:656; *Interstate Industrial Exposition of Chicago, 1879*, 10.

27. Andreas, *History of Chicago*, 3: 655–656; *Interstate Industrial Exposition of Chicago, 1877*, 15.

28. *Interstate Industrial Exposition of Chicago, 1879*, 12; Duis and Holt, "Chicago as It Was," 74, 190.

29. Andreas, *History of Chicago*, 3:222; *City Directory*, 1875–76.

30. Chicago Public Library, "Inaugural Address of the Mayors."

31. Andreas, *History of Chicago*, 3:657.

32. Kysela, "Sara Hallowell Brings 'Modern Art' to the Midwest," 153–54.

33. Whitridge, "Art in Chicago," 50–51, 52; Duis and Holt, "Chicago as It Was," 74.

34. Duis and Holt, "Chicago as It Was," 74; Faulkner, "Painters," 14–17; Whitridge, "Art in Chicago," 50–51; Zolberg, "Art Institute of Chicago," 20.

35. "Its Career Is Ended."

36. Berger, *They Built Chicago*, 95. For more information, see Schabas, *Theodore Thomas*.

37. Pierce, *History of Chicago*, 3:492; Berger, *They Built Chicago*, 95.

38. Lowe, *Lost Chicago*, 126; "Acoustics of the Convention Hall," 64; Berger, *They Built Chicago*, 96.

39. *First Chicago Grand Opera Festival*.

40. Berger, *They Built Chicago*, 96.

41. *Interstate Industrial Exposition . . .* 1875, 2; *Interstate Industrial Exposition . . . 1876*, 12.

42. *Interstate Industrial Exposition . . . 1879*, 11.

43. *Chicago Tribune*, October 17, 1943.

44. *Interstate Industrial Exposition . . . 1876*, 11–12.

45. *Interstate Industrial Exposition . . . 1875*, 7–8.

46. Levine, *Highbrow/Lowbrow*, 11–82.

47. Lowry, *Green Cathedrals*, 126.

48. Ibid.

49. Ibid., 127; "Chicago Base-Ball Grounds," 299.

50. Levine, *A. G. Spalding*, 29–30; "Chicago Nine," 686; Lowry, *Green Cathedrals*, 127–28. For more information, see Faber, *Baseball Pioneers*.

51. Levine, *A. G. Spalding*, 21.

52. Riess, *Touching Base*, 122.

53. Ibid., 111.

54. *National Party Conventions*, 46–47; "Its Career Is Ended"; *Chicago Tribune*, January 19, 1892; Sautter and Burke, *Inside the Wigwam*, 37.

55. *Interstate Industrial Exposition . . . 1879*, 10, 13.

56. *National Party Conventions*, 47.

57. "Its Career Is Ended"; *National Party Conventions*, 49–50; Sautter and Burke, *Inside the Wigwam*, 47, 52.

58. Handy, "Another New Structure," 38–39; "Buildings, Armory, Michigan Ave, (Battery D)," clipping file, Chicago Historical Society.

59. Hannah, "Illinois National Guard."

60. "Buildings, Armory"; Hannah, "Armories."

61. For more information, see Smith, *Urban Disorder*.

62. "Buildings, Armory."

3. The World's Columbian Exposition and Chicago's Cultural Flowering

1. Badger, *Great American Fair*, 13–39.

2. Ibid., 49–51.

3. Ibid., 44–49.

4. Ruby Bradford Murphy, "Works of City's 'Forgotten' Artist Are Discovered," *Chicago Tribune*, October 3, 1966.

5. Burnham and Gookins, *Chicago*, 5–7, 24.

6. Ibid., 5–6.

7. Ibid., 9.

8. Ibid., 21, 24.

9. Johnson, *Narrative*, 1:33.

10. Burnham and Gookins, *Chicago*, 27–28; Larson, *Those Army Engineers*, 109–10; Johnson, *Narrative*, 1:34–35.

11. Berger, *They Built Chicago*, 57; Johnson, *Narrative*, 1:34.

12. Johnson, *Narrative*, 1:35–37; Badger, *Great American Fair*, 56–58.

13. *Public Ledger* (Philadelphia), April 1, 1891; "Chance for Chicago," *Post* (Chicago), December 5, 1890.

14. *Art Institute of Chicago: Information*, 15.

15. Ibid., 15–16.

16. Ibid., 16; Trustees of the Art Institute, *9th Annual Report*, 8–9; Trustees of the Art Institute, *4th Annual Report*, 4, 10.

17. Trustees of the Art Institute, *4th Annual Report*, 6–7.

18. Ibid., 11; Trustees of the Art Institute, *9th Annual Report*, 8; Phipps, "1893 Art Institute Building," 30.

19. Trustees of the Art Institute, *12th Annual Report*, 15.

20. Ibid., 14–15.

21. Johnson, *Narrative*, 1:46–48; Trustees of the Art Institute, *12th Annual Report*, 16.

22. Johnson, *Congresses*, 4:2–3.

23. *Chicago Tribune*, November 7, 1939; Duis and Holt, "Chicago as It Was," 74; "For a Big Art Building," *Chicago Tribune*, August 28, 1891.

24. *Art Institute of Chicago: Information*, 17–18; Trustees of the Art Institute, *12th Annual Report*, 17; "For a Big Art Building," *Chicago Tribune*, August 28, 1891.

25. "For a Big Art Building;" *Chicago Tribune*, August 28, 1891; *Chicago Tribune*, September 16, 1891; Trustees of the Art Institute, *12th Annual Report*, 20.

26. "Plans Adopted for the $800,000 Lake-Front Art Institute," *Chicago Tribune*, November 13, 1891; *Art Institute of Chicago: Information*, 16–17.

27. *Chicago Tribune*, June 2, 1892.

28. Phillips, *Reports of Cases at Law*, 502.

29. *Art Institute of Chicago: Information*, 18; *Chicago Tribune*, June 2, 1892.

30. "To Abate a Nuisance," 5:105.

31. *Art Institute of Chicago: Information*, 18.

32. Johnson, *Congresses*, 4:4.

33. Sautter and Burke, *Inside the Wigwam*, 66.

34. Ibid., 78; *Graphic* (Chicago), June 11, 1892, 445.

35. *Harper's Weekly*, June 25, 1892, 604.

36. *Harper's Weekly*, July 2, 1892, 631; Sautter and Burke, *Inside the Wigwam*, 78.

37. *Harper's Weekly*, July 2, 1892, 631.

38. *Graphic* (Chicago), July 9, 1892, 20; Sautter and Burke, *Inside the Wigwam*, 78–79. For more information, see Wendt and Kogan, *Bosses in Lusty Chicago*.

39. *Graphic* (Chicago), May 6, 1893; *Chicago Tribune*, May 7, 1893.

40. Lowe, *Lost Chicago*, 56; Stover, *History*, 218.

41. Stover, *History*, 217–20.

42. Bach and Gray, *Guide*, 6; Riedy, *Chicago Sculpture*, 46.

43. Ibid.

44. Johnson, *Congresses*, 4:4.

45. *Chicago Daily Tribune*, May 16, 1893.

46. Johnson, *Congresses*, 4:5; Bolotin and Laing, *Chicago World's Fair*, 157.

47. Badger, *Great American Fair*, 100–101; Johnson, *Congresses*, 4:iii–iv, 5.

48. Johnson, *Congresses*, 4:7.

49. "Biography: Henrotin, Mrs. Charles (Ellen Martin)," Minna Schmidt Figurine Collection, clipping file, Chicago Historical Society.

50. Johnson, *Congresses*, 4:5; *Chicago Tribune*, May 16, 1893.

51. Johnson, *Congresses*, 4:11.

52. "General Programme of the World's Congresses of 1893, The." World Columbian Exposition Auxiliary, April 1, 1893, Special Collection, Chicago History Museum; Johnson, *Congresses*, 4:485.

53. Burg, *Chicago's White City*, 328. For more information, see Barrows, "Results of the Parliament," 55–58.

54. Johnson, *Congresses*, 4:13.

55. *Chicago Tribune*, May 1, 1893.

56. For more information, see Lears and Fox, *Culture of Consumption*.

4. Making the White City Permanent

1. Adams, "What a Great City Might Be," 3, 4, 6; Wilson, *City Beautiful Movement*, 1.

2. Bluestone, *Constructing Chicago*, 190.

3. *Inter Ocean* (Chicago), October 11, 1896.

4. *Art Institute of Chicago: Information*, 18.

5. Ibid., 19.

6. *Chicago Tribune*, December 9, 1893; *Chicago Tribune*, May 11, 1894; Clarke, "Art Institute's Guardian Lions," 47–56.

7. Bluestone, *Constructing Chicago*, 164, 166, 168; Horowitz, *Culture and the City*, 98, 103; *Chicago Tribune*, December 1, 1893.

8. *Chicago Tribune*, November 28, 1894.

9. "Too Hasty Action by County Board," 22.

10. Horowitz, *Culture and the City*, 57; *Chicago Tribune*, December 30, 1894.

11. *Chicago Tribune*, December 30, 1894.

12. Ibid.

13. Obituary, Daniel H. Burnham, *Chicago Tribune*, June 2, 1912. For more information, see Moore, *Daniel H. Burnham*; Hines, *Burnham of Chicago*.

14. *Chicago Tribune*, June 4, 1895.

15. Ibid.; Bluestone, *Constructing Chicago*, 189.

16. Bluestone, *Constructing Chicago*, 189.

17. *Inter Ocean* (Chicago), August 10, 1895; "Patton and Miller," Architects File; Bluestone, *Constructing Chicago*, 188, 226. Lake Park also served as the site for a design competition for a music pavilion, which brought additional attention from the architectural community. Many of the entrants demonstrated an understanding of the promise of the site. "Chicago Architectural Club," 8.

18. *Chicago Tribune*, August 10, 1895.

19. Smith, *Plan of Chicago*, 26.

20. Phillips, *Reports of Cases at Law*; *A. Montgomery Ward, Appellant, v. Field Museum of Natural History et al. Appellees*; *South Park Commissioners, Appellant, v. A. Montgomery Ward et al. Appellees*, 503–4; South Park Commissioners, *Report . . . 1895–96*, 6. South Park Commissioners hereafter cited as SPC.

21. SPC, *Report . . . 1902–3*, 8.

22. Smith, *Plan of Chicago*, 26.

23. *Inter Ocean* (Chicago), October 11, 1896.

24. Ibid.

25. Ibid.

26. Ibid.

27. *Inter Ocean* (Chicago), October 11, 1896. For more information, see Osborn, "Development of Recreation"; Tippens, "Synthesis of Reform."

28. Dunham, "Chicago Lake Front and A. Montgomery Ward," 15; Pierce, *History of Chicago*, 3:317; Larson, *Those Army Engineers*, 112.

29. Pierce, *History of Chicago*, 3:317.

30. Larson, *Those Army Engineers*, 112; Schroeder, "Issue of the Lakefront," 13; Phillips, *Reports of Cases at Law*, 502; *A. Montgomery Ward, Appellant, vs. Field Museum of Natural History et al. Appellees; South Park Commissioners, Appellant, vs. A. Montgomery Ward et al. Appellees*, 502.

31. *Chicago Tribune*, October 17, 1890.

32. *Chicago Tribune*, December 8, 1913.

33. *Chicago Tribune*, October 17, 1890; *Chicago Tribune*, December 8, 1913; Schroeder, "Issue of the Lakefront," 13. This phase of Ward's case was decided in *City of Chicago v. Ward*.

34. Phillips, *Reports of Cases at Law*; *A. Montgomery Ward, Appellant, v. Field Museum of Natural History et al. Appellees, South Park Commissioners, Appellant, v. A. Montgomery Ward et al.*, 503.

35. Cronon, *Nature's Metropolis*, 337.

36. Fink, *Grant Park Tomorrow*, 41.

37. Board of Public Works, *Fourteenth Annual Report*, 20.

38. Ibid., 10–11, 31; SPC, *Report . . . 1900–1901*, 11. For detailed information on the filling in of the lake, see SPC, *Report . . . 1895–96*, through SPC, *Report . . . Period of Fifteen Months . . . December 1, 1906*; SPC, *Report . . . 1902–3*, 6–7.

39. SPC, *Report . . . 1896–97*, 13, 18.

40. *Chicago Tribune*, June 13, 1897.

41. *Chicago Tribune*, January 4, 1902; *Chicago Tribune*, November 15, 1901; *Chicago Tribune*, November 19, 1903.

42. *Ceremonies and the Unveiling*, 10–11; Bluestone, *Constructing Chicago*, 191, 193.

43. *Encyclopedia Britannica*, 11th ed., s.v. "Logan, John A."; "John A. Logan Monument—Dedication Program, 22 July 1897," Hamblin Printing, folder 31, box 33, City Wide Collection, 13; SPC, *Report . . . 1896–97*, 28–29.

44. "John A. Logan Monument," 14–15.

45. *Encyclopedia Britannica*, Micropaedia, (1974), 6:298–99.

46. George R. Peck, "Oration Delivered at Chicago, July 22, 1897 at the Dedication of the Monument to the Memory of Major-General John A. Logan," booklet, Chicago History Museum Special Collections.

47. Ibid., 11–12.

48. *Chicago Daily Tribune*, July 23, 1887.

49. Ibid.; *Gazette* (Little Rock, AK), July 23, 1897.

50. Fink, *Grant Park Tomorrow*, 40.

51. Schroeder, "Issue of the Lakefront," 13; *E. R. Bliss et al v. A. Montgomery Ward et al.*, 104.

52. *Chicago Tribune*, December 8, 1913.

53. Schroeder, "Issue of the Lakefront," 13; SPC, *Report . . . 1869–78, 81–1907, 1910–1921*; Dunham, "Chicago Lake Front," 16; *Chicago Tribune*, October 10, 1902. This case was decided in *E. R. Bliss et al v. A. Montgomery Ward et al*, 198 Ill. 104.

54. Dunham, "Chicago Lake Front," 17.

55. SPC, *Report . . . 1902–3*, 7–8.

56. Phillips, *Reports of Cases at Law*, 505.

57. SPC, *Report . . . 1902–3*, 8.

58. Ibid., 9.

59. Ibid., 5–8; SPC, *Report . . . 1902–3*, 10; SPC, *Report . . . 1903–4*, 8–10.

60. SPC, *Report . . . 1903–4*, 11.

61. Fink, *Grant Park Tomorrow*, 42.

62. *Chicago Tribune*, November 28, 1903.

63. *Chicago Tribune*, December 27, 1903.

64. Dunham, "Chicago Lake Front," 17.

65. SPC, *Report . . . 1903–4*, 32, 11, 32.

66. SPC, *Annual Report . . . 1906*, 6, 24, 27, 6, 41; SPC, *Report . . . 1896–97* through *1903–4*; SPC, *Report . . . 1902–3*, 32; SPC, *Report . . . 1903–4*, 34; SPC, *Report . . . 1899–1900*, 15–16.

67. SPC, *Report . . . 1903–4*, 11.

68. SPC, *Annual Report . . . 1905*, 9.

69. SPC, *Report . . .* for a Period of Fifteen Months, 7, 9. The district required the Illinois Central Railroad to construct a wall along the eastern side of its right of way, which separated their holdings. SPC, *Annual Report . . . 1905*, 7; *Annual Report . . . 1906*, 6.

70. SPC, *Report . . .* for a Period of Fifteen Months, 7–11.

71. Ibid., 7.

72. Ibid., 9–10.

73. Schroeder, "Issue of the Lakefront," 14; *A. Montgomery Ward v. Field Museum of Natural History*, 241 Ill. 496.

74. Dunham, "Chicago Lake Front," 17; *Chicago Tribune*, July 14. 1907.

75. *Chicago Tribune*, November 26, 1908.

76. Julia Sniderman and William W. Tippens, "The Historic Resources of the Chicago Park District," *National Register of Historic Places, Multiple Property Documentation Form*, sec. 9:7, 8, unpublished document, 1989, Special Collections, Chicago Park District. The Chicago Park District's Special Collections has a significant number of landscape plans and drawings, including those the Olmsted brothers drafted.

77. Ibid., 11.

78. For more information, see Burnham and Bennett, *Plan of Chicago*; Zukowsky, Chappell, and Bruegmann, *Plan of Chicago*.

79. Condit, *Chicago 1910–29*, 59.

80. Schroeder, "Issue of the Lakefront," 11, 13.

81. Condit, *Chicago 1910–29*, 68.

82. Burnham and Bennett, *Plan of Chicago*, 114.

83. Ibid., 44.

84. Ibid., 121.

85. Ibid., 114.

86. Ibid.

87. Smith, *Plan of Chicago*, 84–85.

88. *Chicago Tribune*, December 8, 1913. This result was reached in *A. Montgomery Ward v. Field Museum*.

89. *Chicago Tribune*, October 27, 1909; Schroeder, "Issue of the Lakefront," 14. This case was decided in *South Park Commissioners v. Montgomery Ward & Co.*

90. "The Multimillionaires of Chicago v. Montgomery Ward," *Chicago Tribune*, July 14, 1907.

91. Van Roessel, *D. H. Burnham*, 15.

92. Ibid., 10, 12, 16.

93. *Chicago Tribune*, December 8, 1913.

94. Schroeder, "Issue of the Lakefront," 14; *A. Montgomery Ward v. Field Museum of Natural History*.

95. *Chicago Tribune*, December 8, 1913.

5. The New Design

1. Fink, *Grant Park Tomorrow*, 82.

2. SPC, *Report* . . . December 1, 1906, 86–88.

3. Ibid., 8.

4. Ibid., 8, 14, 16; Schroeder, "Issue of the Lakefront," 14, 16.

5. SPC, *Report* . . . *March 1, 1909*, 17; SPC, *Annual Report* . . . *February 29, 1912*, 14; SPC, *Report* . . . *March 1, 1909*, 22.

6. Sane Fourth Association of Chicago, "A Few Facts about the Sane Fourth Association (of Chicago) Incorporated," Miscellaneous Pamphlets, Chicago Historical Museum Research Center; SPC, *Report* . . . March 1, 1909, 17.

7. Sane Fourth Association of Chicago, "Reports of the Officers Reports of the Officers of the Sane Fourth Association: Covering the Historical Pageant and Army Tournament of July 4th, 1910," 3, 11–12, 13, Miscellaneous Pamphlets, Chicago History Museum Research Center; Sane Fourth Association of Chicago, "Few Facts."

8. Sane Fourth Association of Chicago, "Reports of the Officers," 13.

9. Ibid., 14.

10. Sane Fourth Association of Chicago, "Report of the President to the Trustees of the Sane Fourth Association," [1911], Miscellaneous Pamphlets, Chicago History Museum Research Center; Sane Fourth Association of Chicago, "Program Sane Fourth Historical Pageant, the Day We Celebrate, July Fourth Nineteen Hundred and Eleven Chicago, Illinois, under the Auspices of Sane Fourth Association," Miscellaneous Pamphlets, Chicago History Museum Research Center.

11. Sane Fourth Association, "Few Facts."

12. Angle, "International Aviation Meet," 1–5; "Chicago Engages World Aviators," *Chicago Tribune*, July 30, 1911; Fink, *Grant Park Tomorrow*, 46.

13. *Chicago Tribune*, July 2, 1913.

14. SPC, *Report* . . . March 1, 1913, 72; Fink, *Grant Park Tomorrow*, 48; *Chicago Daily Tribune*, March 20, 1913.

15. "Preserving Architectural Collections at the Art Institute of Chicago," 7.

16. Ibid.

17. Draper, *Edward H. Bennett*, 16.

18. Julia Sniderman and William W. Tippens, "The Historic Resources of the Chicago Park District," *National Register of Historic Places, Multiple Property Documentation Form*, 15, unpublished document, 1989, Special Collections, Chicago Park District.

19. Draper, "Paris by the Lake," 110; Sniderman and Tippens, "Historic Resources," 15.

20. Fink, *Grant Park Tomorrow*, 48, 53; "Concrete Construction for Park Permanence"; SPC, *Report* . . . March 1, 1914, 16.

21. SPC, "Grant Park." The map "Grant Park, General Plan of Improvements West of I.C.R.R. and North of Jackson St. South Park Commissioners Chicago 1917" delineates the changes in the park that were underway and is between pages 40 and 41.

22. SPC, *Report* . . . *March 1, 1916*, 14, 29, 39–40, 44, 45, 52. For information on the plants introduced to the area, see SPC, *Report* . . . March 1, 1915, 73, and SPC, *Report* . . . *March 1, 1917*, 14, 49.

23. "Ferguson Fund Adds Beauty to Chicago," 22–23; Bluestone, *Constructing Chicago*, 194.

24. SPC, *Report* . . . December 1, 1906, 8, 13–14; Moulton, "Chicago's Dream of Civic Beauty," 123–30.

25. "Dedication of the Ferguson Fountain"; Bach and Gray, *Guide*, 29–30.

26. Bach and Gray, *Guide*, 33–34; Markers and Monuments: George Washington, clipping file, Chicago Historical Society; Mervin Block, "An Institution at Institute: Washington's Statue Shelved," *Chicago American*, June 6, 1960.

27. SPC, *Report*... March 1, 1918, 14; Bach and Gray, *Guide*, 41. The Ferguson fund also paid for Daniel C. French's Statue of the Republic, erected in Jackson Park, and Henry Bacon's Illinois Centennial Monument, situated in Logan Square. Fink, *Grant Park Tomorrow*, 54.

28. SPC, *Report*... March 1, 1918, 50–51.

29. Ibid., 36, 50–51.

30. Folder 1916–17, Miscellaneous Pamphlets, Chicago Band Association, Chicago Historical Society.

31. *Chicago Daily News*, February 22, 1926; folder 1910–11, Miscellaneous Pamphlets, Chicago Band Association, Chicago Historical Museum Research Center.

32. Folders 1913–15, 1916, 1917, 1918, and 1920–21, Miscellaneous Pamphlets, Chicago Band Association, Chicago Historical Museum Research Center. The park district rarely reported in its annual reports about the Chicago Band Association. One exception is, "The Chicago Band gave eight free band concerts in Grant Park at the band stand near Congress Street." SPC, *Report*... March 1, 1920, 24.

33. SPC, *Report*... March 1, 1920, 24, 31.

34. Folder 1918, Miscellaneous Pamphlets, Chicago Band Association, Chicago Historical Museum Research Center; SPC, *Report*... March 1, 1918, 38.

35. Folder 1920–21, Miscellaneous Information, Chicago Band Association, Chicago Historical Museum Research Center.

36. Folder 1922–24, ibid.; *Chicago Daily News*, February 22, 1926.

37. Schroeder, "Issue of the Lakefront," 16.

38. Fink, *Grant Park Tomorrow*, 46, 48.

39. SPC, *Report*... March 1, 1914, 16, 52; *Report*... *March 1, 1913*, 48.

40. Sinkevitch, *AIA Guide to Chicago* (1993), 43.

41. SPC, *Report*... March 1, 1915, 31, 44; SPC, *Report*... *March 1, 1916*, 37; SPC, *Report*... *March 1, 1917*, 38, 44; SPC, *Report*... *March 1, 1914*, 16.

42. SPC, *Report*... March 1, 1918, 36; SPC, *Report*... *March 1, 1920*, 30; SPC, *Report*... *March 1, 1921*, 14.

43. Stover, *History*, 298.

44. SPC, *Modern and Most Valuable*. The lakefront ordinance and amendments are in Chicago City Council, *Reports of the Chicago City Council*, 1919–20, 965–1001, 1837–38, 1922–24, 1962, and SPC, *Report*... *March 1, 1919*, 60.

45. Fink, *Grant Park Tomorrow*, 54.

46. SPC, *Report*... March 1, 1920, 23.

47. SPC, *Modern and Most Valuable*, n.p.

48. Fink, *Grant Park Tomorrow*, 55.

49. SPC, *Report*... March 1, 1919, 25; SPC, *Report*... *March 1, 1920*, 22.

50. SPC, *Modern and Most Valuable*, n.p.

51. Mayer and Wade, *Chicago*, 302.

52. Fink, *Grant Park Tomorrow*, 55; "Automobiles: Parking," clipping file, Chicago Historical Society.

53. SPC, *Annual Report to the Judges*, 19.

54. SPC, *Modern and Most Valuable*, n. p.

55. Fink, *Grant Park Tomorrow*, 55.

56. SPC, *Annual Report to the Judges*, 20–21.

57. Ibid.

58. Glaviano, "Century of Residency," 27–29.

59. In 1955 at the Columbia Yacht Club, a converted excursion boat burned to its moorings. *Chicago Tribune*, May 14, 1955.

60. SPC, *Annual Report to the Judges*, 8, 10.

61. Wacker, "Plan of Chicago," 105–6, 109.

62. SPC, *Annual Report to the Judges*, 1–5.

63. SPC, *Report . . . March 1, 1921*, 34; SPC, *Annual Report to the Judges*, 6; Stadium, Grant Park, Chicago, Ill. for the South Park Commissioners of Chicago, Holabird & Roche, architects, specifications, [1921], blueprints, Chicago Park District Special Collection.

64. Condit, *Chicago 1910–29*, 149; SPC, *Annual Report to the Judges*, 6.

65. SPC, *Annual Report to the Judges*, 6–7; *Chicago Tribune*, October 11, 1977.

66. Fink, *Grant Park Tomorrow*, 60; Paul Gapp, "Soldier Field—54 Years of Spectacles: Mrs. O'Leary's Fire, War Battles Were Staged," *Chicago Tribune*, February 28, 1978.

67. Fink, *Grant Park Tomorrow*, 55, 58, 60.

68. Ibid., 55.

69. "Spirit of Music."

70. Bach and Gray, *Guide*, 26. The South Park District has moved the memorial Spirit of Music several times. In 1941, the district moved it to a peristyle on the north end of the park, put the statue in storage, and demolished the peristyle in 1953 to clear an area for an underground parking garage. After five years in storage, the district placed the monument, without its architectural setting, in the park near the Buckingham Fountain. Ibid. The seven granite panels, however, were put with the rest of the memorial in 1991. *Chicago Sun Times*, July 14, 1992.

71. SPC, *Annual Report to the Judges*, 5.

72. Condit, *Chicago 1910–29*, 187. In 1969, the school ended the student productions in favor of a resident professional company. Ibid. This structure was demolished to make way for the Art Institute of Chicago's modern wing.

73. Draper, *Edward H. Bennett*, 16, 22. The South Park Commissioners agreed to the Buckingham Fountain and paid for construction of its basin. Ibid., 22.

74. SPC, *Modern and Most Valuable*, 19; Fink, *Grant Park Tomorrow*, 58.

75. SPC, *Annual Report to the Judges*, 6.

76. Bach and Gray, *Guide*, 22.

77. Ibid., 21–22.

78. Ibid., 21; Condit, *Chicago 1910–29*, 195; "50,000 See City Given Big Fountain," *Chicago Herald Examiner*, August 27, 1927.

79. Fink, *Grant Park Tomorrow*, 61. The Grant Park Improvement Bonds dispensed in 1927 paid for some of these improvements.

80. Fink, *Grant Park Tomorrow*, 61, 63.

81. Fink, *Grant Park Tomorrow*, 63; Bach and Gray, *Guide*, 19–20.

82. SPC, *Report . . . December 1, 1906*, 7–11.

83. Butler, *Edward B. Butler*, 11–12. On April 27, 1927, the South Park Commissioners obtained the area formerly known as Park Row, although it had been known by some other names as well. This area ran along the southern part of the park from Eleventh Street to Twelfth Street (now Roosevelt Road) west of the Illinois Central right-of-way. It had always been a bit of an anomaly as it was a privately held land within the park. Fink, *Grant Park Tomorrow*, 61.

84. Sniderman and Tippens, "Historic Resources," 7–9.

85. Ibid.

86. Condit, *Chicago 1910–29*, 196.

87. "Parks and Facilities: Shedd Park," Chicago Park District; Fink, *Grant Park Tomorrow*, 63; Hyma, "Looking Backward," 41–45.

88. Condit, *Chicago 1910–29*, 200.

89. *Chicago Tribune*, November 5, 1952; Commission on Chicago Historical and Architectural Landmarks, *Adler Planetarium*; Hill, *Report to the Commission*.

90. Fink, *Grant Park Tomorrow*, 61, 63, 225.

91. Glaviano, "Century of Residency," 33–37.

92. Fink, *Grant Park Tomorrow*, 63.

93. Handy, "Another New Structure," 38–39.

94. Fink, *Grant Park Tomorrow*, 61, 63, 225. For more information of the court case filed by the Stevens Hotel, see *Stevens Hotel Co. v. Art Institute of Chicago*, 342 IL 180 (1930).

95. Bach and Gray, *Guide*, 35. The USS *Monitor* met the USS *Merrimack*/CSS *Virginia* during the American Civil War.

6. Gateway and Cultural Center: From a Century of Progress to Postwar Park

1. The Chicago Architecture Foundation and the Chicago Park District in 2004 and 2005 organized an excellent exhibit, A Century of Progress: Architecture and Chicago's 1933–34 World's Fair. It featured images by the prominent architectural photography firm Kaufmann-Fabry and had an extended run on Northerly Island, the site of the fair.

2. Findling, *Chicago's Great World's Fairs*, 44.

3. "Dever Asks Council to Rival Columbian," *Chicago Daily News*, December 9, 1925.

4. For more information, see Rydell, *World of Fairs*.

5. Findling, *Chicago's Great World's Fairs*, 49–50.

6. *Chicago Tribune*, May 20, 1930; Findling, *Chicago's Great World's Fairs*, 146.

7. Rydell, *World of Fairs*, 50–51.

8. Sinkevitch, *AIA Guide to Chicago* (1993), 46; Fink, *Grant Park Tomorrow*, 18.

9. Rydell, "Century of Progress Exposition."

10. Chicago Public Library, "Chicago's Front Door."

11. Rydell, "Century of Progress Exposition."

12. *Chicago Tribune*, June 19, 1933.

13. Cahan and Cahan, "Lost City of the Depression," 238.

14. Rydell, "Century of Progress Exposition."

15. Rydell, *World of Fairs*, 65–66, 68.

16. Virginia Gardner, "25,000 Italians Join in Colorful Program at Fair," *Chicago Daily Tribune*, August 4, 1933.

17. "General Italo Balbo 1896–1940."

18. *Chicago Tribune*, August 23, 2002.

19. *New York Times*, May 28, 1933.

20. Findling, *Chicago's Great World's Fairs*, 133.

21. *Chicago Tribune*, February 15, 1934.

22. Rydell, *World of Fairs*, 68.

23. Thomas Willis, "Music: The Grant Park Amphitheater: Ward's Ghost Lives," *Chicago Tribune,* July 2, 1972; Richard Christiansen, "Time Will Tell Who Won the Grant Park Shell Game," *Chicago Tribune*, June 11, 1978.

24. Cremin, "Music under the Stars," 4–5.

25. Thomas Willis, "Petrillo and the Battle of Grant Park," *Chicago Tribune*, June 8, 1975. For more information, see Leiter, *Musicians and Petrillo*.

26. "1934 Daily Chicago Symphony Concerts," Samuel and Marie-Louise Rosenthal Archives, Chicago Symphony Orchestra.

27. Mary Trais, "Grant Park Concerts—1935 to 1968—Memorabilia," 1–3, Grant Park Concerts Society, Special Collection, Chicago History Museum.

28. Ibid.

29. John Von Rhein, "Band Shell: 11th-Hour," *Chicago Tribune*, July 2, 1978; "Grant Park Has Cornerstone of Luck and Determination," *Chicago Tribune*, July 10, 1978.

30. Roosevelt, "Quarantine the Aggressors, Address, 1937."

31. Fink, *Grant Park Tomorrow*, 89–91. For more information, see Saarinen, "Project for Lake Front Development," 487–515.

32. Duis, "World War II."

33. Fink, *Grant Park Tomorrow*, 68.

34. *Illinois, a Descriptive and Historical Guide*, 223, 225; *Chicago Tribune*, July 13, 1994.

7. Parking Lots, Protests, and Mayhem: Grant Park in the Daley Era

1. Fogelson, *Downtown*.

2. Ehernhalt, *Lost City*, 47. For more information, see Biles, *Richard J. Daley*.

3. Sinkevitch, *AIA Guide to Chicago* (1993), 35.

4. Ibid.

5. Ibid., 67–68.

6. Fogelson, *Downtown*, 295–308.

7. Sniderman and Tippens, "Historic Resources," 8:19.

8. Hirsch, *Making the Second Ghetto*.

9. "Lake Shore Drive."

10. Wille, *Forever Open*, 127–28.

11. Sinkevitch, *AIA Guide to Chicago*, 1993, 20.

12. Jackson, *Crabgrass Frontier*.

13. *Chicago Daily Tribune*, July 6, 1959.

14. Sinkevitch, *AIA Guide to Chicago*, 1993, 42.

15. *Chicago Daily Tribune*, July 7, 1959.

16. John Von Rhein, "Bandshell: 11th-Hour," *Chicago Tribune*, July 2, 1978; "Grant Park Has Cornerstone of Luck and Determination," *Chicago Tribune*, July 10, 1978.

17. Public Building Commission of Chicago, "PBC Awards."

18. Sinkevitch, *AIA Guide to Chicago*, 1993, 42.

19. Wille, *Forever Open*, 116.

20. Chicago Public Library, "Historical Information."

21. Wille, *Forever Open*, 111–19.

22. *Chicago Tribune*, June 21, 1964.

23. *Chicago Tribune*, June 22, 1964.

24. Ibid.

25. "Chicago and Richard J. Daley."

26. Ibid.

27. *Chicago Tribune*, June 11, 1965.

28. Ibid.

29. *Chicago Tribune*, June 12, 1965.

30. Travis, *Autobiography of Black Politics*, 331.

31. Thomas Fitzpatrick, "Dr. Martin Luther King Rallies Forces to March on City Hall," *Chicago Tribune*, July 25, 1965.

32. Thomas Fitzpatrick, "Suburb Talk Climaxes Rally Series," *Chicago Tribune*, July 26, 1965.

33. Thomas Fitzpatrick, "King Leads Loop March," *Chicago Tribune*, July 27, 1965.

34. Ibid.

35. Travis, *Autobiography of Black Politics*, 341.

36. Ibid., 343.

37. "1965 Watts Riots."

38. Travis, *Autobiography of Black Politics*, 345.

39. Ibid.

40. Travis, *Autobiography of Black Politics*, 347–48.

41. Chicago Public Library, "Martin Luther King."

42. Ralph, "Martin Luther King, Jr."

43. Travis, *Autobiography of Black Politics*, 362.

44. Ibid., 362–63.

45. Ibid., 368.

46. Ibid., 371.

47. Travis, *Autobiography of Black Politics*, 373.

48. Ibid., 386.

49. Chicago Public Library, "Martin Luther King"; Ralph, "Martin Luther King, Jr., in Chicago."

50. Farber, "1968"; Biles, "Daley's Chicago."

51. Blobaum, "Introduction," "Chronology."

52. Myers, "Memorial, Demonstration, and Protest," 6.

53. Ibid., 2–4.

54. "1968 Democratic National Convention."

55. "1968: A Convention in Crisis."

56. Blobaum, "Introduction," "Chronology."

57. Myers, "Memorial, Demonstration, and Protest," 22–23. For more information, see Farber, *Chicago '68*.

58. Schultz, *No One Was Killed*, 96.

59. "1968: A Convention in Crisis."

60. Grossman, Keating, and Reiff, *Encyclopedia of Chicago*, B20.

61. Biles, "Daley's Chicago."

62. *Chicago Tribune*, July 28, 1970; David Thompson, "Newsman Observes Confrontation in Park from Elm Tree Limb," *Chicago Tribune*, July 28, 1970.

63. *Chicago Tribune*, July 29, 1970.

64. "Study Urges Use of Citizens Park Law Aides," *Chicago Tribune*, August 15, 1973.

65. Wetsch, "Harrison, Lester." See also "Murder Is Ruled in Beating in Park," *Chicago Tribune*, October 8, 1972.

66. Meg O'Connor and Harold Remy, "'Wrong Man' Is Set Free by Judge in Grant Park Slaying of Woman," *Chicago Tribune*, August 16, 1973.

67. Wetsch, "Harrison, Lester"; "Murder Is Ruled in Beating in Park."

68. James Elsener and Joe Morang, "Beaten Coed Discovered in Bushes by Boy," *Chicago Tribune*, August 4, 1973.

69. Ibid.; Wetsch, "Harrison, Lester."

70. "Our Unsafe City," *Chicago Tribune*, August 7, 1973.

71. Harold Remy and William Crawford, "4th Woman in Year, New Slaying in Grant Park, Nab Suspect, He's Charged," *Chicago Tribune*, August 14, 1973.

72. George Bliss and Meg O'Connor, "Murder in Garage Is Denied," *Chicago Tribune*, August 15, 1973; Wetsch, "Harrison, Lester."

73. O'Connor and Remy, "'Wrong Man' Is Set Free"; Philip Wattley, "Teen Charged with Slaying in Grant Park Garage," *Chicago Tribune*, January 10, 1974.

74. "Study Urges Use of Citizens Park Law Aides," *Chicago Tribune*, August 15, 1973.

75. Michael Coakley, "What Chicagoans Like Most—and Least—about the City," *Chicago Tribune*, October 13, 1975.

76. Hunter, "Empiricist Tackles Crime."

77. Fink, *Grant Park Tomorrow*, 71–72.

78. Von Rhein, "Bandshell: 11th-Hour."

79. Fink, *Grant Park Tomorrow*, 72; Paul Gapp, "Loop Garage Has Park on Top!" *Chicago Tribune*, October 2, 1974.

80. Biles, "Daley's Chicago."

81. Open Lands Project, home page.

82. Friends of the Parks, home page.

8. The Park Reenvisioned and Renewed

1. Gilfoyle, *Millennium Park*, 49–76.

2. John Von Rhein, "Band Shell: 11th-Hour," *Chicago Tribune*, July 2, 1978; "Grant Park Has Cornerstone of Luck and Determination," *Chicago Tribune*, July 10, 1978.

3. Paul Gapp, "Sweet, Sour Notes in a Design Firm's Band Shell Survey," *Chicago Tribune*, August 14, 1977.

4. Richard Christiansen, "Time Will Tell Who Won the Grant Park Shell Game," *Chicago Tribune*, June 11, 1978.

5. Ibid.

6. For more information, see Wille, *At Home in the Loop*.

7. *Chicago Tribune*, October 4, 1979; *Chicago Tribune*, October 5–6, 1979.

8. *Chicago Sun-Times*, November 24, 2003.

9. McCormick, "City in the Garden," 68.

10. Jarrett, "Council Wars."

11. Kelly, "Chicago Parks Play."

12. *Grant Park Design Guidelines*, 19.

13. Ibid., i.

14. Ibid., i–ii.

15. Ibid., ii.

16. Ibid., iii.

17. Ibid., iii, 1.

18. Sinkevitch, *AIA Guide to Chicago*, 2004, 42.

19. Julia Sniderman and William W. Tippens, "The Historic Resources of the Chicago Park District," *National Register of Historic Places, Multiple Property Documentation Form*, sec. 1, 13–14, unpublished document, 1989, Special Collections, Chicago Park District.

20. Sinkevitch, *AIA Guide to* Chicago, 2004, 42.

21. Sniderman and Tippens, "Historic Resources," 7.

22. *Chicago Tribune*, June 9, 1994.

23. *Chicago Tribune*, April 30, 1995.

24. *Chicago Tribune*, May 1, 1997.

25. Sinkevitch, *AIA Guide to* Chicago, 2004, 47.

26. Ibid., 48.

27. Shedd Aquarium, "Amazon Rising."

28. Sinkevitch, *AIA Guide to Chicago*, 2004, 48.

29. "Mayor Daley Presents."

30. Kamin, *Why Architecture Matters*, 283.

31. *Chicago Tribune*, September 27, 1996.

32. "Mayor Daley Presents."

33. Millennium Park.

34. *Chicago Tribune*, September 27, 1996.

35. Ibid.

36. *Chicago Sun Times*, April 21, 1995.

37. *Chicago Tribune*, October 1, 1996.

38. Greg Kot, "Stunning Skyline: The Setting Is a Jewel That Merits Equally Bookings," *Chicago Tribune*, June 27, 2005.

39. Sinkevitch, *AIA Guide to Chicago*, 2004, 47.

40. Chicago Park District, "Soldier Field: Stadium History."

41. *Chicago Tribune*, March 13, 2001.

42. *Chicago Tribune*, April 26, 2004.

43. Blair Kamin, "Reinventing the Lakefront," six-part series, *Chicago Tribune*, October 26, 1998–November 5, 1998.

44. *Chicago Tribune*, November 11, 1998.

45. Chicago Convention and Tourism Bureau, "Millennium Park."

46. Black, "Shape of Things to Come," 66.

47. Sinkevitch, *AIA Guide to Chicago*, 2004, 37.

48. Heise, *Chicago the Beautiful*, 52.

49. Black, "Shape of Things to Come," 66.

50. Ibid.

51. Ibid.

52. Public Building Commission of Chicago, "PBC Awards Contract to Rebuild Grant Park Garage."

53. Black, "Shape of Things to Come," 67.

54. Twelve organizations signed on to be part of the theater and helped direct the effort. They include Ballet Chicago, Chicago Opera Theater, Chicago Sinfonietta, the Dance Center of Columbia College Chicago, Hubbard Street Dance Chicago, Joffrey Ballet of Chicago, Lyric Opera Center for American Artists, Mexican Fine Arts Center Museum, Muntu Dance Theatre of Chicago, Music of the Baroque, Old Town School of Folk Music, and Performing Arts Chicago.

55. Black, "Shape of Things to Come," 102, 105.

56. Heise, *Chicago the Beautiful*, 56.

57. Black, "Shape of Things to Come," 100.

58. Ibid.

59. Millennium Park Chicago, "Crown Fountain."

60. Black, "Shape of Things to Come," 100.

61. Millennium Park Chicago, "Lurie Garden."

62. Ibid., "Bicycle Parking."

63. Ibid., "Chase Promenade."

64. Ibid., "Boeing Galleries."
65. Ibid., "Exelon Pavilion."
66. Heise, *Chicago the Beautiful*, 56–57.
67. Metra Rail, "Randolph Station."
68. Black, "Shape of Things to Come," 100, 66, 105.
69. Gilfoyle, *Millennium Park*, 81–356.
70. For more information, see Abakanowicz, *Agora*.
71. BBC News, *Full Text*.

Bibliography

Abakanowicz, Magdalena. *Agora*. Chicago: Gray Gallery, 2008.

Abbott, Carl. *Boosters and Businessmen: Popular Economic Thought and Urban Growth in the Antebellum Middle West*. Westport, CT: Greenwood Press, 1981.

"Acoustics of the Convention Hall: Exposition Building Reconditioned by Adler and Sullivan for Music Festival." *Inland Architect* 3 (June 1884): 64.

Adams, John Coleman. "What a Great City Might Be—A Lesson from the White City." *New England Magazine* 14 (March 1896): 3–6.

Allwood, John. *The Great Exhibitions*. London: Studio Vista, 1977.

A. Montgomery Ward v. Field Museum of Natural History, 241 Ill. 496 (1909).

Andreas, Alfred Theodore. *History of Chicago from the Earliest Period to the Present Time*. 3 vols. Chicago: privately published, 1884–87; reprint, New York: Arno Press, 1975. Citations are to the 1975 edition.

Angle, Paul. "Chicago's Second National Convention." Chicago History 7, 1964, 104–15.

———, ed. "The International Aviation Meet Chicago 1911." Chicago History 8, Fall 1966, 1–18.

Architects File. Burnham Library, Art Institute of Chicago.

"Art Institute of Chicago Buildings 1879–1988: A Chronology, The." *Art Institute of Chicago Museum Studies* 14, no. 1 (1988): 7–27.

Art Institute of Chicago: Information about the Art Institute. Chicago: Art Institute of Chicago, 1900. Booklet.

Ayer, Benjamin Franklin. *Lake-Front Questions, Read before the Chicago Literary Club, May 28, 1888*. Chicago: Barnard and Miller, 1888.

Bach, Ira J., and Mary Lackritz Gray. *A Guide to Chicago's Public Sculpture*. Chicago: University of Chicago Press, 1983.

Badger, Reid. *The Great American Fair: The World's Columbian Exposition & American Culture*. Chicago: Nelson Hall, 1979.

Barrows, John Henry. "Results of the Parliament of Religions." *Forum* 18 (September 1894): 55–58.

Bator, Mary Grace, Lisa C. Pesavento, and Barbara Elwood Schlatter. *Reorganizing a World-Class Park System: The Chicago Park District's Evolution from Patronage to Professional Status through Staff Training*. Paper presented at

University of Deusto, Congresso Mundial de Ocio, Bilbao, Spain, July 3–7, 2000. Available at http://www.ocio.deusto.es/formacion/oci021/pdf/P10134. pdf. Accessed December 29, 2005.

BBC News. *Full Text: Obama's Victory Speech.* Last updated November 5, 2008. http: //news.bbc.co.uk/2/hi/americas/us_elections_2008/7710038.stm. Accessed December 2, 2011.

Berger, Miles L. *They Built Chicago: Entrepreneurs Who Shaped a Great City's Architecture.* Chicago: Bonus Books, 1992.

Biles, Roger. "Daley's Chicago." Electronic Encyclopedia of Chicago. Last updated 2005. http://www.encyclopedia.chicagohistory.org/pages/1722.html. Accessed October 22, 2005.

———. Richard J. Daley: Politics, Race, and the Governing of Chicago. DeKalb: Northern Illinois University Press, 1995.

Black, Jonathan. "The Shape of Things to Come." *Chicago Magazine*, February 2004, 47.

Blobaum, Dean. "An Introduction." "Chronology." *Chicago '68.* Last updated 2008. http://chicago68.com/. Accessed September 30, 2012.

Bluestone, Daniel. *Constructing Chicago.* New Haven: Yale University Press, 1991.

Board of Public Works. Eighth Annual Report of the Board of Public Works to the Common Council of the City of Chicago for the Municipal Year Ending March 31st, 1869. Chicago: Jameson and Morse, 1869.

———. Fourteenth Annual Report of the Board of Public Works to the Common Council of the City of Chicago for the Municipal Fiscal Year Ending March 31st, 1875. Chicago: J. S. Thompson, 1875.

———. Ninth Annual Report of the Board of Public Works to the Common Council of the City of Chicago for the Municipal Fiscal Year Ending March 31, 1870. Chicago: Lakeside, 1870.

———. Seventh Annual Report of the Board of Public Works to the Common Council of the City of Chicago for the Municipal Fiscal Year Ending March 31, 1868. Chicago: Jameson and Morse, 1869.

———. Tenth Annual Report of the Board of Public Works Year Ending March 31st, 1871. Chicago, 1871.

———. Third Annual Report of the Board of Public Works. Chicago: Jameson and Morse, 1864.

———. Thirteenth Annual Report of the Board of Public Works to the Common Council of the City of Chicago. For the Municipal Fiscal Year Ending March 31st, 1874. Chicago: J. S. Thompson, 1874.

———. Twelfth Annual Report of the Board of Public Works to the Common Council of the City of Chicago. For the Municipal Fiscal Year Ending March 31st, 1873. Chicago: National, 1873.

Bolotin, Norman, and Christine Laing. *The Chicago World's Fair of 1893: The World's Columbian Exposition.* Washington, DC: Preservation Press, 1992.

Books of the Fairs: Materials about World's Fairs, 1834–1916, in the Smithsonian Institution Libraries, The. Chicago: American Library Association, 1992.

Burg, David F. *Chicago's White City of 1893.* Lexington: University of Kentucky Press, 1976.

Burnham, Daniel Hudson, and Edward H. Bennett. *Plan of Chicago.* Edited by Charles Moore. New York: Princeton Architectural Press, 1993.

Burnham, Telford, and James F. Gookins. *Chicago the Site of the World's Fair of 1892. The Main Exposition on the Lake Front and Special Exhibitions at the Principal Parks, Connected by a Railroad Circuit with All Other Lines of Transportation, and the Heart of the City.* Chicago: Rand, McNally, 1889.

Butler, Edward B. *Edward B. Butler, 1853–1928.* Chicago: Self-published, 1929.

Cahan, Cathy, and Richard Cahan. "The Lost City of the Depression." *Chicago History* 5, Winter 1976–77, 233–42.

Ceremonies and the Unveiling of the Statue of Abraham Lincoln, at Lincoln Park Chicago, Illinois, 22 October 1887. Chicago: Brown, Pettibone, n.d.

"Chicago Architectural Club." *Inland Architect* 27 (February 1896): 8.

Chicago. A Stranger's and Tourists' Guide to the City of Chicago. Chicago: Religious Philosophical, 1866.

Chicago Band Association. Miscellaneous Pamphlets. Chicago Historical Society.

"Chicago Base-Ball Grounds, The." *Harper's Weekly*, May 12, 1883, 200.

Chicago Bears. *Chicago Bears.* http://www.chicagobears.com. Accessed January 28, 2006.

Chicago City Council. Chicago City Council Proceedings. "Lake Shore Protection Plan." August 24, 1844.

———. "Lake Front Ordinance and Amendments." Reports of the Chicago City Council. 1919–20, 1962.

Chicago Common Council. Chicago Common Council Proceeding. April 14, 1837, through 1869/70. Files, Illinois State Archives, Illinois Regional Archives Depository System, Northeastern Illinois University.

———. Chicago Common Council Proceedings. "Petetion of William Crawford to Occupy Public Ground with a Brewery." 1837/37 0313 A 04/14. Microfilm, Illinois Regional Archives Depository System, Illinois State Archives, Northeastern Illinois University.

———. Chicago Common Council Proceedings. "Report of Special Committee on Lake Shore Protection." September 6, 1850. 1850/50 6932 A. Microfilm, Illinois Regional Archives Depository System, Illinois State Archives, Northeastern Illinois University.

Chicago Convention and Tourism Bureau. "Millennium Park." *Chicago Convention and Tourism Bureau.* http://www.choosechicago.com/media/millenniumpark. html. Accessed January 6, 2006.

"Chicago Fire, The." *Chicago Historical Society.* 1999. http://www.chicagohs.org/history /fire.html. Accessed October 12, 2006.

Chicago History Museum Research Center.

"Chicago Nine, The." *Harper's Weekly*, October 17, 1885, 686.

Chicago Park District. "Grant Park Design Guidelines." Office of Research and Planning. July 1, 1992.

———. "Parks and Facilities: Shedd Park." Chicago Park District. http://www. chicagoparkdistrict.com/index.cfm/fuseaction/parks.detail/object_id /28E45F8F-FDAD-45DB-9A0C-021E09CBD482.cfm. Accessed January 15, 2006.

———. "Soldier Field: Stadium History." Chicago Park District. 2011. http://www. soldierfield.net/content/stadium-history. Accessed September 22, 2012.

Chicago Park District Special Collection.

Chicago Public Library. "Chicago's Front Door." Digital collection. Chicago Public Library. http://www.chipublib.org/digital/lake/CFDCOP.html. Accessed January 6, 2006.

———. "Historical Information 1967 January 16—The McCormick Place Fire." Chicago Public Library. Updated August 1987. http://www.chipublib.org/004chicago/timeline/mcormicfire.html. Accessed October 29, 2005.

———. "Inaugural Address of the Mayors of Chicago: Inaugural Address of Mayor Monroe Heath July 24, 1876." Chicago Public Library. http://www.chipublib.org/004chicago/mayors/speeches/heath76.html. Accessed August 1998.

———. "Martin Luther King." Information Center. Chicago Public Library. Updated January 1999. http://www.chipublib.org/003cpl/mlkchifaq.html.

City of Chicago v. A. Montgomery Ward, 169 IL 392. 48 N.E. 927 (1897).

City Wide Collection, Special Collection, Chicago Public Library.

Clarke, Jane H. "The Art Institute's Guardian Lions." *Art Institute of Chicago Museum Studies* 14, no. 1 (1988): 47–56.

Clayton, John. *The Illinois Fact Book and Historical Almanac 1673–1968*. Carbondale: Southern Illinois University Press, 1970.

Cleveland, H. W. S. *Public Grounds of Chicago. How to Give Them Character and Expression*. Chicago: Charles D. Lakey, 1869.

Colbert, Elias, and Everett Chamberlain. *Chicago and the Great Conflagration*. New York: C. F. Vent, 1871.

Colten, Craig E. "Chicago's Waste Lands: Refuse Disposal and Urban Growth, 1840–1990." *Journal of Historical Geography* 20, no. 2 (1994): 124–42.

Commission on Chicago Historical and Architectural Landmarks. The Adler Planetarium: Preliminary Summary of Information. Chicago: Commission, 1976.

———. John G. Shedd Aquarium: Preliminary Summary of Information. Chicago: Commission, 1976.

"Concrete Construction for Park Permanence: Concrete to Beautify Chicago Lakefront." *The Cement Era*. Chicago: Portland Cement, December 1915.

Condit, Carl W. *Chicago 1910–29: Building, Planning, and Urban Technology*. Chicago: University of Chicago Press, 1973.

Conzen, Michael P. "1848: The Birth of Modern Chicago." In 1848: Turning Point for Chicago, Turning Point for the Region. Edited by Conzen, Douglas Knox, and Dennis H. Cremin. Chicago: Newberry Library, 1998. 4–30.

———. "The Historical and Geographical Development of the Illinois and Michigan Canal National Heritage Corridor." In Conzen and Carr, Illinois and Michigan Canal, 3–25.

Conzen, Michael P., and Kay J. Carr, eds. *The Illinois and Michigan Canal National Heritage Corridor: A Guide to Its History and Sources*. DeKalb: Northern Illinois University Press, 1988.

Cook, Frederick Francis. *Bygone Days in Chicago: Recollections of the "Garden City" of the Sixties*. Chicago: A. C. McClurg, 1910.

Cranz, Galen. *The Politics of Park Design: The History of Urban Parks in America*. Boston: MIT Press, 1982.

"Crawford, James and William." Encyclopedia. Early Chicago. 2012. www.earlychicago.com. Accessed November 2, 2010.

Cremin, Dennis H. "Music under the Stars: The Making of the Grant Park Music Festival." Grant Park Music Festival Program, July 15–August 4, 1995. Program.

Crerar Current 4 (April 1957): 5.

Cromie, Robert. *The Great Chicago Fire*. New York: McGraw-Hill, 1958.

Cronon, William. *Nature's Metropolis: Chicago and the Great West*. New York: Norton, 1991.

Cudahy, Brian J. *Destination: Loop, the Story of Rapid Transit Railroading in and around Chicago*. Brattleboro, VT: Stephen Greene Press, 1982.

"Dedication of the Ferguson Fountain of the Great Lakes." Chicago: Art Institute of Chicago, September 9, 1913. Program.

Draper, Joan E. Edward H. Bennett: Architect and City Planner. Chicago: Art Institute of Chicago, 1982.

———. "Paris by the Lake: Sources of Burnham's Plan of Chicago." In Chicago Architecture 1872–1922: Birth of a Metropolis, edited by John Zukowsky. Munich: Prestel-Verlag, 1987. 107–20.

Duis, Perry R. "World War II." *Encyclopedia of Chicago, Chicago Historical Society.* 2005. http://www.encyclopedia.chicagohistory.org/pages/1384.html. Accessed December 29, 2005.

Duis, Perry R., and Glen E. Holt. "Chicago as It Was: Chicago's Lost Exposition." *Chicago* 26, July 1977, 72, 74.

Dunham, Allison. "The Chicago Lake Front and A. Montgomery Ward." *Land-Use Controls* 1 (1967): 15–17.

Ehernhalt, Alan. *The Lost City: Discovering the Forgotten Virtues of Community in Chicago in the 1950s*. New York: Basic Books, 1995.

Einhorn, Robin L. *Property Rules: Political Economy in Chicago, 1833–1872*. Chicago: University of Chicago Press, 1991.

Encyclopedia Britannica. 11th ed.

Encyclopedia Britannica. Micropædia. 15th ed. Chicago: Encyclopedia Britannica, 2007.

E. R. Bliss et al. v. A. Montgomery Ward et al. 198 IL 104.

Faber, Charles F. *Baseball Pioneers: Ratings of Nineteenth Century Players*. Jefferson, NC: McFarland, 1997.

Farber, David. Chicago '68. Chicago: University of Chicago Press, 1988.

———. "1968." Special Features: Year Page. Electronic Encyclopedia of Chicago. Last updated 2005. http://www.encyclopedia.chicagohistory.org/pages/500008. html. Accessed October 29, 2005.

Faulkner, Joseph W. "Painters at the Hall of Exhibitions: 1890." *Chicago History* 2 (Spring 1972): 14–17.

Federal Writers Project, Chicago and Suburbs 1939. Chicago: Chicago Historical Bookworks, 1991.

"Ferguson Fund Adds Beauty to Chicago: Our Trust Department Administers the Estate; Art Institute Receives the Income." *Northerner* (November–December 1948): 22–23.

Findling, John E. *Chicago's Great World's Fairs*. Manchester, NY: Manchester University Press, 1994.

Fink, Theodore J. *Grant Park Tomorrow: Future of Chicago's Front Yard*. Chicago: Open Lands Project, 1979.

Fogelson, Robert M. *Downtown: Its Rise and Fall, 1880–1950*. New Haven: Yale University Press, 2001.

Fox, Richard Wightman, and T. J. Jackson Lears, eds. *The Power of Culture: Critical Essays in American History*. Chicago: University of Chicago Press, 1993.

Friends of the Park. Home page. *Friends of the Parks.* 2004. http://www.fotp.org. Accessed January 6, 2006.

"General Italo Balbo 1896–1940." *Aviation Boom.* February 7, 2003. http://www. aviationboom.com/pioneers/italo_balbo.shtml. Accessed December 30, 2003.

Gilfoyle, Timothy J. *Millennium Park: Creating a Chicago Landmark.* Chicago: University of Chicago Press, 2006.

Grossman, James R., Ann Durkin Keating, and Janice L. Reiff, eds. *The Encyclopedia of Chicago.* Chicago: University of Chicago Press, 2004.

Handy, Edward H. "Another New Structure for City's Front Yard." *Central Manufacturing District Magazine* 14, no. 1 (1930): 38–39.

Hannah, Eleanore. "Armories." The Electronic Encyclopedia of Chicago. 2005. http://www.encyclopedia.chicagohistory.org/pages/1736.html. Accessed October 29, 2006.

———. "Illinois National Guard." The Electronic Encyclopedia of Chicago. 2005. http://www.encyclopedia.chicagohistory.org/pages/873.html. Accessed October 29, 2006.

Harper's Weekly, June 25, 1892, 604.

Harper's Weekly, July 2, 1892, 631.

Heise, Kenan. *Chicago the Beautiful: A City Reborn.* Chicago: Bonus Books, 2001.

Hill, Lewis W. *Report to the Commission on Chicago Historical and Architectural Landmarks on the Adler Planetarium and Astronomical Museum.* Chicago: Commission, 1977.

Hines, Thomas. *Burnham of Chicago: Architect and Planner.* Chicago: University of Chicago Press, 1979.

Hirsch, Arnold R. *Making the Second Ghetto: Race and Housing in Chicago 1940–1960.* Chicago: University of Chicago Press, 1998.

Horowitz, Helen. *Culture and the City: Cultural Philanthropy in Chicago from the 1880's to 1917.* Lexington: University Press of Kentucky, 1976.

Hunter, D. Lyn. "An Empiricist Tackles Crime." *Berkeleyan.* Office of Public Affairs. *UC Berkeley.* 2002. http://www.berkeley.edu/news/berkeleyan/2002/10/16_empir.html. Accessed October 29, 2005.

Hyma, Nora Deans. "Looking Backward: the Fiftieth Anniversary of the John G. Shedd Aquarium." *Chicago History* 9, Spring 1980, 41–45.

Illinois, a Descriptive and Historical Guide. Chicago: P A.C. McClurg, 1939. Reprint, *WPA Guide to Illinois: The Federal Writers' Project Guide to 1930s Illinois.* New York: Pantheon Books, 1983. Citations are to the 1983 edition.

Illinois Central Railroad Company, Report and Accounts, for the year Ending 31st December 1856. New York, 1857.

Illinois Central Archive File 2.7. Chicago Lake Front Cases. 1852–1900. *Newberry Library.* http://mms.newberry.org/html/ICRR.html.

Illinois Central Railroad v. Illinois. 146 U.S. 387 (1892).

Inter-State Exposition Souvenir; Containing a Historical Sketch of Chicago: Also a Record of the Great Inter-State Exposition of 1873, from Its Inception to Its Close, The. Chicago: Van Arsdale and Massie, 1873.

Interstate Industrial Exposition of Chicago. Reports of the Secretary and Treasurer, 1875. Chicago, 1875.

Interstate Industrial Exposition of Chicago. Reports of the Secretary and Treasurer, 1876. Chicago: Fox, 1876.

Interstate Industrial Exposition of Chicago. Reports of the Secretary and Treasurer, 1879. Chicago: Jameson and Morse, 1880.

Jackson, Kenneth T. *Crabgrass Frontier: The Suburbanization of the United States.* New York: Oxford University Press, 1985.

Jarrett, Vernon. "Council Wars." *The Electronic Encyclopedia of Chicago.* 2005. http://www.encyclopedia.chicagohistory.org/pages/342.html. Accessed January 16, 2006.

Johnson, Rossiter, ed. Congresses, vol. 4. A History of the World's Columbian Exposition Held in Chicago in 1893. New York: D. Appleton, 1898.

——, ed. Narrative, vol. 1. A History of the World's Columbian Exposition Held in Chicago in 1893. New York: D. Appleton, 1897.

Kamin, Blair. *Why Architecture Matters: Lessons from Chicago.* Chicago: University of Chicago Press, 2001.

Karamanski, Theodore J. *Rally Round the Flag: Chicago and the Civil War.* Chicago: Nelson-Hall, 1993.

Karlowicz, Titus M. "The Architecture of the World's Columbian Exposition." PhD diss., Northwestern University, 1965.

——. "Notes on the Columbian Exposition's Manufactures and Liberal Arts Building." Journal of the Society of Architectural Historians 33 (1974): 214–18.

Kelly, Steve. "Chicago Parks Play for Keeps with Partnerships." *American City and Country.* September 1, 1995. http://americancityandcounty.com/mag/government_chicago_parks_play. Accessed September 22, 2012.

Kunhardt, Dorothy Meserve, and Philip B. Kunhardt Jr. *Twenty Days.* New York: Harper and Row, 1965.

Kysela, John D. "Sarah Hallowell Brings 'Modern Art' to the Midwest." *Art Quarterly* 27, no. 2 (1964): 150–67.

"Lake Shore Drive." *Wikipedia.* Updated 6 September 2005. http://en.wikipedia.org/wiki/Lakeshore_Drive. Accessed October 29, 2005.

Lakeside City Directory, The. Chicago: Chicago Directory, 1875–91.

Lamb, John. "I&M Canal: A Corridor in Time, 1836–1986." Romeoville, IL: Lewis University, 1987.

Larson, John W. *Those Army Engineers: A History of the Chicago District U.S. Army Corps of Engineers.* Washington, DC: GPO, 1980.

Lears, T. J. Jackson, and Richard Wightman Fox, eds. *The Culture of Consumption: Critical Essays in American History, 1880–1980.* New York: Pantheon, 1983.

Leiter, Robert D. *The Musicians and Petrillo.* New York: Bookman, 1953.

Levine, Lawrence W. *Highbrow/Lowbrow: The Emergence of Cultural Hierarchy in America.* Cambridge, MA: Harvard University Press, 1988.

Levine, Peter. *A. G. Spalding and the Rise of Baseball: The Promise of American Sport.* New York: Oxford University Press, 1985.

Lowe, David. *Lost Chicago.* New York: Wings Books, 1975.

Lowry, Philip J. *Green Cathedrals: The Ultimate Celebration of All 271 Major League and Negro League Ballparks Past and Present.* Reading, MA: Addison-Wesley, 1992.

Lubove, Roy. *H. W. S. Cleveland and the Urban-Rural Continuum in American Landscape Architecture.* Chicago: Jansen, McClurg, 1873; reprint, Pittsburgh: University of Pittsburgh Press, 1965. Citations are to the 1965 edition.

"Mammoth Opera House: Interior Sketch of Chicago Opera Festival Auditorium. Adler and Sullivan, Architects, A." *Inland Architect* 5 (March 1885): 25–30.

Mapleson, James Henry, and S. G. Pratt. *First Chicago Grand Opera Festival: At the Exposition Building, commencing April 6, 1885 under the Auspices of the Chicago Opera Festival Association*. Edited by Pratt. Chicago: Skeen and Stuart, 1885.

Mayer, Harold M., and Richard C. Wade. *Chicago: Growth of a Metropolis*. Chicago: University of Chicago Press, 1969.

"Mayor Daley Presents New Museum Campus to Chicago." *United States Conference of Mayors*. July 31, 1998. http://www.usmayors.org/USCM/home.asp. Accessed January 9, 2006.

McCormick, Kathleen. "Chicago Takes Stock: The Windy City Documents, Preserves, and Restores Its Historic Parks." Historic Preservation 46, no. 6 (1994): 66–68, 97, 103.

———. "City in the Garden." Historic Preservation, November/December 1994, 68.

McCormick v. Chicago Yacht Club. 331 IL 514 (1928).

Metra. "Randolph Station." *Commuter Rail Division of the Regional Transportation Authority*. www.metrarail.com/service_advisories/randolph-station.html. Accessed January 24, 2006.

Millennium Park. "Bicycle Parking." City of Chicago. 2006. http://www.millenniumpark.org/artandarchitecture/bicycle_parking.html. Accessed January 28, 2006.

———. "Bicycle Parking through Lurie Garden." City of Chicago. http://www.millenniumpark.org. Accessed January 24, 2006.

———. "Boeing Galleries." City of Chicago. 2006. http://www.millenniumpark.org/artandarchitecture/boeing_galleries.htm. Accessed January 28, 2006.

———. "Chase Promenade." City of Chicago. 2006. http://www.millenniumpark.org/artandarchitecture/chase_promenade.html. Accessed January 28, 2006.

———. "Crown Fountain." City of Chicago. 2006. http://www.millenniumpark.org/artandarchitecture/crown_fountain.html. Accessed January 24, 2006.

———. "Exelon Pavilion." City of Chicago. 2006. http://www.millenniumpark.org/artandarchitecture/exelon_pavilions.html. Accessed January 28, 2006.

———. "Lurie Garden." City of Chicago. 2006. http://www.millenniumpark.org/artandarchitecture/lurie_garden.html. Accessed January 28, 2006.

Miller, Donald L. *City of the Century: The Epic of Chicago and the Making of America*. New York: Simon and Schuster, 1996.

Moffat, Bruce G. *The L: The Development of Chicago's Rapid Transit System 1888–1932*. Chicago: Central Electric Railfans' Association, 1995.

Moore, Charles. *Daniel H. Burnham: Architect, Planner of Cities*. 2 vols. Boston: Houghton Mifflin, 1921. Reprint, New York: Da Capo Press, 1969. Citations are to the 1969 edition.

Moulton, Robert Hunt. "Chicago's Dream of Civic Beauty Realized in the Symbolic Marble of Lorado Taft's 'Spirit of the Great Lakes.'" *Craftsman* 25 (1913): 123–30.

Museum Campus. 2006. www.museumcampus.org. Accessed January 18, 2006.

Myers, Elizabeth A. "Memorial, Demonstration, and Protest: The Politicization of Public Space in Grant Park, Chicago, in 1968." Paper read at Illinois History Conference Springfield, Illinois, October 2002.

Nash, Roderick. *Wilderness and the American Mind*. New Haven, CT: Yale University Press, 1967.

National Party Conventions 1831–1976. 2nd ed. Washington, DC: Congressional Quarterly, 1979.

"1968: A Convention in Crisis." Parades, Protests and Politics in Chicago. *Chicago Historical Society.* Last updated 1999. http://www.chicagohs.org/history/politics/1968.html. Accessed May 28, 2006.

"1968 Democratic National Convention." *Wikipedia.* http://en.wikipedia.org/wiki/1968_Democratic_National_Convention. Accessed May 28, 2006.

"1965 Watts Riots, The." *University of Southern California.* 2006. http://www.usc.edu/isd/archives/la/watts.html. Accessed April 15, 2006.

Openlands Project. Home page. http://www.openlands.org. Accessed January 6, 2006.

Osborn, M. L. "The Development of Recreation in the South Park System of Chicago." MA thesis, University of Chicago, 1928.

Peckham, Edward L. "Chicago—A Mean Spot." Pierce, *As Others See Chicago,* 166–70.

Phillips, Isaac Newton. *Reports of Cases at Law and in Chancery Argued and Determined in the Supreme Court of Illinois.* Vol. 241. Bloomington, IL: Pantagraph, 1910.

Phipps, Linda S. "The 1893 Art Institute Building and the 'Paris of America' Aspirations of Patrons and Architects in Late Nineteenth-Century Chicago." *Art Institute of Chicago Museum Studies* 14 (1988): 28–45.

Pierce, Bessie Louise, ed. A History of Chicago. 3 vols. New York: Alfred A. Knopf, 1937–57.

———. As Others See Chicago: Impressions of Visitors, 1673–1933. Chicago: University of Chicago Press, 1933.

"Preserving Architectural Collections at the Art Institute of Chicago." *Annotation: The Newsletter of the National Historical Publications and Records Commission* 26, no. 3 (September 1998): 7–8. 2006. http://search.archives.gov/. Accessed January 14, 2006.

Public Building Commission of Chicago. "PBC Awards Contract to Rebuild Grant Park Garage." January 8, 2003.

Quaife, Milo Milton, ed. *The Development of Chicago 1674–1914.* Chicago: Caxton Club, 1916.

Ralph, James. "Martin Luther King, Jr., in Chicago." Electronic Encyclopedia of Chicago. Last modified 2005. http://www.encyclopedia.chicagohistory.org/pages/1438.html. Accessed October 29, 2005.

———. Northern Protest: Martin Luther King, Jr., Chicago and the Civil Rights Movement. Cambridge, MA: Harvard University Press, 1993.

Ranney, Edward. *Prairie Passage: The Illinois and Michigan Canal Corridor.* Urbana: University of Illinois Press, 1998.

Rauch, John H. *Public Parks: Their Effects upon the Moral, Physical and Sanitary Condition of the Inhabitants of Large Cities; with Special Reference to the City of Chicago.* Chicago: S. C. Griggs, 1869.

Riedy, James L. *Chicago Sculpture.* Urbana: University of Illinois Press, 1981.

Riess, Steven A. *Touching Base: Professional Baseball and American Culture in the Progressive Era.* Westport, CT: Greenwood Press, 1980.

Roosevelt, Franklin D. "1930s: President Franklin Roosevelt's 'Quarantine the Aggressors' Address, 1937." *The Public Papers of the Presidents of the United States, Franklin Delano Roosevelt, 1937.* 187–92. Chicago, October 5, 1937. Documents of American History II. American Studies, Institute of International Studies, Faculty of Social Sciences, Charles University. http://tucnak.fsv.cuni.cz/~calda/Documents/1930s/FDR_Quarantine_1937.html. Accessed December 29, 2005.

Roosevelt University. "Chicago and Richard J. Daley, 1960 to 1975." Module 3, chapter 4. History of Chicago from Trading Post to Metropolis. *Roosevelt University.* http://www.roosevelt.edu/chicagohistory/mod3-chap4.htm. Accessed June 5, 2006. Site discontinued.

Rosenthal, Samuel and Marie-Louise, Archives. Chicago Symphony Orchestra, 220 South Michigan Avenue, Chicago.

Rydell, Robert W. "Century of Progress Exposition." The Electronic Encyclopedia of Chicago, Chicago Historical Society. 2005. http://www.encyclopedia.chicagohistory.org/pages/225.html. Accessed January 6, 2006.

———. World of Fairs: The Century-of-Progress Expositions. Chicago: University of Chicago Press, 1993.

Saarinen, Eliel. "Project for Lake Front Development of the City of Chicago." *American Architect* 124 (December 1923): 487–515.

Sautter, R. Craig, and Edward M. Burke. *Inside the Wigwam: Chicago Presidential Conventions 1860–1996.* Foreword by Richard M. Daley. Chicago: Wild Onion Books, 1996.

Sawislak, Karen. *Smoldering City: Chicagoans and the Great Fire, 1871–1874.* Chicago: University of Chicago Press, 1995.

Schabas, Ezra. *Theodore Thomas: America's Conductor and Builder of Orchestras, 1835–1905.* Urbana: University of Illinois Press, 1989.

Schroeder, Douglas. "The Issue of the Lakefront: An Historical Critical Survey." In *Chicago Heritage Committee.* Chicago: Prairie School Press, 1964.

Schultz, John. *No One Was Killed: Documentation and Meditation: Convention Week, Chicago—August 1968.* 1969. Chicago: Big Table, 1998. Citations are to the 1998 edition.

Schuyler, David. *The New Urban Landscape: The Redefinition of City Form in Nineteenth-Century America.* Baltimore: Johns Hopkins University Press, 1986.

Scott, Frank Hamline. *In Memoriam, John H. Hamline.* Chicago: n.p., 1904. http://www.worldcat.org/title/in-memoriam-john-h-hamline/oclc/270763636.

Sheahan, James W. Chicago Illustrated. Part 1, January 1867. Chicago: Jevne and Almini, 1867.

———. Chicago Illustrated. Part 2, February1866. Chicago: Jevne and Almini, 1866.

———. Chicago Illustrated. Part 10, October 1967. Chicago: Jevne and Almini, 1867.

Shedd Aquarium. "Amazon Rising." *Shedd Aquarium.* http://www.sheddaquarium.org. Accessed January 6 and 18, 2006.

Sinkevitch, Alice, ed. AIA Guide to Chicago. New York: Harcourt, Brace, 1993.

———. AIA Guide to Chicago. 2nd ed. New York: Harcourt, 2004.

Smith, Carl. The Plan of Chicago: Daniel Burnham and the Remaking of the American City. Chicago: University of Chicago Press, 2006.

———. Urban Disorder and the Shape of Belief: The Great Chicago Fire, the Haymarket Bomb, and the Model Town of Pullman. Chicago: University of Chicago Press, 1995.

South Park Commissioners. Annual Report of the South Park Commissioners for the Fiscal Year 1905.

———. Annual Report of the South Park Commissioners for the Fiscal Year 1906. Chicago, 1907.

———. Annual Report of the South Park Commissioners for the Fiscal Year Ended February 29, 1912. 1912.

——. Annual Report to the Judges of the Circuit Court of Cook County, Submitted by Edward J. Kelly, President, South Park Commissioners December 31, 1924.

——. "Grant Park, General Plan of Improvements West of I.C.R.R. and North of Jackson St. South Park Commissioners Chicago 1917." In-house report. Ca. 1917.

——. Modern and Most Valuable Park Development in the South Park District of the City of Chicago; Progress made in Large Undertaking by the South Park Commissioners Following the Burnham Plan and the City Plan Commission. Chicago, 1923.

——. Report of the South Park Commissioners to the Board of County Commissioners of Cook County. 1895–96. 1896–97. 1899–1900. 1902–3. 1903–4. Chicago.

——. Report of the South Park Commissioners for a Period of Fifteen Months. December 1, 1906 to February 29, 1908. March 1, 1909 to February 28, 1910. March 1, 1913, to February 28, 1914. March 1, 1914, to February 28, 1915. March 1, 1915, to February 29, 1916. March 1, 1916 to February 28, 1917. March 1, 1917, to February 28, 1918. March 1, 1918, to February 28, 1919. March 1, 1920, to February 28, 1921. March 1, 1921, to February 28, 1922.

South Park Commissioners, Appellant, v. Montgomery Ward & Co., et al. Appellees, 248 Ill. 299, 93 N.E. 910 (1910).

Spiess, Philip D, II. "Exhibitions and Expositions in 19th Century Cincinnati." *Cincinnati Historical Society Bulletin* 28 (1970): 170–92.

"Spirit of Music" Theodore Thomas Memorial . . . Unveiled April 24, 1924. Chicago: South Park Commissioners, 1924. Dedication program.

Stevens Hotel Co. v. Art Institute of Chicago, 342 IL 180 (1930).

Stevens Hotel Co. v. Chicago Yacht Club, 282 US 875 (1930).

Stover, John F. *History of the Illinois Central Railroad*. New York: Macmillan, 1975.

"Thoroughfares." *Putnam's Monthly Magazine* 7 (June 1856): 606–13. In Pierce, *As Others See Chicago*, 157–70.

Tippens, William W. "Synthesis of Reform: The Development of the Small Parks in Chicago's South and West Park Commissions." MA thesis, Columbia University, 1988.

"To Abate a Nuisance." *Art Institute Scrapbook*, 5, 105.

"Too Hasty Action by County Board." *Inland Architect* 25 (October 1894): 22.

Travis, Dempsey J. *An Autobiography of Black Politics*. Vol. 1. Chicago: Urban Research Press, 1987.

Trustees of the Art Institute of Chicago. 4th Annual Report of the Trustees of the Art Institute of Chicago. Chicago: R. R. Donnelley, 1883.

——. 9th Annual Report of the Trustees of the Art Institute of Chicago. Chicago, 1888.

——. 12th Annual Report of the Trustees of the Art Institute of Chicago. Chicago: Knight and Leonard, 1891.

Van Roessel, Annemarie. *D. H. Burnham and Chicago's Loop*. Architecture in Context. Chicago: Art Institute of Chicago, 1996.

Wacker, Charles H. "The Plan of Chicago—Its Purpose and Development." *Art and Archaeology* 12, no. 3–4 (1921): 105–6, 109.

Wendt, Lloyd, and Herman Kogan. *Bosses in Lusty Chicago: The Story of Bath-house John and Hinky Dink*. Bloomington: Indiana University Press, 1967.

Wetsch, Elisabeth. "Harrison, Lester." *Serial Killer Crime Index*. 1995. http://www.crimezzz.net/serialkillers/H/HARRISON_lester.php. Accessed October 30, 2005.

Whitridge, Eugenia Remelin. "Art in Chicago: The Structure of the Art World in a Metropolitan Community." PhD diss., University of Chicago, 1946.

Wille, Lois. At Home in the Loop: How Clout and Community Built Chicago's Dearborn Park. Carbondale: Southern Illinois University Press, 1997.

———. Forever Open, Clear and Free: The Struggle for Chicago's Lakefront. 2nd ed. Chicago: University of Chicago Press, 1991.

Wilson, William H. *The City Beautiful Movement*. Baltimore: Johns Hopkins University Press, 1989.

Zolberg, Vera Lenchner. "The Art Institute of Chicago: The Sociology of a Cultural Organization." PhD diss., University of Chicago, 1974.

Zukowsky, John, Sally Chappell, and Robert Bruegmann. *The Plan of Chicago*. Chicago: Art Institute of Chicago, 1979.

Index

A page number with an italicized *f* following it refers to the location of a figure.

Dennis H. Cremin is a professor of history at Lewis University. He is the director of the Lewis University History Center and has served as the academic director for the Lasallian University Center for Education (LUCE) in Rome, Italy. He has extensive public history experience with award winning exhibitions and grant funded projects. His research includes topics related to art, pilgrimage and spiritual travel, and the pedagogy of place-based learning.